KANT 2022

Twenty Five Thousand Days of Memories

Acknowledgements

I would like to use this space to extend my greatest thanks to a long list of friends, colleagues, and random kindred spirits without whom this book would never have been completed.

I cannot name everyone, but I'll mention the following at least: thanks to all those who transcribed dozens of hours of sound recordings, Pavla Pokorná, who – as always – resolved heaps of problems with a smile, and I'd also like to thank my best friends Kačenka Amblerová, Aleš Voverka, Luboš Loibl, David Kubík, and Tom Kosnar.

My thanks also go out to those who provided their photographs: Alice Štechová, Andrea Thiel Lhotáková, Radka Ciglerová, Milan Pitlach, Tonda Kratochvíl and many others whose names the dear reader will find in the photo credits.

I'd like to thank Míra Masák for his valuable advice and excellent pointers, Johnny Eisler for his help in preparing the English mutation of this book, Tom Plzenský, who stood at the very beginning of this enormous piece of work, Jakub Cigler and the entire A1 studio, Boris Jirků for the lightness with which he created the portrait of me used in this book with so little time left before the deadline, and finally, huge thanks go out to Tom Machek, who, with his tirelessness, artfulness, and fantastic ideas, far exceeded the usual role of the graphic designer.

Over a period of more than a year, me and Magda became such a good team, we created a fully fledged writer's unit, which we gave the working title of "MagMa". Me and Magda would like to thank each other mutually for having gotten through it together.

Finally, I cannot forget three people who are often mentioned in the book, all of whom were instrumental in the book's creation: my dad Ivo, my fantastic friend Pavel Štecha, and Blanka Plzenská. I'm sure they would all be very happy about this book coming out and I would like to thank them today, over the chasm of space and time but with all of my heart…
M. R.

Twenty Five Thousand Days of Memories

Martin Rajniš
Magdalena Šebestová

Kant

KANT, 2022

ISBN 978-80-7437-366-4

The authors have made every effort to acquire the appropriate information and permission to reproduce the image materials whose authors are listed in the photo credits. In case of error, the authors will gladly receive word from the copyright owners omitted here and arrange a correction.

Table of Contents

I'd been toying with the idea of getting started on my memoirs – delimited to include 25 344 days of my life – for a long time. But what would it be about?

And how would I put it together, seeing as I'd never written anything like that before and I don't use a computer?

Then, I got a sign that this might just be the right time to start reminiscing: I met Magda – still Magda Křížková back then – when she interviewed me for a magazine. I enjoyed working with her – she's cheerful and talking to her is a joy.

We agreed that if we were to work on this together, it would have to be totally un-academic. In short: over seventy years of impressions and anecdotes about my love for sailing and travelling, for dogs, and for certain women. Reminiscences of my family, of butchers in the procession at President Beneš's funeral, the gorgeous ass of my aunt Milena, and, of course, my life-long love: architecture.

I also thought about what I wanted to say with my book and who I was writing it for. Well then: first of all, I want everyone to realise that if a nobody like me can become a university professor with a world-renowned architecture prize to his name, practically anyone can do the same! This book, however, will not be a technical treatise on architecture – I'll write that later and it will be called Almighty Architecture. This will be about my life with architecture, with which I am in an almost sinfully dishonourable relationship.

But what I want most is to tell people who have been struck by the many injustices of fate that even someone who was almost put in a special school; even a nobody like me can live a fabulous life. I wish that the reader lets their hair down, starts speaking in slang, and enjoys the wonderfully enunciated swearwords that glitter like the cherry on the proverbial cake. To flush all their pills down the bog, let loose, and, when the time comes, to depart with the blissful feeling that they lived those last few days, years, or decades to the full. In short, to ruffle up the calm waters of our homeland and feel like a champion.

Oh my, I'd like to smash quite a few things to pieces! I'd really wish for all this to come true...

There are two other things I'd like to quickly explain: my diligent and systematic father, Ivo, wrote a memoir near the end of his life. This inspired me to do something similar and also served as a repository of information. This is why I occasionally allowed myself the luxury of blending my own memories with his. Reading through this text, I realised again why the two of us could never agree on anything, but even so, this reminiscing was like a late cleansing bath for our relationship...

I owe the kind reader another explanation – regarding the dating: in the contents, I list the year 2034. There are several reasons for this: my father, just like many of my closest relatives, only died after turning ninety. I therefore decided that fate would grant me a similarly long life, so I planned it out until the year 2034, including my finances. You can therefore take this is as a preemptive announcement of my death. And if I survive the year 2034, nothing crucial will probably happen – unless I get married.

In short, dear reader, it would make me truly happy if you enjoy this book, just like I enjoyed making it.

One last thing:
Some years ago, the first to record my reminiscences was Blanka – my friend and the wife of my close pal Tom Plzenský. She was the first to give me courage, and she herself recorded and transcribed several hours of interviews. Unfortunately, she died before she could see this book in print, but she definitely left her mark on it and I remember her with enormous gratitude.

Let's get started, then, and rewind back to the year 1945...

My Sweet Childhood (1944–1951)

—

In the summer of 1943, the newspapers are full of the Battle of Kursk. Hitler tries to reverse the setbacks on the Russian front with his new Tiger I tanks. Nevertheless, the Germans – massively outnumbered by the Russians – are forced to retreat with huge losses. After several weeks, the battle ends in a decisive German loss – a crucial twist after Moscow and Stalingrad.

My father and his friend Franta Rachlík, a writer and communist, decided this was cause for celebration. But the war was in its fifth year, and the supply of decent booze had long since dried up.

They walked around town until they arrived at a bar kept by a friend: "Lads, you can see I've got nothing here, but if memory serves, something good should be buried in the coal cellar. But you'll have to dig it out yourself!"

They took off their party clothes and started digging. And indeed, after several hours, they uncovered three bottles of cognac – Marie Brizard, my father's favourite. Withsome friends, they decided to celebrate the Russian victory at Kursk so thoroughly, that when my father came home late that night, he and my mother added my conception to the bill.

As my grandmother later told me, my father immediately began referring to me as the "alcoholic foetus" that had to go. Because my mother was approaching forty, however, both my grandmothers went on bended knee to beg for my birth. In the end, my father gave in.

My Childhood in Římov

I was born nine months after the victory at Kursk, 16 May 1944. My father's feelings are best documented in the following extract from his diary:

"My son was named at the town hall in the presence of two lawyers who attested that he was born of matrimony and that he would bear the name Martin. Just like that, I had discarded my plans for wandering the world and began attempting to discover the shades of warmth in the family hearth. I had to reconsider many of my positions, which was not easy in the slightest.. ."

My poor mother had a difficult labour, leaving her considerably marked. She suffered from hypothyroidism and often spent long months in a sanatorium. Thus, it came to pass that I spent part of my early childhood in the beautiful village of Římov, which was, I think, the second stop on the old horsecar track from České Budějovice to Linz. In this little Catholic village, my aunt rented a beautiful house with a crenelated tower and a garden on the rocks overlooking the Malše river. This is more or less how I imagined paradise, as Professor Žák later described it to us at the Academy.

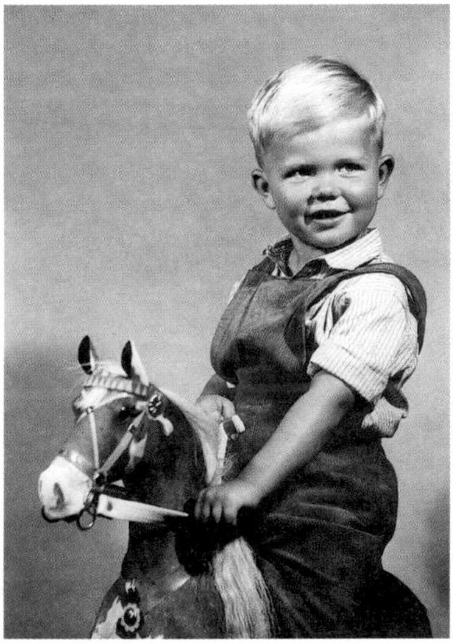

Beautiful Aunt Milena

The garden was full of parasol mushrooms that reached almost all the way up to my knob. I spent a lot of time there with my mother's sister – Aunt Milena. Her effect on men (myself included) was truly magical. But she was clever, well-read, and funny too. To me, she was truly a beauty. Long waves of honey-gold hair fell to her waist, and she knew how to throw it beautifully around. She enjoyed sunbathing naked and I, a three-year-old squirt, could crawl around her and examine all the gifts nature had granted her. Her stunning beauty influenced me throughout my life.

Aunt Milena was a very sociable woman. She survived her husband, a German actor at the German theatre in Prague and a handsome man of aristocratic blood: von Ströhlin. On the occasion of the final referendum on Hitler, they were living together at a family château somewhere near the Rhein Falls.

It must be said that Milena was among the minority of four million Germans who voted "NO"

My father crossing Černá hora on horseback (1934)

Me on horseback, Prague (1946)

to Hitler when balloted, and was appropriately proud of it. But of course, she couldn't boast about it much to her new German family. When her husband joined the SS and left to fight for Hitler at the front, Milena asked for a divorce.

He, however, loved her madly, and in 1942, brought her a dog he had saved from a minefield. He gave her this little boxer bitch hoping it would mollify her, and perhaps she'd take him back. It did not. With defiant pride, Milena gave it a Jewish name: Judita.

I lived in the dog-bed with Judka, as we called her, and I screamed my head off whenever someone tried to carry me away. Put simply, she was my best friend. We ate from the same bowl, but as a child I was already gluttonous, so I fought for the grub, hard. Once I was found with blood smeared on my face and poor Judka was beaten for biting me. As it later transpired, the opposite was true: I'd bitten her.

Judka was a water-dog. All you had to do was walk down to the Malše river and she'd leap into the water from a distance and spend hours swimming in circles. We'd be getting ready to leave for dinner, but she had no intention of getting out of the water, so Mr Fiala, the beautiful tanned bee-keeper, would have to step in. Although he was almost twenty years younger than my aunt, he would almost put his eyes out staring at her. Into the water he would leap, dragging the defiant Judka up to the tower.

Mr Fiala would visit often, bringing the most wonderful things – forest strawberries with fresh cream, for example. Once, when it was pouring down with rain, Mr Fiala arrived completely dry. When I asked him how, he said he was able to move in "interdroplet space".

Overall, the people in Římov were wonderful – for example Leopold Knapp, known as Poldíček, a German who avoided expulsion after the war, would do amazing magic tricks for me and my friend Maruška Kyselová. Suddenly, he could stick two scraps of iron together, then cut them in two

Aunt Milena, just married to Gerhard von Ströhlin, Prague (1935)

The house in Římov (2016)

The house on the corner of Rašínovo nábřeží after the fatal air raid, Prague (1945)

with a knife, then join them again – we couldn't believe our eyes.

Everyone loved Poldíček. Ivan – a Russian deserter hiding in the woods – also came to visit him. After a year, the locals took pity on Ivan and began giving him food and clothing. In short, he became part of the community.

Ivan, Poldíček, and my grandmother – whom we called Big Nana – Aunt Milena, and the beekeeper Mr Fiala – they were all lovely, and they all contributed to my idyllic childhood.

Living Memories

No one can believe that I remember so much of my early childhood. Years later, I found myself near Římov and recounted my story to Kačenka (in fact Kamila Amblerová, of whom more later). She just laughed at me: "Nonsense!" So, I told her: "Every place we go into, I'll describe the door, the stairs, the banister, the door handle..." I hadn't been there since 1947, so it was a leap of about fifty years.

Believe it or not, it all fit, except for the somewhat flaky paint and the giant parasol mushrooms. Perhaps that is why I became an architect – as a child, I was already fascinated by that gorgeous, mysterious house, as it remains in my head to this day...

Like I said, I have always liked to eat, so the following memories are linked to the delight I felt at the local pub where we ate lunch. Dozens of house martins' nests were crammed under the roof of the large hall, with a shelf under them to stop the birds from pooing on the customers.

The house martins would catch flies for their young, making a racket, and I was in heaven – observing my beloved animals while stuffing my tummy. As well as my spoon, I had a kind of pusher – a handle with a little flat bit, like a miniature snow shovel – which I'd use to push the food onto my spoon with my left hand.

When my mother was in better health, she took poor unwanted baby Martin for a walk around Petřín Hill, where she was caught outside in the

Allied air raid that destroyed the house next to the Havel's. Today, it's Milunić's Dancing House. ItThe Allied forces also damaged Jirásek Bridge and bombed the spot on Národní třída where, three decades later, together with Míra Masák and Johny Eisler, we designed and built the Máj department store – now MY – which became a cultural monument. During the attack, my mother said, she lay over the pram to stop any stray shrapnel from piercing my little body.

Shortly after the war, a number of childhood diseases did a great deal of damage in Czechoslovakia. In 1945, half of all under-twos contracted tuberculosis, but I was lucky – I only got rickets. The treatment at the time was interesting; every day, I had to drink two glasses of raw whipped liver, washing it down with a big shot of fish oil. I fell in love with both – compared with the idiotic spinach and noodles the adults usually forced into me, it was much more adventurous. I've loved raw meat ever since.

My Mother's Family

My mother Věra, born in 1905, and her sister Milena, five years older, grew up very well-to-do. Their father, my grandpa, was the headmaster of the agricultural school, a deputy at the Imperial Council in Vienna, and the author of approximately twenty-seven academic publications on agriculture. He bought a farm of over three hundred hectares, a small brewery, and a forest, and travelled all over Europe studying the most modern developments in agricultural technology.

Milena, born in 1900, and my mother, five years her junior, lived with all the agricultural workers, brick-makers, but also with the teacher and mayor – my grandfather had established a tradition that everyone should eat at the same table. Since this was more than eighty people, my grandmother and her two staff helpers had their work cut out. From their stories, I understood it to be a strange, olde-worlde kind of life.

Grandpa died at the beginning of 1914, when Grandma, who had married him as a widower with

an adult son, was just a little over thirty-five. After he died, she tried to run the farm on her own, and when it proved to be beyond her, sold it with the help of her friends. She got seven million Gulden – a huge sum of money at the time – and deposited it in the bank on the so-called "orphan's security" scheme.

My mother and aunt should thus have been financially secure for life, but thirty years later, in 1953, came the currency reform, and suddenly it was all gone. My grandmother, aunt, and mother had not expected to face so scandalous a proposition as working for a living. (I viewed this part of my family history with a certain acrimony, because I had had to work for a living from the age of fifteen.) Aunt Milena, however, took an entirely pragmatic approach to the situation: she studied at night school and became a nurse. Eventually, she rose to become the director of diagnostics at the hospital in Motol. She began working at fifty-three, and continued to do so for twenty-five years, when, aged eighty-eight, she finally made it to retirement. In short, she showed herself to be a true child of her extremely hard-working father. I have to say I have always admired her for it.

Dad's Family

From a Bolshevik perspective, my father's background was not in his favour. His father – my grandfather – had a factory in Roztoky near Prague, where he made excellent cast-iron goods: scales, corkscrews. I still have one in use, it's the best of them all. This grandfather, poor sod, was not as successful as the other, and the factory went bust, so although my father was likewise born with a silver spoon up his ass,he still had to work for a living. There was even a question that grandpa wanted to commit suicide – apparently, he threw himself off a ferry into the Vltava, but to his humiliation, they rescued him. In the end, he died before the First World War. This is how my dad remembers those times in his diary:

"Our idyllic childhood days in Roztoky were at a close when the signs of financial ruin came to the doorstep. My father, probably a diligent

At the cabin in Maxov (1949)

Me and Tomík Plzenský, Maxov (1950)

LANGHANS
PRAGVE

bureaucrat, was certainly not a competent businessman. From an early age, I heard the words at home: due date, insolvency, decline, bankruptcy, like barbed wire strewn across the lawn where we played."

My other grandmother was of slighter stature, but very sprightly. We called her Little Nana. She started a dormitory for university students in Karlín, a district of Prague where my father began studying at the Realschule. Little Nana took impeccable care of the students – she substituted their families' nurture and prevented them from running wild. Various painters came under her care at some point, Joža Úprka – a painter with a keen interest in South Moravian folklore – among them.

My grandmother gave her son, my dad, an education in prudence towards life and money. He enrolled in the technical university and became an engineer. He worked organising international trade and industry, and in the nineteen-thirties, deep in the Great Depression, established Dorka with Franz Novotný:

Grandma Marie and Grandpa Alois Rajniš
(1898)

"Little Nana", my father Ivo, and Aunt Lída
(1911)

"In addition to providing me with a hiding place and an income, Dorka gave many a job and saved a number of young people from work in the Reich. But the factory was not just a profitable business afloat on the waters of the wartime boom. It was also established and run with an aesthetic focus and a social mission."

Mr Novotný might have been German in descent, but he was not a Reich German. He distanced himself from Nazism during the war, which was rightly judged as an act of courage. My father later told me how he had to steal him away to the American zone in the spring of 1945, because here, his German heritage put him in danger of lynching by a horde of informants trying to appease a rotten conscience. Franz Novotný then became the commercial director of a little company called Volkswagen. He helped me a lot, but the kind reader will have to wait a little longer for the details.

My father and Franz Novotný were very successful in Dorka, implementing Czech inventions, so that while others hung their heads and suffered unemployment, my father's business began to thrive. He wasn't even thirty when he began making decent money, in the 1930s, and shortly before 1948 he had even made it to the position of commercial director in the nationalised wood industry.

German Lessons with Nietzsche and Schopenhauer

Dad proved to be a very resourceful experimentalist with a propensity to invention, so, as soon as I was born, he began applying it with me. He said I needed to know foreign languages, German, if possible, and grasp the foundations of philosophy, and so, beginning at the age of three, he read to me for half an hour every day: one day in Czech, and the second day, the same material in the original.

To this day, I remember how the incomprehensible babbling scared me so much I developed a stutter. Needless to say, I did not learn German, and they had to take me to Professor Seman because of the stutter. Thank God, there is almost no trace of it left.

Around 1947, a beautiful young law student called Milda appeared in our house. My father had taken her on as my nanny. Although I was three and a half and she was twenty, we were instant friends. I loved her with all the might of my three-year-old heart, and Milda became a permanent part of our family for several decades.

She later lived with an avant-garde actor (apparently a communist, but I knew nothing about that then), and I was particularly charmed by the fact that he lived on a houseboat moored on the quay directly across from UMPRUM (known in Engilsh as the Academy of Art, Architecture and Design, UMPRUM is a prestigious university for applied and fine arts). Milda often took me for walks around there. She'd put me to sleep in the cabin so that I wouldn't disturb them, and the quacking ducks and croaking frogs formed a beautiful lullaby for me. Even today, I cannot imagine a better way to fall asleep.

Housing as a Reflection of Lifestyle

At the time, we lived right by the National Theatre in a house by the builder Radimský in Ostrovní Street. We occupied the entire mezzanine, which was very expensive, but my father never hesitated to stump up for a luxury lifestyle. I found the following passage about housing in a text of his:

"One's apartment and housing reflect a standard of living. When I got married, I rented an apartment in Ostrovní, and twenty-eight years later, I moved to a fantastic attic apartment in Malá Strana, originally adapted for E. F. Burian." (Burian was an innovator in music and theatre; one of the most important figures of the interwar avant-garde.)

We had a live-in maid and housekeeper in Ostrovní, and every two weeks, a laundress would come. I loved her. She was large, beautifully plump, with large breasts and a beautiful voice.

In the basement of the house was a huge laundry room with a massive drum washer, tubs, and a mangle. I spent a lot of time there – there was the centre of my universe, my rock. The mighty laundress with her beautiful shapes sang as if into

My childhood home, Ostrovní Street no. 7 (2016)

With my father, Prague (1947)

a forest, the clothes smelled of Helada-brand soap, with a deer on the packaging, and I was in seventh heaven.

Family Rituals and Taboos

Up to 1948, food was a ritual affair in our household. We barely cooked at home, but care was always taken to dine with all the appropriate gentility. Soup was always served from the soup bowl, there was always at least a small appetizer and dessert, and cutlery for every course, which really came in handy later on.

As a child, I was fascinated by the serving table with its wheels strung like a bicycle. I think my father's account of the table's repair, which I found in his notes, is worth retelling:

"During the Protectorate, I secretly bought a sheet of eighteen-carat gold, which would've gotten me the death penalty back then. I had considered that the 'reliably secure' hiding spots are usually discovered right away, so I threw the gold into a toolbox. Checking on them later, I was surprised to find that part of one of the sheets had been cut off. I racked my brains for the answer, which finally turned out to be quite simple: Some time ago, my wife asked the husband of a certain lady to repair the broken wheel on our serving table, which he did in our absence. He used a sheet of metal and then returned what was left over. And so it happened that we had a serving table with a solid gold wheel."

We barely ate Czech cuisine – sauce and dumplings – with only one exception: my father's favourite food was buřtguláš[1], which I still love to cook and eat today. I'd say that both my parents exhibited an almost obstinate intention not to succumb to the times. They were terrified of resembling a working-class family.

But in fact, my father was a passionate socialist! He believed in planning, equality, fair labour conditions, annual leave, pensions – the whole

1 A coarse sausage goulash, with added bacon. (Editor's note)

repertoire we know so intimately from years past. Because of his conviction, I had to watch him closely after the revolution and make sure he voted ODS. Thankfully at that time, he also accepted that I was the head of the family.

Mother was not accustomed to cooking daily and my father respected this, so we mostly ate at restaurants. We were regulars at Mánes and I was allowed to go into their kitchen: fragrant schnitzels floating in an enormous roasting pan full of lard seemed to me one of the wonders of the world.

Every morning, my grandmother took me to Café Slavia, where I admired the pinkish fountain, which in 1947 still had three fish swimming in it. After the victory of the people, one disappeared, and the last one snuffed it in '49…

There were a number of things that were simply not done in our family. Singing, for example. In order not to fail singing at school, I had to recite the anthem. Other than that, it was truly cultural despotism: I had to attend operas and concerts from the age of twelve and we were at the theatre every week. After a few years, I avoided the theatre at all costs, as a form of rebellion against my father.

My Father Ivo (1905–1995)

I feel like I should write a little more about my complicated relationship with my father. Today, I see our conflicts with different eyes, and I'm ashamed to have caused this difficult but in his own way exceptional person such torment. We're supposedly quite alike, after all – egocentric, competitive mules.

The building of the Mánes Union of Fine Artists, Prague (1932)

Mánes, the original interior design of the French restaurant, Prague (1930)

The empty fountain in the foyer of the Slavia café, Prague (2016)

My entire life, Dad never let me prove myself to him, to show that I was perhaps better at anything than he was. The more he denied it, the more vigorous my efforts were. On the one hand, he supported my confidence, but only when it didn't concern him – then he'd compete with me to the death! Our conflicts came to a head when I was around fifteen.

Looking back, I know I acted like an idiot and I'm not proud of it at all. But at fifteen, one has

a certain right to be immature. Shouldn't it be the adult who displays reason and understanding in the face of youthful imprudence and arrogance?

My father reprimanded me for behaving poorly: I threw cigarette butts on the carpet, my room was a mess, I napped after lunch... How should I have not, having just put down three beers? Apparently, I would not see a penny from him until I started behaving with some decency.

I didn't, and I really didn't see a penny from him for the next fifty years. Partly because I didn't need it. Truth be told, dad helped me in all the important ways. What he naively considered punishment was in fact a somewhat tougher form of the school of life. He was willing to cause himself serious medical issues in his obstinacy. Once, when I was about fifteen, he around fifty-five with a sick gallbladder, he had to prove to me that he could take the heavier backpack up a mountain. Halfway up he was struck down with terrible colic.

It's a sad and somewhat embarrassing admission, but up to the age of forty, I thought my father to be an idiot. Reading his diary today,

My father and his schoolmates, the Italian Riviera (1924)

My father Ivo, Prague (1985)

Ivo with Andulka, Maxov (1979)

I am once again convinced that the two of us could never have gotten along, but I also realise that he was very well-educated, one of the factors that allowed him to meet such excellent people. One of the groups he frequented was the Pátečníci, 'the Friday Club':

"What most sticks in my mind from the intoxicating age of the First Republic was an invitation to join the group which called itself the Pátečníci – every Friday, notable figures of public life would meet in the Čapek brothers' villa in Vinohrady. The president, T. G. Masaryk, would often join them. On that occasion, sadly, the president was absent, his chair near the door – as it always was in his absence – left empty. It was rumoured that the old man came from the Castle on foot, and even took an interest in how long it took him!"

My father never awakened natural respect, affection, and love within me. Now that I alone survive him, it makes me terribly sad. When I remember how arrogantly I laid into him about making more money than him, I feel ashamed.

Only at a very advanced age was my stubborn father able to admit that I am quite good at a number of things – and that I am physically more capable than him. He saw that despite my tragic school record, I am quite sharp, I can take care of myself, I can direct people, and, most importantly, I can make money, which was always particularly important to him.

Only in his final years did the demon within him subside, the demon that commanded him to triumph continually, even to crow over his opponent! He was incredibly well-read and had a photographic memory, so that he remembered entire encyclopaedia pages. He always enjoyed putting me down: "You're talking nonsense! The correct information is given on such-and-such page of so-and-so's encyclopaedia, please do look it up!" Wouldn't you just kill him? And I – what an idiot – couldn't rise above it! We wasted thirty-five years of our lives on this bickering, thirty-five years we could have spent so much better...

In principle, what I hated was the class elitism that flourished in our family. At the time, I almost gleefully observed how the Bolsheviks took us down a peg or two. I saw it as retribution for my family's hubris.

At the same time, I took great joy in trying to sabotage the Bolsheviks backstage, and at times I succeeded. I took my revenge for school, and despite all the injustices at home, also for the wasted lives of my parents: for my poor mother, her life burdened by disease, and finally, even for my father. Our parents' generation had it awfully tough. This is my father's succinct formulation, part of his meditation on the need to be born on a lucky planet.

"Chance plays a considerable role in human life. In other words, one should know to be born on a lucky planet. I'm afraid that I and my generation were born into bad times. Our youth was marked by the First World War. The revolution in 1918 and national independence was like the sunlit morning of a new life, but soon came the depression, followed by the

Second World War and communist dictatorship. Just as during the Protectorate, we were scared they might come for us at any time – formerly the Gestapo, then the StB[2]. When the Prague Spring broke out in 1968, it was a little late for our generation. We were already old and grey, plagued by the ailments of old age. Not to mention the revolution in 1989. . ."

Despite all this, my father was unbreakable. I observed him getting fired from his job again and again, until he ended up as a labourer on the factory belt. He never lost his energy and good spirit. Despite his occasional snobbery, he was a socialist and the people from the factory were his friends. He stuck to the motto: Everyone has the same stomach, so they deserve equal amounts of food and drink! This is how he put it:

"Since my youth as a poor boy, I tended towards socialism. It was the result of limited possibilities, my secondary school education, and to a considerable extent, the influence of literature. I lived with so-called lefty opinions, which is why I was sometimes referred to as the Little Bolshevik. However, I never identified with communist dogma, and of course I entirely rejected communism, particularly of the Soviet kind."

When my father's time came, he died at home. I arranged for nurses, a hospital bed, intravenous drips, doctors... He spent a long time in a kind of half-coma, absolutely terrified. As he neared the end, he spoke only German, which I understood, or French, which I pretended to.

This confirmed my conviction that life on Earth can be hellish. Why should we go through this? I am not bound by some higher being to serve my time in Hell on Earth and then enter up into heaven through the pearly gates, where I don't even want

My parents at the harbour below Vyšehrad
(1959)

My mom with Andulka, Maxov
(1970)

2 The StB, "Státní bezpečnost", were a secret police force to deal with any activity considered against the Communist Party of Czechoslovakia or the State.

to go. The thought of getting to a boring heaven full of angels really puts me off. If someone were to come up with a punishment for me, they'd send me to heaven. What goes on there, anyway? Could I work? Probably not.

In short, I refuse to allow fate and the whims of my body of late drag me around from hospital to hospital. Just in case, I have an escape planned out: apparently, it's enough to push a box of dry ice under your bed, and by morning, you're in complete calm and silence, with beautiful pink cheeks, dead.

In short, I believe both in a free life and a free death. My body, soul, and brain were not assigned to me. They simply came into being, and I alone bear responsibility for them. I am the spawn of billions of years of nature's development and I'm not about to let anyone tell me how to handle myself. I can't say I was born in complete freedom, but they could let me die the way I want. I am, of course, speaking only for myself...

Nevertheless, we needlessly demonise death. It's a natural part of life, so we should know how to cope with it. I believe that a time will come when people will depart surrounded by their family, friends, and acquaintances. They'll be invited to a party, they'll sit, drink, be merry, and say: "Well, Pepa is gone, may the earth rest lightly on him." I just hope it doesn't play out that modern medicine swallows up the entire GDP on keeping people alive to the age of a hundred and eighty. What an awful vision!

Films and My Father's Encounter with Otakar Vávra

I have mentioned the cultural despotism I was subject to, up to a certain point. Thus, I despised theatre, classical music, and opera, but I adored film – another thing I seem to have inherited from my dad. We were both fascinated by cinematography from a tender age. My father speaks about his friendship with the famous film director Otakar Vávra. :

"I became close with Ota Vávra back when he used to visit us in Ostrovní. Once, over a glass of cognac,

he spoke about being a true film director. To him, it meant that even the producers would go silent when he walked into the studio. Our friendship ended after the revolution, when I asked him in jest who he'd work with now, since both Mandlová and Baarová were locked up in Pankrác prison. He replied that he was no longer interested in the fate of individuals, but in the problems of the collective. Back then, he was already preparing to climb the social ladder as high as possible, and indeed, he became first a Distinguished and later a National Artist.. ." (These were titles which the communist regime conferred upon their favourite artists.)

Just like Dad, I was ready to go to the cinema three times a day, and I've still got that in me. The cinema helped me in my studies too, because, truth be told, I didn't give much time to revision – I studied a record seven days for my maths state exam at university.

Everything important was contained in this beautiful thick blue book full of mathematical definitions, formulas, and problems, and I worked out the following study regime: I'd get up in the morning and study for an hour, then go to the cinema at half past ten, then another hour and a half of studying, followed by the cinema at three. Then another hour and a half and the cinema again at eight.

Everything that happened on the screen touched me deeply – I remember cursing aloud when it all ended badly. This was before Hollywood had established the institution of the happy ending, so there were loads of films with sad endings.

To this day, a certain magical mood overtakes me in the cinema. My brain comes alive. You will not be surprised to learn, dear reader, that television was also banned in our household – perhaps that is partly the reason I still enjoy it today

I Don't Like Institutions

Religion was another one of the family taboos – both my parents were rigorous atheists. My mother studied at the French lyceum in Grenoble and she recounted to me how she struggled to talk her

The entrance to the Lucerna cinema, Prague
(30s)

classmates into going skiing with her on a Sunday – to them, missing Holy Mass was simply unthinkable.

My father was a proud fourth-generation atheist, and I am the fifth. It gives me no pride, but ending up in church is just as unacceptable to me as ending up in the drunk-tank – I am incredibly irritated by any and all institutional manipulations.

If I were to categorise myself, I'd say I'm a libertarian, anarchist, and right-wing-oriented bloke who believes in the power of human freedom and individuality guarded by internal controls, by which I mean laws, justice, fair trial, and fair treatment. That's what I have embraced, and I'll never give up on it.

My father believed in institution, so that the head of state was sacred to him – thank goodness he was no longer around for the recent presidential election, in which I, of course, vehemently supported Schwarzenberg – a member of a famous Czech aristocratic house who became the chancellor to my own president, Václav Havel, and later ran for president himself, losing to Miloš Zeman. I still have a poster in a window at my studio which proclaims that Zeman is not my president.

Schwarzenberg is an educated, kind, and good-humoured person. I have one sweet memory of him. Shortly after the revolution, I met him on the Orlík Dam and I said: "My friend named his dog after you."
"Schwarzenberg?" he asked.
"No, Karel."

I believe that most institutions – from schools and universities, prisons and the police, to entire platoons of bureaucrats, up to the government and the president – have failed tragically. Their dysfunctionality does much more harm than good, which led me to create my own solutions to certain questions of human society.

Because I have no illusions about the likelihood of implementation, I will take the liberty of sharing them with the kind reader.
First, in place of lengthy and toothless trials, I'd apply complete exclusion. I'd simply allocate

a part of the country to the thugs. There, they can commit their atrocities on one another.

Prison is a school of crime, and I don't see why we should spend such tremendous resources on the further education of thousands of rogues in the field. They'd simply be thrown into their enclosed ghetto in which their harsh laws apply, so they'd probably have a pretty shit time. There'd probably be a high death rate, which seems to me like a pretty logical punishment for what they did to decent people.

I admit my idea of life in a community is much looser than most. For example, I think schools are built on educating average, orderly, obedient citizens that the state can easily manage. But that isn't my ideal at all!

The most agreeable and educated kids I met were on ships and in ports, where families on their way around the world were anchored. Their children don't go to normal schools – their parents teach them in the cabin. But they learn most from what happens around them. And a mighty lot happens in ports. A capability to combine imagination with courage, to come up with one's own solution to any situation – nobody can do it better than they can. Those are people of my tribe – I like them.

It was a tribe of this kind that we tried to establish with Jakub Cígler at the Architecture 1 studio at UMPRUM, where I taught many years later. We advocated the idea that nothing was impossible. "Don't say something can't be done! Say right away that you can't do it!" In the spirit of this motto, we organised wild trips with minimal budgets for the students, because we tried to make these trips available even to the poorest students. That's the best way to form a team.

The Nordic Heroes of My Childhood

Most little children have their favourite fairy-tale heroes. I had none – I was the hero of all of my stories. There was no television, so my real heroes were the arctic explorers father talked and read

Roald Amundsen (1899)
National Library of Norway
photograph by Daniel Georg Nyblin

to me about. Dad was always drawn to the Nordic lands – resisting the cold seemed to him manlier than facing tropical heat.

My father got me into the stories of the young Amundsen, who during a winter crossing of Jostedalsbreen (the closest wild mountain range to Trondheim) spent the night in an igloo, but his beard froze to the ice overnight. He couldn't move and very nearly died there. However, he was a tough and ingenious guy – he breathed and huffed with such intensity that, over the course of a few hours, he managed to melt the ice that had frozen on his beard and break free. Another hero of mine was the explorer Sven Hedin. At first, I listened breathlessly to my dad, but once I could read, I devoured these travelogues myself.

Even so, I must say I was most fascinated by looking out of the window of our country house. As a little boy, I imagined walking through the infinite forest to Poland, along the Pomeranian lakes to the Baltic and on past the Arctic circle, where the forest turns to tundra. Then comes the Arctic Ocean, which in my imagination I always overcame with a leap to land somewhere in the midst of a large herd of reindeer. Then I ran on until I reached the Tian Shan mountain range and entered the Gobi desert, where I nearly froze to death at night and expired in the heat during the day. This is something I later experienced for real, not in the Gobi desert but in Bolivia's Altiplano.

The Incident with the Locomotive and the Ashtray

Between 1945 and '48, my dad travelled around Europe, closing deals for the nationalised wood industry and bringing me fantastic toys. Among my absolute favourites were a real steam engine; you'd light a fire, the boiler would pressurise, then you'd open the tap and it wheezed and spun like a devil. Then a Swedish metal locomotive you'd wind up with a key, and finally a Merkur (Meccano) building set, which is probably the reason I am such a keen builder to this day.

I spent virtually all of the summer in Římov, with Aunt Milena taking care of me. My father would take me there on the express train. Once, me, my dad, my little rucksack and the metal locomotive boarded in Prague and raced off to see Aunt Milena. There was a girl in our compartment, who immediately seemed to me to be suspect. My dark misgivings were soon confirmed: she touched my locomotive, which I saw as an attack on my person.

As I was already cunning back then, I waited for a tunnel and then lunged in the dark and bit her. She began screaming her head off and her mummy got us kicked off the train. My father, an upstanding citizen whose copious respect for state institutions included the railway, was in complete shock. I had brought terrible shame upon him, and I don't think he ever forgave me.

But the episode had one positive effect – dad stopped reading me the German classics. In fact, he was beginning to suspect that despite his upbringing, I would probably never be a genius. This suspicion was confirmed by the following incident.

Franta Rachlík (my father's friend) had a son, Mikuláš. We were really good friends. Today, he is the renowned Italian painter Mikula Rachlik. Back then, Mikuláš was celebrating his sixth birthday and our entire family was on the guest list. I didn't really want to go. I had a weird premonition that the visit would go badly.

We set out from Ostrovní into the misty autumn evening all the way to the Petřín funicular, where the Rachlíks lived in a modern apartment house. The door opened and I froze: the birthday boy was wearing a white-and-blue sailor's outfit, with the classic square collar and sailor's cap! It was my dream of dreams.

That was far from all I longed for. He also had long johns. Yet still, this was not everything: he sat down at the piano – we didn't have a piano – and sung in his falsetto and accompanied himself and everyone smiled and praised him. In short, he was the centre of attention.

The Škoda PV15 steamroller (20s)

The Škoda Sentinel with its lowered floor for transporting rubbish bins (1930s)

The funeral of president Edvard Beneš, parade on Národní třída, Prague (September 8th, 1948)

It was too much for me. I grabbed a huge ashtray made of dark green glass and shot Mikulka down, down from his piano stool with a single well-aimed shot to the head. It was a miracle that I didn't kill him, merely splitting his lip and knocking a tooth out. Everyone went numb with amazement. But I got my way – they took Mikulka's cap off, he stopped playing and singing, and I became the centre of attention.

I'm sure the idea crossed my father's mind that he shouldn't have yielded to the grandmothers; that he should have got rid of that damned alcoholic foetus. They hurriedly stuffed me into my coat and off home we went. I vividly remember =, my father telling my mother that this would need institutional treatment. I didn't know what it was; I imagined it might be some healthy canned fruit they'd force down my throat. My mother comforted him: "Relax, Ivo, it'll even out."

Mikula Rachlík forgave me. My parents also forgave me, and – after a longer period of hesitation – so did the Rachlíks. And me and Mikula remain best friends to this day.

Life in the Centre of Prague

The surroundings of Ostrovní and this entire part of central Prague influenced me greatly. There were very few cars back then, but you could see my beloved steamroller and the Sentinel steam cars. But my favourite was the post, with its horse-drawn blue cars. The post coachman was sat in the front. At the back was a small seat you could grab onto and ride along, but the coachman hated this. He was able to crack his whip behind his back with brilliant precision, stinging the intruder on the back of their neck – awfully painful. At the time, only two private cars were parked in Ostrovní Street and no others appeared over the course of the next ten years.

Living in the centre of Prague was also fantastic because everything appeared to us first-hand. When President Beneš died, for example, I observed the funeral procession snake its way along the river past the National Theatre. I was most impressed by the butchers. They walked past in their chequered clothes wielding huge axes – under the strength of this impression, I wanted to become a butcher for some time.

I was also fascinated by rubbish collection vehicles, so that following my butcher phase I wanted to be a binman. My boundless admiration for these strong fellows has never disappeared.

My careless pre-school period was full of kind adults willing to talk to me about picture books, transformers, machines, and also to laugh at the political anecdotes I recounted with gusto and without comprehension.

There was this joke, for example: There are many asses in Bohemia – most are edible (jedlý) but one is inedible (Nejedlý – Nejedlý was the communist Minister of Culture, and responsible for many of the socialist realist reforms in the 1950s). I would let that out in some select company or other, adding what I'd heard at home – that they'd lock up my father. Everyone laughed, but it later turned out I wasn't so far from the truth.

With Pavel Frieb and his sister Marta at the Točná airport (1953)

With my schoolmates (1955)

School – A Factory of Suffering (1951–1962)

—

Elementary School

In 1951, I started first grade. In short, I couldn't imagine something as disgusting as school, not even in my worst nightmares. I suddenly found myself among unknown screaming children I wasn't accustomed to and towards whom I felt only disgust.

I didn't have any friends. The only boys I spoke to were Pavel Frieb, Franta Císař, and Bréťa Ackermann – I still remember their names, but I've tried to block out most people and events from elementary school. The exception is a jolly memory of a school trip to the zoo which went particularly well.

The school I attended in Ostrovní Street had been (and is now once again) administered by the order of the Ursulines, who were then kicked out, rounded up, thrown in jail, and replaced by the most trusted of cadres, among which was our deputy principal. We all despised him, but worse than that, I was terribly afraid of him. Often, while falling asleep, I imagined how one day, when I grew up, I'd grab him, knock him down to the ground,

School photograph, third grade, M.R. is the third from the right in the third row counting from the bottom (1953)

School photograph, sixth grade, M.R. is in the middle of the first row (1956)

jump around on his body, stomp on his neck, break his fingers one by one, then his arms and legs, and generally inflict every evil in the world on him,that I could think of.

Our teacher was called Lupínková and I didn't make the best first impression. You see, my good friend Tom Plzenský had taught me how to pee over a bus. For those for whom no mental image springs to mind, I append an explanation: One grabs one's penis at the end, fills it with wee, and then pushes down while letting it loose like a fountain so it can fly over a tram and reach someone on the other side. I was trying to get the boys' respect by demonstrating practically that I could piss up to the ceiling, and of course Lupínková came in at the worst possible moment.

You can imagine what followed. I'll say right away that – to my father's utter despair – I never received a report card that was not marked down for behaviour in my entire time as a schoolboy.

These terrible times also contain the one cheerful memory of my school years: the trip to the zoo, imprudently organised by Lupínková. It's important because, exceptionally, I wasn't the idiot – it was that imbecile Ouhrabka – but also because I (together with the monkey and the elephant) really wiped the floor with Lupínková...

This educational excursion to the zoo began – particularly for us boys – with something very interesting: the mating of the ostriches. We didn't know this polite bird had an almost metre-long dick reminiscent of a sewage pipe. This act left a profound impression on all those present. To the great joy of the students, a monkey then stole our stupid teacher's glasses, hid them in its lair, and refused to surrender them – even to the caretaker.

The imbecile Ouhrabka crowned the trip. While we were on the tram, someone sat on the cake his mother had made him, so he offered it to the elephant, who inhaled it and then delivered a mighty sneeze. A revolting mixture of crumbs and slime flew out of its trunk, covering Ouhrabka from head to toe. The humiliated teacher, still without her glasses, convinced one of the caretakers to make Ouhrabka human again by hosing him down, and only then could the jolly class and the furious teacher return to school. How beautiful!

Later, me and Ouhrabka got into a fight. I ate dirt while his great big arse crushed me victoriously. From then on, I noted that fist-fighting was not my strong point,and talked my way out of every fight that followed – I can do a lot more with my mouth than my fists.

I detested school from the depths of my infant soul. I was terrified of it, but it was the cruel and evil Bolshevik deputy principal who scared me the most. He used teaching methods that were truly Gestapo-like. I remember that he once punished us five boys for an innocent snowball fight by making us stand at attention facing the wall for four hours.

When I remembered him during breakfast, I began vomiting immediately, and since after a certain point I was always remembering him, there were few breakfasts at our table that would go by without retching. Thankfully I developed some sort of eczema, and the doctor – under my understanding mother's kind pressure – concluded that I was infectious and could not go to school. Put plainly, this institution made me an entirely poorer human being, and try as I might, I could not succeed. Because I was not able to fulfil the bizarre criteria which divided the successful from the failures, I learned to circumvent everything through tricks and scams.

It took me a long time to realise that in fact, school wasn't so important. The spectrum of knowledge required is an artificially and notably deformed sector rid of autonomy, freedom, and a number of other things without which life – at least for me – is unthinkable.

It took me eight years to understand that if they were playing dirty, I'd have to do the same. Eight years of concentrated suffering, trying to find out what it was they wanted from me. None of what I could do counted, and the other way around: the things I couldn't do due to dyslexia and dysgraphia were crucial to them.

I couldn't come to terms with the stress of my first failure and my father's disappointment. He was desperate when he saw his son failing in comparison to other children from working families. I couldn't write, read, count, or communicate, meanwhile the sons and daughters of doorkeepers and cleaning ladies increased their lead on me up to light-years.

Grandma with Little Nana; School Gets Worse

Put plainly, elementary school caught me entirely unprepared for institutional tuition. There was even a suggestion that I go to a special needs school. When I failed to learn to read even in third grade, Little Nana intervened and began reading Božená Němcová's Grandma with me. I think back to those times when I was terrifically interested in the stories of the people from the book, and for a long time, I was able to narrate entire long passages by heart. I had liked Němcová, until school made her perfectly disgusting to me.

After two months of gruelling daily sessions lasting several hours, I finally began to understand how the little squiggles related to my native tongue, and behold, I learned to read. I had only relatively got a grip on spelling by the age of around twenty-five – for a left-handed child forced into right-handedness, with dyslexia and dysgraphia to boot, this was a huge burden! Perhaps this is part of the reason all teachers seemed the personification of all evil to me.

My father had a hard time accepting that our doorkeeper's Pepička put me to shame almost without effort. His son wasn't even capable of the most basic tasks! Once again, his notion that I was an unsuccessful specimen was confirmed, and though he probably did not see it as a punishment, at around the same time, he introduced another of his educational experiments – polar training.

Deep in the 1950s, my elementary school experiences were a chasm in my life, a catastrophe from which I spent decades recovering. I was used to grown-ups, and one of the things that shocked me about school was being forced to take part in this boundless boredom. A tired and poorly paid teacher bellows out things the children cannot digest, without interest or an opinion.

It seemed to me that in a whole day at school, nobody said anything that would lead to me becoming reasonably informed about anything I enjoyed. And if something interesting did come up, or something great and beautiful, they reliably managed to fuck it up for me – like Karel Hynek Mácha. Whenever I'm feeling shit I say a few stanzas from May to myself, and I'm comforted. School even managed to ruin this fine thing for children.

I was recently filling in a questionnaire in which I declared that I'd prefer to abolish the school system along with a number of other institutions. I'm dead serious about that. For a number of people such as myself, school – at least up to the age of fifteen – was an utter, almost a wilful waste of time, intellect, creativity, will to live, and motivation to work.

Attending school was like cholera or the plague. I didn't like a single teacher. Some of them I hated so much that if I'd had the power, I would've killed them. They aroused a fear in me that was close to panic.

Only much later did I realise that school, really, is more of a charade From the incredibly varied world-perspectives possible, school infallibly selects the murkiest of narrow, bureaucratically processed segments. And the bored child's mind takes in nothing. In a way, it's good that the brain is set up this way, and whatever doesn't conjure up strong emotions is practically impossible to remember. I remember the hours of fear and boredom, but I remember nothing of what they tried to teach us, so I had to learn a number of things from scratch later.

Education hurt me so much I thought about suicide almost every day. Later, this became more of an urge to kill them. With hindsight, I know they weren't actually bad. Just not very clever. If I had had at least had some experience from nursery school, it might have gone better. But on the other hand, without this childhood torment, my total rebellion would probably not have reached its full dimensions.

It was my hatred of school that made me an unbeliever in the standard forms of teaching. And the fact that I ended up being a successful pedagogue – I consider that one of the greatest paradoxes of my life.

My Tormentor, Twenty Years Later

Once, when I was about thirty, I was walking down Národní třída, and suddenly, I saw him from behind, his hunched back. Don't be surprised that I recognised him straight away – throughout my childhood, he was the incarnation of all evil to me. My heart beat harder: "That's him!"

I sped up, and in a flash, I was hobbling along right up beside him.

He suddenly stopped. His hands started shaking. I don't think he could have recognised me – more than twenty years had passed. "I probably hurt you, right? I've hurt so many people..." he said in the scared tone of a hunted animal. "Don't hurt me, please, don't hurt me!"

Glacier, the Arctic (2016)

The Stalin monument, Prague (1955)

The demolition of the Stalin monument, Prague (1962)

I'm not a big guy, but his bowed head barely reached my shoulder. Although he had turned my tender years into hell, I could not enact my revenge. I just couldn't. From that point, I decided that if ever some asshole wronged me, I'd settle the score there and then.

Polar Training

The year was 1954 and I was nine years old. Because my father had run out of money, we had to make do with half of our original floor space. Our home was suddenly a squeeze and I moved into the room once inhabited by the housemaids.

I've mentioned my father's polar training. What did it consist of? My father opened the window and hammered in huge nails that fastened the shutter to the frame so no one could close it. Regardless of the season, the window was always ajar. He turned the heating off and confiscated the black control wheel. He took my duvet and replaced it with an itchy military blanket. He even confiscated my pyjamas and said: "You'll be sleeping naked from now on." I was alright with this last point; I quite enjoyed being naked, just like I do today. And so I lived, for a number of years.

But I have to say I didn't feel particularly bullied. I thought that was how everyone lived, and it never occurred to me that other children had duvets, pillows, pyjamas, windows which closed, and the heating on. Mum didn't protest because she was also used to a tough upbringing. Grandpa was a rich but hard entrepreneur, and he also gave his children a Spartan upbringing, so it must have seemed perfectly normal to Mum that her child should be used to the cold.

I was fit as a fiddle and only started getting sick when we stopped with the polar training. Then I had several bouts of tonsillitis and they had to remove my tonsils. But I remained fit except for the occasional injury here and there. I practically had no need for a doctor until the age of forty-five. Around me, colleagues thirty or forty years younger would get ill several times a winter, but I held out.

Later, in Iceland, I even bet on a crate of whisky with some of my students: could I swim around the glacier? The cold was terrible, but I made it, so we spent several weeks getting wasted on the excess of whisky I'd won. I was so used to the cold I could wear only a shirt in ten degrees below zero. And gloves? I didn't even know what they were.

So, when I finally learned to read, my father gave me the biographies of all the polar explorers. Nansen, Amundsen, Sverdrup, General Nobile... Alone – the great novel by Evelyn Byrd... I'm really awfully thankful to Dad for the polar training. It was more than useful many times in my life. And although I said goodbye to my father for thirty-five years, I always considered the polar training one of the greatest victories of my life.

Childhood Memories of the Bolsheviks

After finishing first grade, I came to dad and said I had another daddy.
"What daddy is that?"
"His name is comrade Stalin," I replied. "He's my daddy now, he thinks about me, he loves me very much, and I am to think of him every night when I fall asleep. And then I'll be a Jiskra and then a Pionýr." (Jiskra – "Spark" – and Pionýr – "Pioneer" – were the communist equivalent of the Scouts.)

My father was petrified. He put me on his lap – not a usual occurrence with him – and he said: "Well, dear boy, now listen to who this daddy of yours, Stalin, is."

I found the following letter in my father's memoirs:

"I remember an incredible story from the early '50s. My son, then a first-grader, came back from school and asked his grandma whether it was true that his grandpa, who used to own a factory, shot the factory workers with a rifle, like comrade teacher had told them."

The funeral of the mass murderer Klement Gottwald, Prague (1953)

A Gottwald postage stamp (1953)

My father was very well informed, so he knew about the gulags, the tens of millions dead, about hunger in Ukraine... He told me everything and then added: "And now you have to strengthen yourself with patience, get your wits together, and pluck up your courage. You have to realise the teachers are paid to lie to you. But you can't let them know that you know."

"And what would happen?" I pried.

"Nothing to you, but they'd lock me and mum up and then you'd have to live in a home and go to school all the time."

This petrified me, so instead of going from a Jiskra to a Pionýr, I went from Jiskra to a Dissident.

This was a formative moment, and believe me when I say that I remember every word Dad said. So when, say, Professor Šik's boy – born in Switzerland with a silver spoon up his ass – is yelling at me, spewing lefty theories at me, it falls off me like mud off a sturdy elephant.

My other childhood memories relating to the Communist regime were also hellish. It was the autumn of 1953, after the currency reform, and we were on our way to school as normal. A few metres from the window of our classroom was this small balcony, and on it swung the hanging bodies of an elderly couple who had lost all their savings. Ms Lupínková, that revolting, cowardly hyena, commented: "Children, take a good look! Those are profiteers – finally struck down by the fist of the working class! finally

The trial of the conspiracy around Rudolf Slánský had the following epilogue at school. We received an order: "Children, open your reading books, grab your glue, and stick page seventeen and page eighteen together. Then take your ink and black out lines eight through twenty-one on page nineteen." And so, we edited history as instructed by comrade teacher.

When mass murderer Klement Gottwald kicked the bucket in '53, my father spent his last money on a bottle of wine and he and my mother celebrated. I guess it'll come as no surprise that when the first protests against the communist regime took place, I was among the first by Mácha's statue on

Petřín Hill. Nor could I miss, much later of course, November 17th, when the cops broke my nose and gave me a concussion.

Another grand event of my school years involved policemen – me and my friend, Honza Duda, built a two-stage rocket. We used a saturated solution of sodium chlorate in which we submerged blotting paper from our schoolbooks. Dried up, these created powerful fuel for our rocket. We called it Vega 3, after the Americans.

Take-off was on Střelecký Island, but the rocket exploded prematurely. There was an explosion and policeman began gathering by the National Theatre for a raid. We saw ourselves in juvenile hall, but in the end we managed to slip out. We climbed onto a narrow ramp on a pillar above the water where the policemen couldn't see us. But they set up camp, and we had nowhere to run. After three hours, my legs could no longer carry me and I slipped silently into the water. I managed to hold with only my hands.

When the police finally gave up and left, we made a fire from chestnut leaves to dry me off a little, but it only served to make me smell awful. "Mum, I fell into the water and I wanted to dry out," my unconvincing explanation went. "I understand!" – Mum understood a young man's occasional need for discretion.

Rockets held my attention for a long time, but in the end, I took a different path. But it's true that almost all of the lookout towers I designed later are inspired by the shape of rockets. Moreover, the most perfect tower in the world – the Eiffel Tower – is probably just a well-camouflaged spaceship that will one day fly off into space.

Maxov (1949–2034)

—

In 1949, dad bought a cabin in the Jizera Mountains for two thousand crowns. This is how he described his feelings at the time:

"I kept walking up the hill and away from the road, away from other people. Clouds chased across the sky in the bleak weather, and when the mist finally cleared, I saw her – the last lonely cabin on the very tip of the hill. It had a fantastic view. I said to myself: 'That's her!'"

I perceive a certain Zen principle in his selection. At least from one side, one keeps one's eyes on the horizon – the large world – whilst also observing the small world. Only then can one achieve spiritual balance. Poor dad had so little money at the time, he divided the sum into a hundred equal payments of twenty crowns. In place of school, then, me and Mum could go to our cottage in Maxov, where I experienced permanent holidays. There were cows grazing under our windows, fragrant pastures – in short, everything was nice there.

We would travel to the cabin in Mr Bubla's truck, as the Germans took dad's car (a fantastic six-cylinder Ford which my father loved, just as he loved fast driving) during the occupation, so we were left without a car. Just like the others, we had to make do with rattling along under the tarp of Mr Bubla's truck. The stench was unbelievable – partly due to the punctured exhaust pipe, partly due to the vomit of poor sods like myself.

The journey from Prague took four hours or more, depending on how well we managed to overcome the hill near Sychrov: It was nicknamed the Magnetic Mountain, because people believed something weird was going on with the magnetic fields there. That was usually where our truck would pop its lid and we had to wait for it to cool down.

Cottage Regime

Visits to the cabin, or 'cottage' as Czechoslovaks called them, had a routine in the 1950s. Back then people still worked on Saturday mornings, so my father whizzed home by two while my mother packed two large sacks of supplies. The hits of the summer back then were: halasle, which was a very good fish soup for three crowns, and then

a crab called chatka (known in English as the red king crab or Kamchatka crab). Today it costs over a thousand crowns, back then, it was five. Oh, and roast aubergines with garlic from Bulgaria.

Bubla left Prague around half two and we only arrived at our destination after dark. We dragged the sacks into the cottage and started taking things out of their hiding places. We had to hide everything – the riffraff around there had burgled our cabin three times.

In order to protect the cottage, my father installed bars across the windows and – him being an electrical engineer – an alarm on the doors and windows too; simple battery-operated switches. But the first thing the burglars took was the battery. The alarm system's second failing came to light when Dad lent the cottage to his friends without instructing them to disarm it. When they opened the door, the alarm began wailing furiously. Labourers armed with axes ran out of the woods and beat our guests until everything was explained. So finally, it came to it that we simply hid things.

Football at the cabin (1952)

The Maxov cabin (2014)

After arriving, then, we spent up to three hours getting the duvets out of their hiding places – they were wrapped in military tarps – so we only sat down to eat after midnight. In the meantime, my mother would usually make buřtguláš (by that time the sausages were actually made of meat) which my father and I desperately looked forward to. We mashed the potatoes and, even seven years after the food shortages of the war, ate slowly and ritualistically, with cries of bliss.

Here, my parents created a beautiful world for me, of light, warmth from the stove, filled stomachs and boundless affection, and I enjoyed it fully. But the weekend was short and back in Prague, the hellish world of elementary school still awaited. We woke up on Sunday morning and around noon began to put everything back in its hiding place, because Bubla left at five. There were at least thirty of us holidaymakers in the back of the track, shivering like chihuahuas in winter. For me, the experience was further coloured by the fact that I had to fight for a place from which I could vomit over the side.

True, the trips to the mountains were a little over our budget, but we wouldn't have given up walking on the meadows, eating breakfast and dinner together, and all those beautiful cottage moments for anything in the world. And when the worst came to the worst financially, dad sold individual volumes of his Encyclopaedia Britannica, or jewellery and paintings...

Part of the reason we worked so well together as a community in the mountains was because my father and his friends had all bought cabins in the same place. They were also like-minded in opinion, so we lived very happy lives there.

Different cottages were inhabited by different families. The most prolific was the Záhora clan, so that the fourth and fifth generations no longer fit in the cabin. Then, there was the Tobolka clan, stemming from the famous secretary of the First Republic senate, PhDr. Tobolka. Their family branched out into other cottages outside Maxov, but the weight of this clan was indisputable. Only I am alone in my extensive cottage. I often feel like a Russian in Siberia, inhabiting an enormous,

empty country while the Chinese procreate next door, in order to probably one day beat us to death with their caps.

Jára Horník, a few years my junior, was an excellent friend. At first he came to Maxov to visit his uncle, but later inherited the cottage from him. Jára moved here and began farming. He took meticulous care of his rabbits and goats, he even started breeding ponies. For us, he was something like a mayor, though I'm sure if we'd cast votes at the time he'd have been the actual mayor, and an excellent one at that. Tom Plzenský, my best friend, is the son of one of Tobolka's daughters, who also married – what else – a lawyer. Then there was JUDr. Rón, who lived in the next cottage over.

The older kids in our group came up with the idea of holding an Olympic Games, each of us representing a different country. Everyone wanted to be America, France, England, or Canada, and I can proudly say that among us, the Soviet Union did not even qualify!

The event, however, was cut short by my participation in the archery event, because I shot an arrow into my friend Tom Plzenský's head –

With Tom Plzenský in Maxov (2012)

We from the Scholzberg cabin, Upper Maxov. We've been here for sixty-five years! By the Brechschmied chapel.
J. Dostál and his daughter Linda, S. Dostál, O. Dostálová, K. Čepková, O. Čepek and his daughter Bára, J. Plzenský, M. Rajniš, T. Plzenský, B. Plzenská, R. Tobolka sr., E. Tobolková and her granddaughter Raja, J. Čepková, P. Čepek, J. Tobolka, Z. Tobolka, V. Tobolková, R. Tobolka jr. and his son Emil, D. Plzenská and her son Vojta, L. Tobolka, J. Horník with Čert
(October 28th, 2005)

thankfully, only skin-deep. He ran screaming into his parents' room, stuck like a redskin in a game of Cowboys and Indians. He was captured, the arrow extracted, and the Olympics stopped. And I was banned forever from participating in shooting contests.

Other than that, the Olympics were great – more than twenty children from eight families competed, and the disciplines included running, throwing, jumping, archery, cycling, rope-climbing, tug of war...

Another favourite activity of ours was battling in bunkers. The Germans had left piles of stones on the meadows. We made bunkers in these. We'd run out in parties of varying sizes, brandishing soil and stones and attacking each other. The pieces of soil were softer weapons, but when the going got tough, stones wrapped up in mud would fly through the air. Our sweatpants were soaked but we didn't stop running around until night-time.

In order to have as much time for my gang as possible, I'd force up to seven slices of bread into me for breakfast and only returned in the evening. We ran through the forests, built dams on the stream, inflated some unlucky frogs and made zoos of salamanders – paradise, in short.

These were the beautiful years of 1957 and '58. In the winter, we'd climb up the hills so that we could ski down, and the trips! – I still admire my parents' courage – they let me, a twelve-year old boy, visit my friend Láďa Rufr in Svatý Petr in the Krkonoše Mountains.

I'd take my skis and rucksack on the bus to Harrachov, then climb up Lysá hora so I could ride down Labský důl to Horní Mísečky and onwards to Špindlerův Mlýn. Quite a distance! I set out at dawn and got there at dusk. People were terribly surprised when they saw a little boy by himself, but my parents knew I was fit, so they weren't scared. Perhaps they weren't aware of the danger of avalanches. I barely managed to keep my pants dry sometimes, but I was always proud of having made it.

Thanks to my polar training, I didn't need gloves, and if it were necessary, I could easily have slept in the snow. My body had been trained to sleep in temperatures bordering on freezing – my room was only about five degrees warmer than outside. It went so far as the neighbours complaining about the cold affecting their apartments. The director Čeněk Duba, who knew I walked over half of Krkonoše on my own, even invited me to a casting for his film about Václav Vrbata, but I could not get a single word out in front of the camera. No film career for me.

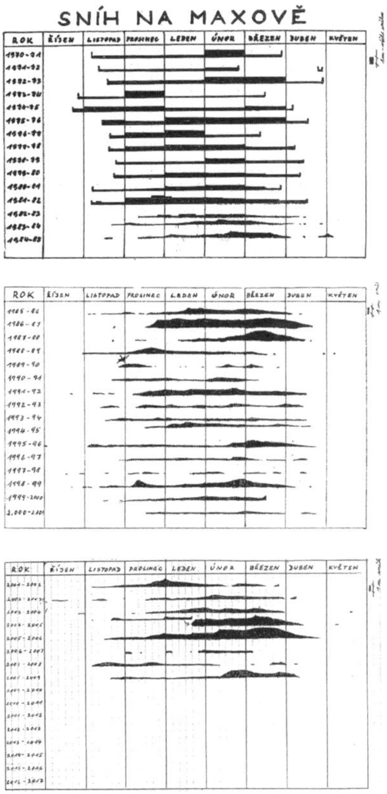

There were often film screenings near our cottage, on Bramberk Mountain. I remember how I once saw Sorcerer with Yves Montand. Unfortunately, the projector stopped working several times during the screening, the sawdust stove exploded, and there was a snowstorm to boot, so the event stretched out long past midnight.

My father was worried, so he came to pick us up. We saw his flashlight approaching, and we went "Hooo!" This got my father – who was already quite pissed-off anyway – riled up to the extent that he lost control and gave me a few smacks, the only time in my life. He lay into me, screaming: "I'll show you 'hooo'!" Afterwards he felt very guilty to have broken his own rule. Whenever I did anything, I wouldn't get a beating – instead, I would receive a lecture lasting several hours on the topic of what I'd done, what the cause was, what the consequences could have been, and how I needed to go deep within myself and search for my inner strength... It was a hundred times worse than a beating.

Perhaps that's why I'm so chatty – just like dad, I can talk for hours and hours, which can be a problem for other people. And so, I am understanding with my students: I throw cans of Red Bull at them to stir them into action.

Poster for the film *Salair de la Peur le; The Wages of Fear* (1953)

Graphs of snow cover at Maxov as recorded by Jaroslav Horník (1970–2009)

My father spent a long time apologising to me after the beating. I didn't understand. Back then, I didn't know that his world was full of rigorous rules of behaviour which he could not violate under any circumstances. I was never a stickler for rules, though, so my later rebellion was an escape into freedom where not only did his rules not apply – almost no rules applied.

When I escaped this straitjacket, I ran wild. It took a long time before I understood that I had to set my own rules. I did so by trial and error, until I found a way to organise my life without (I hope) harming others too much.

I was infinitely grateful to dad for buying the cottage, and I still am today. We were all happy there, it was good for Mum; and for me, it was an absolute boyhood paradise. To this day it is my refuge, my nest, where I most like to be. Dad loved it too:

"Staying at the cottage was good for my wife's illness, and when the time came, she found eternal peace by a large stone on our meadow, under a forged metal tombstone made by the sculptor Kurt Gebauer. My dates, as well as my son's, are also ready.. ."

The decision to place my father's name and my own on the tombstone despite the fact that we were very much alive had a somewhat tragicomic epilogue. People would visit and ask me: "Dear God, Martin, are you going to commit suicide or what? Why did you put your name on the tombstone with only the date of birth?" "It's obvious! If we're getting this fantastic tombstone done by Kurt Gebauer, do it all in one go. For all three of us! I'm sure it'll be cheaper..."

High School (1958–1962)

—

When I was fourteen, I wanted to go to a SVVŠ – gymnasiums, at the time, were called střední všeobecně vzdělávací škola; general education high schools. But getting in when you came from a branded family was a tough nut to crack. That was the only time my mother implored me to get good grades, and especially: no problems with conduct.

I was intending to oblige, but then we went on the elementary school skiing trip. Thanks to mum and her lessons in Maxov, I was a much better skier than the instructor, so I showed off and my friend Láďa Rufr paid the price (the poor sod jumped off a railway bridge later in life, due to unrequited love).

Back to the trip: we were rowdy, playing tag, and somehow, I accidentally closed a glass door right in front of Láďa's face. He fell through it and cut his nose open. There were streams of blood and any chance of a clean report card was lost.

My grades improved towards the end of the nine years of elementary, as I began feeling that the going was about to get tough. The task of deciding which school they'd shove me into and whether I'd manage secondary education at all had arrived. My parents were very nervous about it, because a vocational school would have been shit.

Unfortunately, it turned out that here too, I had bad luck in teachers. The principal of the high school in Braník which accepted me used to be the principal at the school in Štěpánská. She was feared, a communist harpy, and having a child placed under this swine's skirts was considered a family tragedy.

Her zeal is well-illustrated by the following episode: two boys, chasing each other around the school corridors, knocked over the busts of Stalin and Gottwald. Following an investigation by the monstrous woman, aimed at sending the kids to juvenile hall and their parents to jail, one of the poor young bastards was so stressed that he jumped out a window and died on the spot. In 1958 this was too much, even for the Communists, so they relocated their tribeswoman to the school in Braník where people were sent as punishment. That's where I ran into her.

The building of my high school in Braník (2016)

High School in Braník

At the time, Braník was a gardeners' periphery with a slowly decomposing ice factory and a number of local suburban characters. The only fun thing was the tram; you could jump on and off while it was in motion. At first, I felt desperate, but in the end, it was actually pretty amazing.

I was sat next to Milan Vaněček, who became a member of the Academy of Sciences at the department of solid matter. I was safe in the knowledge that he was cleverer than me, but I wasn't jealous. A certain Magda was just as clever. Then, the strengths of one Renata Bartoňová were a gorgeous pair of breasts and a beautifully round bum. There were few other places in the centre of Prague where I could have found female associates who wouldn't hesitate to stick a match in their pussy horizontally and have their picture taken, just to make the boys happy. There were also few places where I could visit a chocolate factory, then exchange my stolen bar of Tuzex chocolate for three beers.

We'd go skiing at our cottage with the boys from school. A favourite pastime when none of us

wanted to get up in the frosty room in the morning to get the fire started was to take a pellet gun and chase the other lazy sods out of bed. Then we'd fight for the rifle. Once, we shot through dad's posh chandelier. Thankfully, he took it in good spirits – probably because I told him we were shooting mice. I remember another excellent game: every time someone would fart out loud, if they didn't say "Arab, caravan, camel" and whistle, they'd be thrown out into the snow from the first floor. Let me tell you, it's quite hard to whistle when you're laughing your head off. Thanks to my appetite, I ended up in the snow many times.

Stolen History of Art as a Gift from Pedro

And so, I slowly began taking school quite lightly. Some boys were pretty rough: Petr Kocům, for example, known as Pedro, who'd walk around with a plank he'd ripped out of a fence. When he didn't like someone, he'd smash them over the head. He always had a C in behaviour.

Me and Pedro were great friends. Once, he brought me a box he'd stolen, full of Matějček's History of Art, which I read in its entirety out of gratitude to him – perhaps it was because of him that I began to take an interest in visual art.

A number of teachers at my school were there to be punished. Some of them had let their mouths run off, others had trouble with alcohol or girls – various characters. But the worst was the principal. My father declared that I needed to do the unthinkable, yet necessary to get into university, so I, the coward, joined the Czechoslovak Union of Youth (ČSM – Československý svaz mládeže). I am deeply ashamed of it to this day. As a member of ČSM, I even wrote some school twaddle for the radio every week. In short, it was disgraceful.

High school class, M.R. third from the right at the top, Petr "Pedro" Kocům fourth from the right at the top (1962)

High school tableau in Martin Rajniš's graphic layout (1962)

They Don't Want me in the Pioneers, I Tutor Maths

Even though everyone was in the Pioneers, they did not accept me, a bourgeois boy. But Dad's opinion? – "Thank God." Interesting times, however, began in high school. My head suddenly sparked up an interest in maths and physics, and in tenth or eleventh grade, I was tutoring the girls.

I'll tell you right away that tutoring dear Esterka was the pleasure of all pleasures. As Ester was hanging between a C and D, her daddy paid me fifty crowns an hour and suggested that if I made her a B student, I'd get two hundred as a bonus.

Ester had prodigious tits – not too soft, not too hard, just pointy enough, perfectly pointy, perfectly rounded. And a round little ass, just the right size. Not the kind that black women in the Caribbean have – little fucking machines. In short, a beauty. But her father was careful, constantly watching me through a hole in the curtain. Esterka would always wind her thigh towards me, shake her body, and off we went with the maths. And, you won't believe this, she started enjoying it. I had these childish explanations for dummies that anyone I ever taught understood, so Ester made it to a B and I cashed in my bonus.

I also taught Majda Rachlíková, Honza Horníček, and a number of others. At the time, fifty crowns an hour meant forty ten-degree beers in the pub, or three visits to a wine bar with a girl for dinner and a bottle. Who gets that now?

At the time, my father was slaving away in the factory making a measly twelve hundred crowns monthly, while I taught three or four hours every week. That adds up to two hundred crowns a week and the occasional bonus, so as a sixteen-year-old dandy, I made good money every month and I could booze, stay up late, rebel, smoke...

I began smoking and drinking aged thirteen. My parents, who both smoked like factory chimneys, could hardly reprimand me for smoking. My drinking worried them, however, even though it wasn't excessive – I rarely made it past four beers, and it wasn't even every day.

But the disgusting principal was the greater threat, continually stretching her claws out further towards me. To her, I was an unreliable, imposturous, bourgeois element. Apparently, she'd read my essay on "The Principles of the

Life of the Socialist Man" and found bewildering ironies contained within it. Apparently, these were "extortionately socialist and spitefully place the idea of communism into a bizarre and absurd world". She was right about that. I was taking the piss and my essay bordered on a farce. After that, I began watching my back – I endured it all, and finished school.

I have to say that throughout my long years in school, I only met one teacher I liked. It was at the gymnasium and her name was Vasiljuková. Incidentally, her son is quite a good architect.

Ships (1954–2034)

—

How could I have been such a lunatic and suspected my father of not making clever decisions? He felt that even though Communism held us in the fist of its hand and banned us from travel, we had to follow the example of Jack London's Star Rover and escape into another world. Our escape was in ships.

Mistral

The list of ships on which I served, or which I owned, even, is of considerable length. It all started in 1954, when my father's friend, the engineer Mr Topinka, bought a German cutter – a common sailboat used for fishing. He converted it and arranged it with my father so that our family would act as crew, which put me in the midst of a harbour full of ships and people who loved them. Our kingdom was in a bay, in the so-called "Vyšehrad Hafen", and we sailed on the Mistral – twin masts with Luger sails.

Topinka was not a particularly gifted captain. Once, we were riding the tailwind along the Barrandov Rocks, it picked up a little, caps appeared on the waves, and the captain started screaming: "Tornado!" Thanks in part to this affair, he got our Mistral nicknamed "Mistr sral" ("the master shat himself").

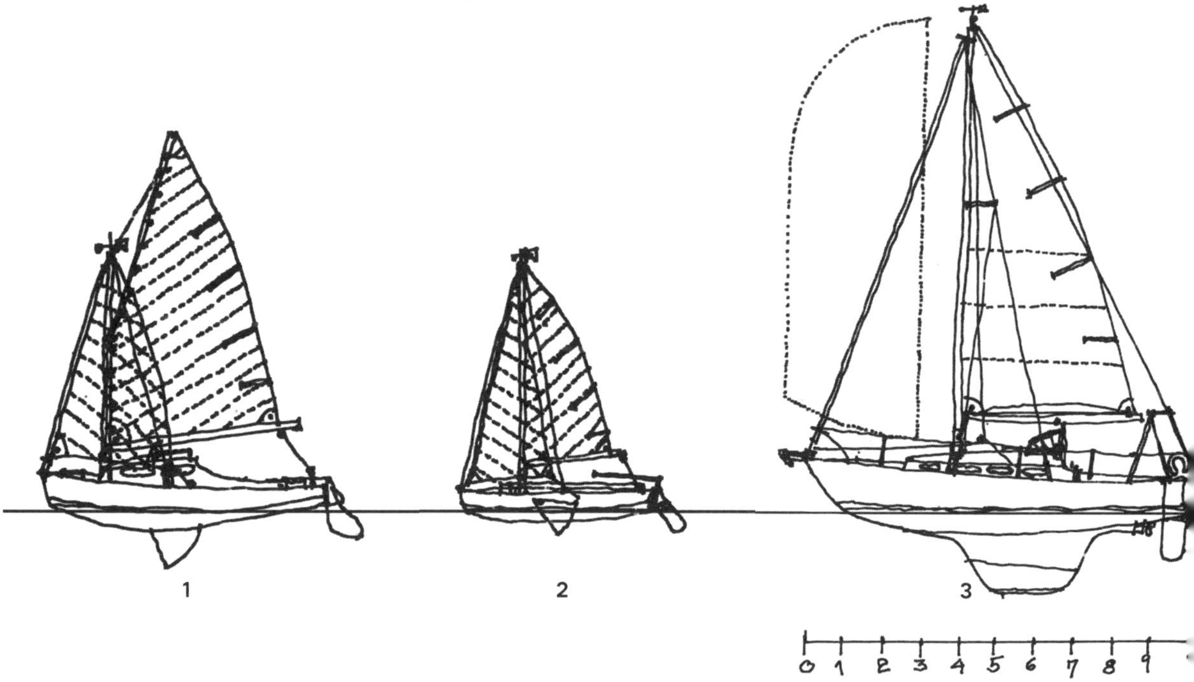

Wandr Jola *Skua*

Then my father found an old, partly cracked and putrid little ship which the Germans called Wanderjolle and convinced the owner to sell it to him. We finally had our own boat, then, with a small mast, a large spar, and an old outboard motor from 1920, which you put into a hole called "the pit".

Then dad's friend, the Jiřička, taught us to fix boats. First you steam oak slates to make new ribbing. Then you shave down mahogany boards until they fit into the hole that once housed the now rotten mahogany lining. You can also make homemade rivets from copper nails.

My father called our ship Skua, which, as we later discovered, means a scavenging seagull, but the name stuck with our beauty and I loved her. I learned to sail with great zeal, so from the age of eight up to this day, I've spent more than four years of my life and over twenty-thousand nautical miles on water of all kinds.

Captain Hlinomaz was anchored nearby. In addition to being a real captain who took Czech

4 5 6

1 Beluga
1a St Helena, 1967–1969
1b Odetta, 1970–1975
2 Pirate, 2011
3 Maia, 1993–2004
4 Wander jola Skua, 1956–1980
5 Salamander – Daisy, 1957–1977
6 Mistral, 1950s

archaeologists and Egyptologists along the Nile, he also had a terrifically beautiful daughter. She was a year older than myself and had a certain contempt for me, but it was bearable. To my great joy, our fathers agreed to buy us a small sailboat of the Mlok type. It was about four metres long and just over a metre wide, so you couldn't fit more than two people.

And now imagine this: thanks to the fact that fate took me to the gymnasium in Braník, when I managed to wake up early and there was a northerly wind, it took me an hour and a quarter to drop anchor by the ice plants, and then I could take the boys (and sometimes girls) out on the boat. Such bliss! First on the Mlok, but then more and schoolmates wanted to come, so I'd take the Skua, which could hold up to eight people.

A Captain's Duties…

Over time, I discovered that sailing and designing buildings have many elements in common. The stubbornness you need to sail is very similar to the stubbornness that helps resolve problems on a project. But the most important consideration

is this: Every time you leave port, you have to think very hard about what you might encounter on the water and prepare for three possibilities: 1) everything's fine, 2) only a few things fuck up, and 3) everything fucks up. Everything is collapsing, people are screaming in fear, but the captain has to know how to get out of it. It is expected of him to land all of you on solid ground, everyone alive. When I led an office later on, I had three things I knew I could rely on: my father's arctic training, my hard-bitten money-making, and the experiences I had on the water.

Sailing Around the World on the St. Helena

In the 60s, my friend Pavel Linhart inherited part of a villa from his father, the famous architect Evžen Linhart. He sold it and we bought a beluga yacht called St Helena for 12 000 Czech crowns.

Just like her predecessors, she was also at an advanced stage of use and putrefaction, so we changed out the worst inlays and decided we'd go on a tour of Europe, make some money on the way, and turn it into a journey around the world, waitering on ocean liners.

We did not take the political situation into account when planning, but the incredible became true: the only year in which this could be done was 1968, which was exactly when we'd planned the trip for. Because, back then, university studies could not be intermitted for a year, I had to ask my friend Vláďa and his girlfriend, the daughter of a famous psychiatrist, for help: I stuffed myself full of LSD and went to see the shrinks. They were pretty terrified and wanted to lock me up in the madhouse right away. I managed to weasel out of it, however, and thanks to my total "exhaustion", I received a year off.

At first, me and Pavel worked as stagehands in the theatre to save a little money, and in March 1968, we were off. I had no interest in Dubček and the other communists, so I left with complete peace of mind. We sailed out from our apartment on the Čertovka canal – full of excitement, my father fired his flare gun in celebration.

The motor took us out of port, but Pavel soon fell ill with a viral infection. When we got to Podbaba, where a confluence of all of Prague's sewers come together to create a stench reminiscent of a funeral of skunks, Pavel's nose started bleeding and his temperature rose towards the forties. And as if that wasn't enough, our Soviet Vyetorok motor also gave out, so we had to anchor down for a few days.

Slapy Reservoire
(mid-1970s)

At the helm, Slapy
(mid-1970s)

Tailwind, Slapy
(mid-1970s)

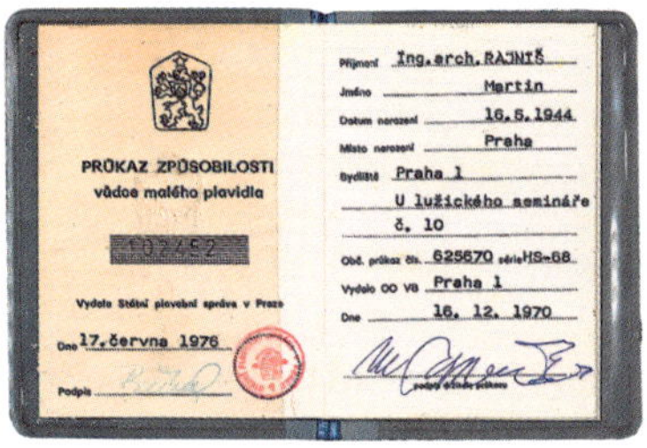

PRŮKAZ ZPŮSOBILOSTI
vůdce malého plavidla

102452

Vydala Státní plavební správa v Praze

Dne 17. června 1976

Podpis

Příjmení Ing. arch. RAJNIŠ
Jméno Martin
Datum narození 16.5.1944
Místo narození Praha
Bydliště Praha 1
U lužického semináře
č. 10
Obč. průkaz čís. 625670 série HS-68
Vydalo OO VB Praha 1
Dne 16. 12. 1970

podpis držitele průkazu

I spent three days brewing huge buckets of tea for Pavel and attending to him intensively. Then, I borrowed some cash from my father and bought an East German Tümler motor, and we finally sailed out on the Vltava River towards the Mittelland Canal. The next step was anchoring in front of the Volkswagen factory in Wolfsburg, where dad's former partner at Dorka, Franz Novotný, was now commercial manager. He immediately found us some well-paid work on the production line. It was a pretty good plan: we had no rent to pay, and to get to work we simply had to go out onto the towpath and take a few of the tunnels under the Mittelland Canal to get to the factory.

An old German captain had his ugly aluminium boat moored next to us: "Boys, I spent thirty years as a captain in the South East Pacific, and I taught those niggers German – so what couldn't I do with two clever students from Prague?"

We shook hands on it and every day, after we came back from work, he'd have a pot of tea ready. He'd give us three hours of German. After three months, I could chat down the pub – about anything, even politics. The captain even invited us to his home – his son, a former SS lieutenant, was clearly not particularly pleased...

We sailed through the Dortmund-Ems-Kanal and Frisia to the city of my heart, Amsterdam, where we spent a month on the Prinsengracht before departing for Gouda via Rotterdam where our friend Zdeněk Zavřel was working in the studio of the world-famous architect Jaap Bakema. Zdenda – dean of the faculty of architecture after the revolution, and ex-husband of our friend Helena Jiskrová, known as Jiskrovka – then showed us around town, we shared a few rounds of shots, and went to sleep on the boat.

Early the following morning – knock, knock, knock – a policeman appeared on deck. "Are either of your parents members of the Central Committee of the Czechoslovak Communist Party?"

We were sleepy and thought he'd gone nuts. He continued: "The Russian secret police came with the army and they're locking up the children of all the Central Committee members to blackmail their parents. We've been instructed to gather them up and protect them from the KGB." Still, we understood nothing. The date was August 21st, 1968 and our private battle with the Soviet Union had just begun.

I instantly made my way to Bakema's studio to see Zdeněk Zavřel. I have to say, Bakema showed great character – he immediately gave us two offices so we could begin preparing our operation against the occupying forces. I, the weathered revolutionary, immediately took action: I gathered our savings while Pavel found a sales catalogue of army surplus goods; we discovered we could afford either a machine gun or a mortar. We were waiting for the Europeans to get sufficiently pissed off with the Russians that they'd get hands-on in sorting it out. As we all know, none of that came to pass. So, we began preparing to attack the Russian embassy instead.

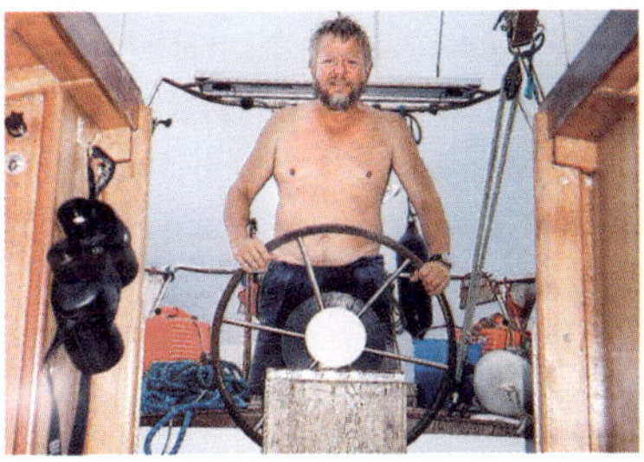

The local left-wing socialists soon got wind of our plan. Theirs was similar, so they invited us to join them. Who could resist an offer like that? They were all keen to get in on the action; they had a unique opportunity to tease the police a little with their cobblestones and Molotovs – starting a revolution is a high-adrenaline activity. I was recently convinced of this again at a protest against the Chinese and their sidekick Zeman – boy, did my blood get flowing!

It's also sexy, as Pavel learnt first-hand. He established the headquarters of the struggle against the USSR in a beautiful whorehouse in Amsterdam, so while I was engaged in a fierce struggle at the centre of the action, he made posters with the girls, who gladly added their own contribution to the struggle – thus, Pavel has quite fond memories of the fight against the occupiers.

My certification to navigate small ships (1970)

Lunch with Kačenka somewhere in the Atlantic (1999)

Me at the helm in the Atlantic (1999)

An Enemy of the Russians is a Friend of Ours!

Kind and decent Zdenda then surprised us with a humane gesture: he announced himself at the Russian embassy and proclaimed we were gathering forces to take them out. Seeing as we were very aggrieved, he said, we would probably succeed; he would be very sorry for any victims on their side, and pleaded with them to withdraw. The Russians were so nonplussed they didn't even take a picture.

Of course, they took no heed of him, so the day of the attack came to pass after all. The socialists arrived armed with long sticks, at the end of which were little signs, thirty by twenty centimetres, with metal horns and images of their heroes: Mao, Che Guevara, Trotsky, Stalin – a variety of left-wing heavyweights. They asked us if we minded, but we said: "An enemy of the Russians is a friend of ours!"

The purpose of these strange signs became apparent immediately: the police were on horseback, and when you slam a stallion across the dick with an armoured rod, it hurts him so much he'll run away from the battlefield with the policeman still on his back. We fought like lions and overcame four barbed-wire fences. We were stopped before we could scale the fifth.

Immediately after the occupation, there was a huge wave of solidarity. A productive group of friends organised itself in Europe. Their efforts were largely responsible for the glut of states opening the floodgates to Czechoslovak refugees, with a number of incredible benefits: Swiss and American citizenship within twenty-four hours, three-year scholarships to Harvard... But I didn't want to become one of those people. Not one bit.

We continued travelling by "hitch-boating". How does that work, you ask? You sail out onto the wide river Meuse, which flows through the largest port in the world – Rotterdam – and, just like a hitch-hiker, you stick up your thumb to show you're looking for a ride. If a ship responds, you throw them a rope and sail up against the flow of the Rhine.

But it's no joke. Steering a small ship hitched behind a big one is a truly awful ordeal. Our rope broke twice, but both times they came back for us. It took two and a half days to sail against the current from Rotterdam to Leverkusen. They were nice lads. They even sent bottles of beer down to us along the rope.

We continued our journey in a Ford Taunus we had bought for 250 Marks. We were making eight Marks an hour, so between the two of us, we had the car in two days. For a student from behind the Iron Curtain, this was like a dream – back home we'd have to work perhaps for years even for an old piece of junk like that.

This car carried us some fifty thousand kilometres from Orkney to Sicily and back, so in addition to German, I also learned to drive. In the end, Pavel had sold the boat for six thousand Marks, or about seventy thousand crowns – more than five times his original investment of twelve thousand. Not bad, right?

The "friendly" armies in Prague (1968)

With the boys from the Liberec Collective of Engineers and Architects (SIAL) and some other friends, we later established a nautical society. We bought ourselves a gorgeous blueblood of boats, Odetta – another beluga yacht. She was fast and light, the proud recipient of a number of gold medals and blue ribbons – simply put, a champion ship.

Honza Malina, who worked at the Vinohrady Theatre, had a beautiful creek on the Orlík Reservoir which we called Malina's Creek, and we'd take turns there all summer. I'll admit that not much compares to the feeling of quietly sailing on a featherlight boat through the translucent morning mist, becoming a part of the water. That is why I still treat myself to it every once in a while.

My next boat, Maya, was fantastic. Once in 1993, Tom Plzenský called me up: "I'm establishing a company, Czech Windsailing Inc. – I've got a wonderful boat picked out; someone just has to buy it. We'll have a charter company and we'll make loads of money. You can count on it." I said to myself: If we have a boat, at least I can sail it sometimes. And why wouldn't I support a friend?

We bought the boat, paying a little over the odds, perhaps, but it was a truly beautiful yawl. A classic maritime yacht, designed and built by van de Stadt, a Dutchman and the ultimate expert in small yacht design. At times, Maya became more important than family to both Tom and myself.

As I suffered from the delusion of thinking I knew everything best, I said: "Tom, I'll do the accounts and you find the clients!" No entrepreneurial success story followed. Reality turned out to be quite different from our business dreams, but I don't regret it in the slightest.

I had to pay the upkeep every year, so we decided to sell the ship, but since it cost three quarters of a million and nobody was offering us more than fifty thousand, I ended up keeping it. I spent a year and a half repairing it, and when it was good as new, I set out for a trip around the world.

We repaired it with sailor Petr Maslín, Tom, and anyone else who'd help. The christening was rather moving: I bought a Norwegian dictionary in an effort to deliver my incantations to Odin and the other gods in Old Norse. Just for the record, the original budget for the repair was six hundred thousand and it wasn't supposed to take longer than six months. It took three times as long and the expenses slowly inched up to one million six hundred thousand. It follows that the love of boats seems to cloud my judgement.

Maya was beautiful; in the autumn of 1999, we set out from Barcelona on our voyage around the world. In a classic twist, the motor was fucked before we even left the Spanish coast, so we had to stop off for general repair in the Canary Islands. After that, everything ran smoothly, and we set off in the tracks of Christopher Columbus – from the Canaries to Grenada. It took him twenty-three days in the 15th century – it took us half a day longer. But Columbus had much bigger ships: even his smallest Niña was twice as long as our Maya...

I later sold Maya, co-investing a modest sum in the beautiful 56-foot Lady Blue, which anchors at

a particular spot in the Antilles, the very best spot in all of the Caribbean. She has five cabins, several saloons, and her own captain, Jirka, who has been chartering her successfully for over ten years. I ride along sometimes, but only as a paying passenger. Maya was, in a way, beautifully reincarnated as Lady Blue.

And then there's Pirate – a ship belonging to a company of sailors: Voverka, Amblerová, Kubík, and Rajniš. We occasionally take Pirate to the Expo or the Venice Biennale. Pirate was also at the Kyje Pond when we erected our stickman lookout tower with its design based on a lady's behind. In short, she's a darling. Just as I live for dogs (more on this shortly), my love for boats will never cease. I am incredibly grateful to my father and fate in all its mercy that I was able to spend a considerable part of my life on the water...

Boxers in My Life

—

If I talk about lifelong companions, I couldn't miss out my dogs. All my life, I have kept boxers. I already mentioned Judita, Judka for short, into whose bed I forced myself as a one-year old so we could become best friends. I bought Andulka while I was at university, but because I was running around all the time, I wasn't able to be with her much of the time.

When the DA studio was getting started, my secretary Nora Geislerová told me there was a boxer breeder in Vinohrady selling a few puppies. She dragged me over there. One climbed out of the tangle onto my lap and immediately fell asleep. They'd named him Arnold, but I changed it to Arnošt.

He was a wonderful dog with whom I had several wonderful adventures. He was a specialist in architecture –the most educated dog in human history, I believe he could analyse the quality of an

Maya by the northwestern coast of Mallorca (1994)

Our training sailboat in Davle, Pirát (2016)

architectural project. When I walked to UMPRUM, which was only a few steps from U Lužického semináře, Arnošt would march with me right into the studio. The works would hang on the wall, and if they sucked, Arnošt would sit under the project and bark. The despondent author would trudge along: "So, what do you think, Martin?" "Me? Just listen to Arnošt!" Arnošt started barking even louder and that was that. He either sensed my own feelings and expressed them out loud, or perhaps, who knows, he just understood architecture. Maybe I take after him...

He often escaped the school building through the basement, making straight for the butcher's on Kaprova Street, where he made himself appear the very image of misery. His eyes seemed to say, "I am on the verge of perishing of hunger..." and the result would be the same: he got an incredible quantity of cuttings. The nice butcher lady would smile at him and say: "He finally beat the worst of the hunger, poor little thing."

Arnošt also liked fighting and I felt as if I owed it to him: he helped me appraise architecture, and I helped him to recognise a dog he could fight from one it would be best to avoid. Humans see better than dogs at a distance, so I could assess the competition about five seconds before Arnošt. If the adversary seemed dangerous, I'd start out and grab Arnošt by the hind legs – we didn't own a leash, because a dog, just like a person, needs freedom.

True, my assessment was sometimes wrong, while at other times the opponent appeared suddenly from the bushes, and the going got tough. But I developed tricks to insert my knees between the two screaming dogs – never hands or legs, which both dogs would bite.

Once, I took Arnošt out for a walk around 3 a.m. and another fight started. After it was all over, I reached into my pocket, but my keys were nowhere to be found. It was pitch black and the keys were evidently somewhere on the grass by the

Lužice Seminary. I started running my hands along the ground; I hit fresh dog poo about twenty times, but still couldn't find the keys. I ended up sleeping on a bench and Arnošt, perhaps to make up for what he'd done, warmed me up. Before dawn, we were both shaking with the cold.

Arnošt accompanied me everywhere, even on my journeys, and one of them proved fatal – a snake bit him in Kara Denis Dahlari in eastern Turkey. He departed as a proud, brave partner and excellent friend. Everyone cried over it and I'll never forget him.

I missed him terribly, so I ended up getting Andulka no. 2, but she died too. Her bed, bowl, and Mr Zindulka, the stuffed toy she liked to play with, are still at my cabin in the same place. When we were working on this book, Magda's dog Mánička used them, and now they're probably waiting for a new buddy, because I really miss having a dog and I probably won't make it much longer without one...

University (1962–1969)

—

For someone who was considered a second-class citizen for political cadre reasons, getting into university was no mean feat. I applied for construction, because back then, architecture was still part of the construction faculty and students were only divided after the second year. Several thousand people took the entrance exams; two and a half thousand were accepted, and then elimination brutally continued. I really wanted to get in, and unlike my high school graduation exam (which I was terrified by) I took the entrance exams in my stride.

I had a holiday job in Šumava with this socialist fellow who spent most of his time stealing. I left at four in the morning, jolting along in my car to Prague, and around nine, made straight for the

Judita
(1942–1950)

Arnošt
(1993–1999)

Andulka II
(2007–2015)

Andulka sick at the cabin
(2014)

exam. I was grimy, my hair tousled – I must've seemed a right vagabond.

Thankfully, the somewhat bored gentlemen on the panel were more interested in maths and physics than my destitute appearance, and when talk turned to calculations, I told them I don't have the formula in question in my head at the moment, but if they wait just a little moment, I'd derive it. Naturally I could derive it – I taught those poor girls how to do it several times a week. Then the conversation moved to the history of art – to this day, I am thankful to Pedro Kocům for stealing those thick tomes by Matějíček for me. Thanks to him, I read them, and even remembered something, so the gentlemen arrived at the conclusion that I could become a university student.

They were adamant, however, that since I knew maths, I should study geodesy and cartography. My heart skipped a beat and I pleaded: "Don't put me there, I want to be an architect."

"But there's so little maths in architecture. With your talent, you should be calculating flight paths for Soviet satellites!"

In the end I talked them round, and became a student at the construction faculty.

I kept expecting someone would start teaching me in earnest. This didn't happen in elementary school, though this was partially due to my obtuseness, dyslexia, and so on. I branded high school a mockery, and using only a few tricks, I secured the straight A-grades so desired by my father (except for behaviour, of course). I expected to get proper teaching here at university, at least.

That subjects like "Scientific Communism" and "The History of the Labour Movement" were shit came as no surprise. And I can't say that maths or descriptive geometry were taught badly. The lecturers were pretty reasonable men, and there'd even occasionally be a woman, one of whom we called Breccia after a geological compound.

Then architectural teaching began, and I grew desperate: Jesus, they're not teaching us! Again! My third school and another disappointment! At

The photograph in my student index at the technical university (1962)

Self-portrait (1965)

The photograph in my student index at the Academy of Fine Arts (1969)

that point, I decided that the only reason to attend university is to obtain enough free time for the pub and all manner of mischief, particularly sex, which I had neglected considerably in the past.

But the most important thing of all was to spend time with the friends I'd keep for the rest of my working life – at least in this respect, fate was merciful to me. What I neglected in sex, I made up for in friendship.

The colleagues who joined me after graduation with Hubáček and Masák in the so-called SIAL Nursery were the shining stars of our generation. I grew closest to Emil Přikryl, a good boy from a good family who speaks with a funny north-Moravian accent, I thought.

Our friendship lasted a lifetime and Emil truly showed himself to be the superstar of our generation. Not that I wasn't a little jealous, but I was mostly happy for him. He was handsome, funny, the girls loved him, and he had God-given talent as well – fuck, isn't that enough for one guy!?

Dalibor Vokáč was also in the group. He later became a partner in Zeidler's huge studio in Canada and built a number of skyscrapers in South East Asia. Then you had Zdenda Zavřel and Jirka Suchomel. Jirka Suchomel was this sort of Wise Old Man, he knew everything, he could do everything, and fate would have it that after Hubáček's departure, he led SIAL for a time and then established the architecture department at the technical university in Liberec.

Finally, Mirko Baum joined us – a troubadour from Mladá Boleslav who married our mutual friend Mina Koine. Mirko had several children with Mina, but then she was tragically run over by a car. Still handsome and young, Mirko remarried, having another batch of offspring. This chap, blessed with so many children, is now a professor of architecture in Aachen.

And I can't forget our wonderful friends Helena Jiskrová (Jiskrovka) and Dana Zámečníková

(Zámejda), and also Jarmila Očenášková. Me and Jarmila had this exchange going on. Just as Mr Třeška used to say, "Give me a bow and arrow and I'll give you a bear pelt", Jarmila was great at construction and I was much better at maths, so we'd work together.

The cleverest of all was Petr Vaďura. He was encyclopaedic and everyone placed their best hopes in him, but even so, the poor guy died of cancer before he was thirty. Nevertheless, the few things he had the time to give and to teach us live on within us. Petr Vaďura left a legacy.

As a testament to what a strong group we were, we only need to look to the fact that out of fourteen people, nine of us became professors or studio leaders, or deans in the cases of Zdenda Zavřel and Jirka Suchomel. Even though it took a long time, my friends from university meant that I did eventually learn architecture – by looking over their shoulders. I'm the sloth of architecture, you might say.

Perhaps a story from descriptive geometry is worth relating here. I liked the subject, so I had no problem learning it. But I did have enormous problems not forgetting my pencil, eraser, compass, and rulers.

I was also always clumsy, and I drafted slower than the others, so I decided to take a scientific and methodical approach. We were to choose a task and complete it, and I opted for the toughest option in existence – a toroid (like a tire; a round circle) and its shadow projected onto the surface of a wreathed column. You might know these from some Baroque altar columns.

When I was halfway through my calculations, I was really getting into trouble, so I went to see the assistant about it. She acted tough for fifteen minutes and then told me to see the professor. Professor Secr, with a brow like Brezhnev's, stood up in all his toweringly tall majesty and said: "The shadow of a toroid on a wreathed column, we haven't seen that in a long time!" He jumped at it, and after two hours, he was excited to have solved it. When I later had an exam, I only had to appear in

Church of St Martin in the Rock, one of my first projects. The sketch was destroyed by the 2002 flooding, following a wish expressed by Benjamin Fragner, I drew it again in 2010
(1965)

The Last Judgement, one of my ancient paintings not destroyed by the flood
(1967)

the door of his office for him to say: "Ah, you're the one with the wreathed column, aren't you? Give me your index, you've got an A."

I enjoyed my freedom to the full at university. I didn't attend many lectures or seminars, I copied what I could, and for the rest, me, Dalibor, and Emil had a system: when we wanted to go to Germany to make some money, buy a car, and spend a few weeks driving around, we needed to get our exams out of the way fast. So, each of us chose a subject, wrote out a cheat sheet, and poured it into the others' heads. This way, all our exams were done in a week and we could set out. We barely gave it a thought; only once did I have to say to myself: "The going's getting tough, boy, you really have to put the work in now."

It was the end of our second year, when the school determined who'd be a civil engineer and who'd be an architect. Of the original two and a half thousand, there were only six hundred left. Of these, the vast majority wanted to be chosen for architecture, where they had sixty places. Thirty of them, however, were reserved for communist brats, so in consequence, six hundred of the unanointed scrabbled for thirty places.

There was one more obstacle on my path to architecture, which was my dream: I was simply incapable of getting geology into my skull – the damn rocks just wouldn't go in. Dad helped. One of his boat friends, Bojan Záruba, who drafted the Slapy Reservoir, had a brother, Quido Záruba, who was, miraculously, the head of the geology department. Bojan told Quido to find someone to tutor me because I needed an A, and who took me on? Poor Breccia, whom I've already mentioned. She hammered it into me, I got an A, and with that, straight A's, and because only seven other students out of two and a half thousand also had straight A's, they couldn't refuse me.

When the Socialist Union of Youth organised a conference and I had to share with the comrades how you get straight A's, I said: "You just come back from the pub sooner, have a look at it, and when your eyelids start getting heavy, you take one or two Phenmetrazine and by morning it's all inside you. It all hurtles out of you during the exam, and two days later, your head is clear, you know nothing of it. And on you go." The comrades got properly pissed off that I was making so light of it. Yes, honesty didn't get you anywhere in socialism...

To celebrate achieving my dream of studying architecture, I decide to swim the length of the Slapy Reservoir, which is about forty-five kilometres. I planned it out over two days, hitchhiked to Slapy, prepared three plastic bags, put all my clothes in the first one, wrapped it up with rubber bands, put it in the second one, rubber bands, third one, rubber bands, then I tied my belt around it and wrapped it around my neck so it swam behind me like a rescue buoy. It was awfully cold, so I made a fire the first night to warm myself up a bit. There was a huge storm on the afternoon of the second day, so I walked the last two or three kilometres. That was my celebration of my acceptance into the study of architecture.

And I started doing projects. I have to laugh when I remember my first family home. Back then, this was two months of work, while today, I'd have it done in twenty minutes. Yeah, once you learn something, of course it seems as obvious as breathing. As if your whole body functioned automatically; it draws itself.

Back then, though, it was all awfully hard, and I really can't say my talent thrust its way to the surface. Quite the opposite – it was resting somewhere deep inside. But by observing the other talents, I was getting there – slowly. I'll be very honest: the professors and associate professors had no particular part in this. However, I have to admit that good pedagogues existed too, like František Cubr from the famous Cubr – Hrubý – Pokorný trio. Boy, was he some architect!

If we're speaking of exceptional professors, I can't leave out Mr Ladislav Žák from AVU. I unfortunately only caught him towards the end of his fantastic career, but his lectures were a huge influence on me. This educated and entertaining gentleman could make fun of everything – including himself – and say things that were completely out of the usual academic framework. It is no accident that I've borrowed certain terms from him, such as, for example, "habitable landscape".

Žák often dwelled on the topics of paradise and original sin, on which he could charm up a number of theories. One of them said that the snake which offered Adam and Eve the sinful fruit spoke Czech. The way he got his name – reptile in Latin – was by grumbling (reptal in Czech) about the Lord. When a lecture of mine occasionally goes well, I always remember Mr Žák with love and gratitude.

Let my mention of him be at least a partial balance to the fact that I found no words of praise for the vast majority of my lecturers. And I have to say that not even in my wildest dreams did I imagine that I would ever find myself in their shoes...

Military Service and Jail (1973–1974)

—

I dodged the madness of compulsory military service under socialism in any way I could, until I was suddenly twenty-nine years old and leaving school, and the military administration got on my case straight away. My last hope was "the blue book", awarded only to those found physically unfit to serve. So, I started rousing the doctors – my stomach hurts terribly, and I'm losing weight. One friend had suggested that if, before an x-ray, I drank three egg whites and ate twenty raisins, the buggers would stick to the stomach wall and look just like an ulcer. And I had better start actually losing weight.

I began, even though I was always awfully hungry. One week, I even covered over three hundred kilometres on cross-country skis, so I lost some weight, but I also never looked healthier – tanned, red cheeks, chiselled muscles... Nevertheless, I stubbornly insisted that my stomach hurt more and more, so they x-rayed me again and again until they discovered that the ulcers seemed to be migrating. In the end I was enlisted, comforting myself with the idea that even the most stupid experience can be good for something.

A Private Graduate, with Wind Between the Bars

We went through military service while studying – we had one day a week for two years. Then, we had one year of "full" military training. We were graduates with our rank expressed on our epaulettes, known as "bars on the shoulder". I had what was called "wind between the bars", which means there was nothing – no rank. I was a Private and a university graduate, which was rare because, as was common in Stalinist armies, graduates were usually trained to be commissioned officers.

We were filling out forms which included a column: parents' class origins. I wrote down the truth: father – bourgeois, mother – bourgeois, grandfather – bourgeois. The green idiot who was sat there stared at me in disbelief: "Private – you can't write it like that, comrade. That's not how you write it. You have to write clerical, or

somethinglike that. Otherwise, you just have no future in the army." I responded naively: "But I'm the honest type." I left it like that, which turned out to be a tremendous trick.

At that point, I already had one attempt to illegally cross the Iron Curtain on my record, so I thought: "Well, I'll scrub toilets. Screw it." But no! The big shots got together and discussed it, because there were three of us whose class origins were fucked: two civil engineers and I, an architect. The green cadres lamented: "What will we do with you, comrades? You're off the charts. We can't train you to be officers. Poor fellow, what did you write in the form? You must be suicidal!" So, while the others were training, we loitered about in uniform and nobody expressed the least bit of interest in us.

With my friends Honza and Ivan, we established the ASIA studio – the Army Studio of Engineers and Architects, which was an unauthorised paraphrasing of SIAL. We immediately had a stamp and headed paper made. I appointed myself director of the Institution project, and went to see the lieutenant with an offer:

"Do you want to be famous? Do you want to be the best-known lieutenant in the Second Army? We're ready to do projects for you that will earn you a pat on the back from the generals. I need only one thing – a room. We'll go to Prague, find our tools, and then we can do useful work for you. We'll set up an audio-visual room with the most modern technology from the Soviet Union where you can school the Privates. And we'll also build a new parking lot and petroleum hydrocarbon separator..."

I blabbered on and on until he said: "Okay! You can have it. We don't know what to do with you anyway."

So, the good times in Kamýk nad Vltavou began. We got together with the doctors right away and they supplied us with an excellent cocktail: a mix of fatigue medication and B12 with sixty-percent alcohol. All you needed was three shots and you'd flail around like a Christmas tree.

Military jail in Příbram
(2016)

The barracks in Kamýk upon Vltava
(2016)

The dam in Kamýk upon Vltava
(2016)

We decided we'd work Tuesdays, Wednesdays, and Thursdays and leave the barracks from Friday to Monday. I'm an anarchist, after all, and I couldn't just accept this servitude I'd been forced into. I'd disappear, for at least half the time.

We'd do unbelievable things, like going to the Headquarters of Army Audiovisual Technology in Moravia, always bringing back two bottles of slivovice – traditional Moravian plum spirit. The local boss – a mighty alcoholic – would send telegrams to our division claiming that the meeting had to be postponed and that we should report at this and that division where they have such and such a specialist who could not leave there. We were to return in three days. In short, wonderful.

Military Prison

One time, we decided we'd go skiing, and since all three of us were good skiers, we'd lead the girls' teams from the nearby high school in Třešňová. The esteemed reader will certainly have surmised the direction of our desires. We had arranged for the high school to request us, but since nothing was happening, I went over to nudge things along in person.

I gave the teacher the address of the commanding general who made the decision, and just to make sure, I also gave her his secret home address. The strange thing was that this address had no rank, only a name, a mailbox, and a four-digit number. Under no circumstances could these two addresses be found together.

"You have to swear you won't get it mixed up!"

I should have known women wouldn't have a feel for the military world. Despite my lecture on it, the teacher wrote one address above the other, so that within the hour, counter-espionage officers were on her, scaring the poor girl so much that she pointed the finger at me as the perpetrator. "You've set yourself up for five years in jail," they told me. I was angry, but mostly at myself – Setting myself up like that! But since our colonel needed a villa drafted, he managed to talk them down, and I only went to jail for three weeks.

They demoted me at once. I was once again a Private and I arrived in jail in my civvies, so I was immediately given a broom and I spent the rest of the day sweeping leaves. Then the prison director came up to me in the barracks courtyard: "You're an architect, right?"

"Yes I am!"

"Look, we have a partner nursery. Can you do a nursery? Can you do interiors?"

"Of course, colonel."

"And what do you need?" he asked.

"Any room. I'll go get my papers, drawing pins, pencils, erasers, rulers. I have cash. And I'll whip it right up!"

"Can you do it in three weeks? Of course you can. And if you can't, I'll throw in some extra jail time," he said. That was a strong argument.

The interiors for a socialist school can be done in three days, and that's with a fair few peaceful coffee breaks thrown in. I'd go sleep in my cell, but one of my friends from university was head of construction, so we quickly found a way to sidestep jail a little.

I said to myself: "I've been getting paid for my labour for fifteen years, I'm almost thirty, so why should I serve for free like a slave?" We went to the firms that realised our projects and proposed we could make the project documentation. They could barely get this done if they tried their best, and as this was an extra from us, they'd pay us for it. It'll be part of their consignment, so the army would compensate them for it, and they'd simply mail us part of the money.

It was a promising idea and they had no objections, but they wanted it signed by our lieutenant colonel. When I went to see him, he nearly screamed the roof off. He ripped the folder out of my hands and threw it out the window. I excused myself in the appropriate manner and went outside to collect the papers. I was back in five minutes.

I thought I'd talk him over, but no dice. He threw himself at me as soon as I was through the door, ripping the papers apart and throwing them out of the window again in a rage. However, this pissed me off so much I didn't hesitate to return with the crumpled up, muddy documents a third time. Now, I too was pissed off beyond reason:

"How dare this little green shit speak to me like that? To me, the architect whose building stands on Národní třída?"

When he launched himself at me again, I slapped him. He froze – this clearly hadn't happened to him in a long time – and I got another three weeks of jail time.

My third military jail was in a garrison detainment facility in Příbram. My reputation preceded me, so I was escorted by men armed with AK-47s mounted with bayonets. The warden (no longer the one I had drafted for) said to the escort: "Ah, the famous recidivist, Graduate-Private Rajniš. When he starts running, forget about warning shots in the air! Go straight for the knees! Or better yet, his head!"

Blunt Saws and Sweet Revenge

Everyone was awfully scared of this guy. "And tomorrow – the forest," the swine said. They took me and some others to the woods, where I found out this asshole had blunted everyone's saws. We used wood for heat at the cabin, so I'd cut down enough of it in my life to know that cutting fresh wood with a blunt saw is a terror beyond all terrors. What a pitiful man!

The rage welled up inside me and I felt immediately that revenge would be sweet. As soon as I got out, I asked a Czech-speaking Swede to write a letter of approximately this wording: "Dear sirs, your information about the location of ballistics and combat equipment belonging to the Fifth Army was appreciated in the United States, particularly by the espionage officers. We would like to thank you very much and ask you to continue in your supply of first-rate information."

The warden got this letter at both his private and secret addresses, and the contras then didn't leave the asshole alone for years. He couldn't blunt anyone's saw now.

I had three stints in military jails: for the teacher, the slap, and for an escape. And civil incarceration? I've had that experience too. In 1965, they locked me, Emil Přikryl, and Dalibor Vokáč up in France. We were dirty, we stank a little, and we were caught cooking soup in the forest in a big pickled cucumber can. On another occasion, I was captured by the transport police when jumping off a freight train. And in 1968, I was in jail in the Netherlands and England for vagrancy. I firmly hope that I've thus done all my time...

When the entire army is against you and you've got nothing, when you're the zero of all zeros while they have all the power in their hands to destroy you every day, you get enormous relief when you realise any and all means of opposing them are allowed. They deserve no compassion.

My trick rested in the improvers' movement. We drafted a project whilst also drafting several steps of improvement – the first version was for thirty million, then we lowered it to twenty-five, then twenty, and we'd finish up on eight. And we always sent it to our friends in the construction bureau along with a good bottle. We found out in advance what a realistic price was, then made a ridiculously exaggerated budget, from which we then arrived at the real price, collecting half a percent of the money saved by the army.

I was still receiving money from the military treasury two years later and our division became the best improver in the entire people's army. In the end, the colonel said: "Private, I've forgiven you. I get praise and you get your money." Much later, when I started a business, all my tricks from the military were terribly useful, because the modern state is often reminiscent of the old Bolshevik army.

SIAL and the SIAL Nursery (1969–1979)

—

The SIAL Nursery studio, Jedlová (1970s)

SIAL – the Liberec Association of Engineers and Architects – was established in the '60s by

the architect Karel Hubáček. At the time, the situation had loosened up somewhat, so this was the first time something like this was possible since the Bolshevik putsch. SIAL quickly became enormously important, and it often seemed that that was where the crucial developments in Czech architecture took place.

In 1969, when I finished school, I got a telegram from Miroslav Masák with an offer to join SIAL. I felt like a Greek javelin thrower being invited to Olympus. The SIAL Nursery – thought up, founded, and built up from the ground up by Míra – was based on an interesting concept: to create a group of young architects who would operate alongside SIAL as a kind of permanent study workshop. The original idea was that everyone would spend some time in the Nursery, later leaving for practice hardened by tough treatment of the utmost sophistication, making space for others.

The selection process was fascinating: our friend, Zdenda Zavřel's future wife, Jiskrovka, was from Liberec, and she was doing some temp work at SIAL. She met Masák, who asked her who was good at school. So, it was mostly her – though supposedly Mirko Baum supplied some names

Karel Hubáček, Míra Masák
(late 1970s)

E. Přikryl, J. Suchomel, Z. Zavřel
(1970s)

Mirko Baum at Jedlová
(1970s)

Milan Pitlach and Johny Eisler under a painting by Jiří Sopko
(1970s)

too – who created the group of twelve boys and two girls who spent years as the Nursery under Míra's direction.

In those times, though, you couldn't plan very far ahead. The political situation continued to deteriorate, and if you were clinging on to the life-raft called the Nursery in order to float through the stinking waters of Normalization in the 1970s, you'd find it hard to leap out into the void too...
I was one of these people.

Míra Masák had this fantastic idea to put us all together so that we could learn from one another. What the SIAL Nursery demonstrated – and all the esteemed gentlemen at the world's architecture universities should realise this – was that the students are the most important element. If they're stupid, even super-professors can't teach them anything. But fantastic students who are clever, interested, who want to study and try to barge forward cannot be prevented from becoming excellent architects, not even by the stupidest lecturing staff.

After all, nature taught us to copy and we do it with everything important: we learn language by listening and sex by looking – and architecture is the same. It's a somewhat absurd admission, but unlike the other gentlemen professors of architecture, I don't know precisely what architecture is.

It's probably absolutely everything around us, but it can disappear completely, like a cloud covered by sunlight. It's an elusive thing, so how can it be taught? It can only be copied. When you have the opportunity, day and night, to watch people who know how to do it, to compare their performance on paper with their performance on the construction site, and observe, millimetre by millimetre, how dozens – or, in the case of the SIAL Nursery, hundreds – of projects are born, you'd have to be cursed if nothing stuck...

Personally, I boarded a moving train. As was the custom at the time, Hubáček kept a full studio with all the professions, and he led it excellently.

We from the Nursery seemed more like subversives than assistants at first, as we were not ready to address the pragmatic problems that always come up when planning.

I have to admit it's no coincidence that I much later established an office I called Huť architektury, which could loosely be translated as the Architecture Guild – that's how it was in the Middle Ages, and that's how Hubáček did it too: working on a project, everyone was on one boat – the people who draft, invent, chisel, mason, dig, but also the women who cook for them and without whom no proper work can survive. I have to say we're still missing the women in our office, but who knows what might happen...

Hubáček believed that money corrupts, so he paid himself and us poorly. That didn't change over the years. Decades later, I was arranging a fee for him for some lecture or other, and he says: "You fix it, you're better with money." I got him a fee that nearly made the poor man collapse.

To a large extent, SIAL's renown came from Hubáček's charm. He was like a torch – he had a gift from God to inspire people to strength, conviction, and courage. And while courage is truly a precious good in the Czech lands, Hubáček had so much that he could give it away.

It wasn't screaming-barricades bravery, but the calm, factual, and persistent courage of a man who believed in decency and abiding by the rules. He felt that if one speaks the truth, he has a God-given right to speak it at full volume. The following anecdote attests to his character and bravery.

Hubáček Complains at the Gestapo

Karel Hubáček was born in 1922, and in 1943, was doing forced labour in the German Vergeltungswaffe salt-mine-cum-factory underground, which was part of a concentration camp. They had been sentenced for one year, which had long run out, but they were still in the mines, so Hubáček and a friend of his ran away, tied themselves to the bottom of a freight train,

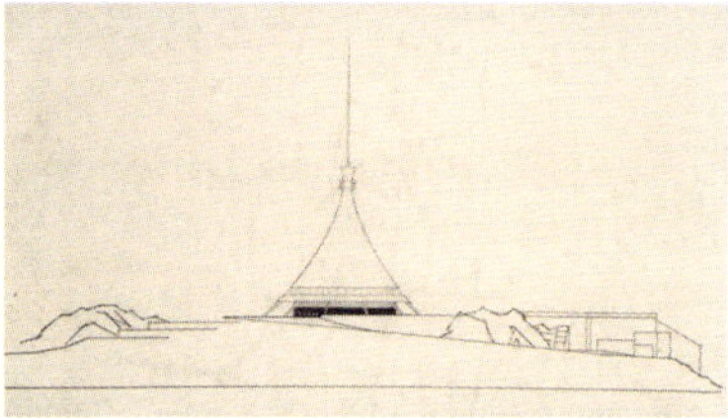

and went to the Magdeburg gestapo headquarters, where they presented – in perfect German – their complaints about the German Reich, which had failed to fulfil its commitments towards them.

The gestapo chief was so dismayed that he didn't shoot them or have them locked up but instead loaded them onto motorbikes with sidecars, took them to the concentration camp commander, and arranged for all the Czechs to be released within a few days. But the camp commander says: "But I'll keep these two here because they ran away." The gestapo man agreed: "Ordnung muss sein!"

The Czechs departed, but their train was unfortunately shot apart during an allied raid and nearly all of them perished. Hubáček then managed to escape and get back to Bohemia safely. That was Hubáček. My dears, I'm a stuck-up only child and I am not in the habit of going around admiring people, but I'll admit to having one guru. His name is Karel Hubáček. There are very few people like him!

That's not to say Hubáček handled us with care. We took home twelve hundred crowns per month and we paid for our accommodation ourselves. When we complained, he pointed towards the large drafting table and said: "There's plenty of space there."

It's true that when we worked long into the night, that's exactly where we slept. But then Masák found an old, partly abandoned pub close to Liberec, near Jedlová. He completely redesigned it and placed us in little booths, two people per booth, the levels divided only with a plywood partition: we slept upstairs and worked downstairs. I was with Emil Přikryl, who probably regretted this bitterly, as even at that age I snored and farted in my sleep terribly.

Jedlová became this strange beacon of normal life where all manner of friends would visit us, including Václav Havel, Pavel Štecha, various painters and sculptors. It was fantastic – which of course could not escape the communists' attention, so they arranged for a so-called delimitation and SIAL was absorbed by the state

Karel Hubáček, competition plans for the Ještěd communications tower (1963)

Karel Hubáček's birthday party, from left to right: Z. Zavřel, K. Hubáček, M. Rajniš, J. Cigler (1993)

company Stavoprojekt Liberec (Construction-Project Liberec).

In ten years, the SIAL Nursery gave rise to forty wonderful projects, but only four were realised – the Bolsheviks just didn't know how to build these brilliant things. And since drafting couldn't make us a living, our lives were financed by "Pyrok", a special anti-flammable material that would be sprayed onto steel structures, and a very well-paid adjacent production. SIAL bought the rights to use the English patent, and as fire regulations were getting stricter and stricter back then and recently built steel structures couldn't be made compliant in any other way, this was quite the business.

Hubáček had received one of the most prestigious architecture awards, the Auguste Perret Prize, and his Ještěd was justly described as the best Czechoslovak architecture of the 20th century. Alas, even God is right sometimes. When the original Ještěd (a lightly romantic cabin sitting atop a hill) burned down, God was probably looking at Hubáček trying to think of what to build there, and decided to inspire him with a brilliant idea: "Now look, Hubáček: what if you were to pull up Ještěd by the tip, say, a hundred and eighty metres into the air, concentrating the entire force of the volcano into a simple structure?" He also must have said to himself: "I've been following him for a long time and I know he deserves it..."

The First-Republic Hero Míra Masák

I also have to say a few words about Míra. The fact that the inconspicuous term "SIAL Nursery" became a legend is doubtless due to Miroslav Masák's ideas and dedication. None of it would exist without him. He was the boss of the Nursery and we had to address him in the formal manner – I understood this, but I also realised I can start liking my bosses only when they stop being bosses and become friends, which, thank God, was the case both with Míra Masák and Karel Hubáček.

Mirek is a person straight from the period of the First Republic (1919–1939) – he is well-mannered, he stands up when a lady joins the table, he speaks in clear, well-built sentences, he's clever, he knows a lot about many things, and we can really only envy him the depth and breadth of his erudition. His character is firm, and when he decides something is atrocious, nothing and no one can convince him otherwise.

It was he who constantly told me what the Bolsheviks were like, making me firmer in my belief that things must return to the right track – it is no coincidence that he was a good friend and important collaborator of Václav Havel. Hubáček and Masák created a famous duo and made SIAL and the Nursery famous.

I was extremely lucky to have met them both. The more I got to know them, the more I respected them. The only think I would say is that Míra should have made the walls at Jedlová at least a little bit thicker...

Máj (1972–1975)

—

Hubáček was such a good guy he would occasionally pass on commissions that any famous architect would leap at, which occasionally got us fantastic work. He always said: "Well, lads, come here, take out your violins and bows and start playing. It's yours!" This is how he passed the call for the Máj department store and the House of Technology on to Masák, Johny Eisler, and me.

In the spring of 1945, back when me and Dad used to go there to eat lobster canapés, a bomb fell on the corner of Spálená and Národní třída. Back then, it was only a wooden temporary building (oh, how gladly would I now build something like that there). And that's where a new department store was to be built, as well as something the Bolsheviks boastfully called the House of Technology. Míra Masák, a man of grand gestures, said: "Gentlemen,

Míra Masák at Jedlová (1970s)

Johny Eisler at Jedlová (1970s)

Drawing Máj at Jedlová (1970s)

we're going to the High Tatra Mountains to think it over."

The call was invitation-only, and like I said, Hubáček gave us his invitation. Another five famed teams participated, including Prager and his young helpers Línek and Milunić, but it was our design that won! Why? Thanks to Míra Masák's foresight and experience. He repeated from the start: "Gentlemen, it's obvious the Communists don't have enough cash for two buildings. They'll only build one. The second is a wild goose chase – so we have to put all the fundamentals into the shopping mall!" This cunning calculation was later confirmed. Make no bones about it – Míra is a visionary strategist.

As the kind reader will surely remember, I was born on Ostrovní, around the corner, and I lived there for twenty years, until 1965. This was my childhood stomping ground, and suddenly I was to design a huge building for it!

Máj and Kotva were intended to resolve a massive shortage of retail space in the centre of Prague, so building them was a political priority. If I'm honest, I always felt that Máj was too big for its location. Its dominant position is emphasised even further by the fact that it's on a street corner. It occupies a stronger position than a shopping mall should.

Even so, I think we made a beautiful building – or at least we tried as hard as we could. Suddenly, we were thinking in Czechia in a manner you could see in magazines in London or Scandinavia. It wasn't tired; it was crystal clear. We longed for architecture that would show strength, decisiveness, life without limits... no aestheticised boxes! We wanted a dynamic building, and I think we achieved that, at least partially.

After all, if you take up a thick architecture textbook, turn to the section labelled Czechoslovakia in the second half of the 20th century, and you'll find only two projects: Hubáček's Ještěd and our Máj. That means Máj's not bad, quite the contrary – it has many great qualities. But it's still just a department store! I think it's right that you can see on the face of it that it's just a box into which a lot of poor people walk in order to exchange their hard-earned cash for practically worthless goods. The people want it and the building gives it to them. It's no cathedral of consumerism!

We have to appreciate one more thing: Máj was built at the beginning of the 1970s, but our assignment was more like an assignment from the '30s – things like this hadn't been built in an entire generation! The Bolsheviks were slow, just like in everything else. The comrades who decided to commission it had just seen something from the '30s abroad and wanted to bring it over here.

And what's more: how do you make a fantastic shopping mall at a time when there are virtually no goods available? The philosophy of trade in a society of abundance and plenitude is entirely opposite to that in so-called socialism (a society of poverty and scarcity). The socialist investor takes care that the customers won't get in the way and will leave the building as soon as possible. In contrast, the capitalist wants to keep them in the mall as long as possible so that they buy more.

I have very profound memories of everything surrounding Máj, but I have to say that I was the weakest link in our trio – however hard I tried, I couldn't compare to the genius of Johny Eisler and the rational and experienced Míra Masák. What's more, my frequent spells in military jail took me out for more than a year, so Máj is really more Míra and Johny's work. Rajniš hides somewhere in the back behind a girder, riding along. But just like with brainstorming sessions – whoever participates is a co-author!

I learned a lot from my more talented colleagues, and I later used a lot of this knowledge in Smíchov – such as how important it is to try and incorporate the rough shopping mall into the structure of the city as softly as possible.

Illustrations for the project documentation submitted to the territorial committee deliberating on the Máj department store (1970s)

Máj department store (autumn 1974)

Something interesting happened with Máj: this building, scorned by many people, became protected cultural heritage. Of course, I consider this an irony of fate, as the conservationists – to whom I was the worst vermin in their district – had once sworn to kill me. The vermin has become a show-weasel! This situation was brought about by Professor Švácha, who's trying to protect modern buildings – unfortunately including the Paneláks[3] – as cultural heritage.

Well, it would be insolent of me to add anything... But it led to another situation. The owner of Máj, Tesco, wanted to demolish the original structure because they had somewhat different ideas of what a modern mall should be like. Thanks to this protection, though, they couldn't, so they came to us as the original architects and asked us to improve it.

Our Thwarted Innovations to Máj

However, we knew that Jakub Cigler was drafting Quadrio right next door, which would be of the same height, and we realised that Máj would need bolstering; raising up, aesthetically. We also wanted to make it into a magnificent public space, so we came up with the idea of raising the terrace by two storeys and installing a moveable roof, entering Máj into the latest dynamic game in the public spaces of the city centre. We drew it and congratulated each other – we really liked it.

But, as usual, the Tesco bosses couldn't see past the 840 million crown price tag, so Máj stayed the same as when we built it. It's a real shame that our innovation for Máj wasn't realised. Not only would it have been beautiful, and a success with the public too, I believe – it would have been a rare event: all three authors meeting again after forty years in full flight, to revisit and improve upon their original project. Our Máj terrace would certainly have become another of Prague's attraction...

When I walk through the area today, I feel that having Quadrio next door helped Máj, and not only in substance. Jakub is practically my blood

3 Tower block estates built by the Communists as high-density housing

brother, and I believe he'll forgive me if I say that Máj's architecture is drawn from a different pail, and a comparison of the two finds in favour of Máj. Furthermore, now that two buildings of equal size are next to each other, Máj's over-assertive presence on the corner is a little less of an eyesore.

An Appendix to Máj – A Memento of Socialist Business

Under socialism, the only two department stores in Prague, Máj and Kotva, had to have huge storage space because suppliers were unable to deliver regularly. Regular delivery is normal practice in market economies, and it couldn't work any other way, but Czech socialism couldn't manage it, and if we are to believe the news from North Korea, it still can't. So, the Trade Project Planning Institute was tasked with drafting plans for a huge warehouse – ten thousand square metres.

The ambitious deputy trade minister responsible for Máj and Kotva kept thinking about the storage coefficient, which establishes how many lanes the warehouse has available to store however many goods. This communist fiend then proposed a measure to save the national economy a few crowns (he even got a Volga for it or something), and came up with an idea to make the lanes in the warehouse narrower.

In his fit of innovation, he then went even further: "No concrete, asphalt's good enough for the floors!"

What do you think happened? The reason I mention it is that this is a situation typical of socialism: only one a single type of forklift truck would fit into the new, narrower lanes, and it had to be imported from England.

What did the supplier do? Knowing that their competition had been cut off, they tripled the price. Grinding their teeth, our comrades populated the lanes with expensive forklifts. But the legs of the tall shelves began digging into the asphalt, the shelves tilted and trapped the trucks in the lanes, creating a structure of products, shelves, and forklifts which hundreds of soldiers had to sort through with ladders, running around the warehouse extracting goods.

Dear children, would you wish for a repeat of these absurdities? I'm not sure if they took comrade deputy's Volga away, but I know for certain he wasn't fired...

Exhibitions (1979–1989)

—

Studio Shape

My exhibition period is indelibly linked with Studio Shape and Art Centrum. During Communism, Art Centrum was the international export office, armed by the state with a licence to export Czech and Slovak art around the world.

It was created following an incentive from doctor Matějíček. He was looking for a way to cooperate with professor Frič, who had enchanted one of the wives of the last Iranian Shah, Mohammad Reza Pahlavi, which created an opportunity for considerable profit. As a hole opened in the Iron Curtain, a curious situation was born – the communist dictatorship had to agree to a number of compromises. And since this office was the only option for the entire field, it's no wonder that it was the meeting point for top artists and all kinds of regime riffraff. In short, if there's only one watering hole, that's where everyone comes to drink.

I remember a moment in 1979 – I was sitting in my studio above the Čertovka canal, it was drizzling, narrow trickles of acid rain were running down the slanted windows, and I was thinking about the fact that I would never have what one becomes so easily accustomed to – a regular salary. The thought that I was leaving the zoo for the jungle, as a free creature, brought tears to my eyes. I soon found out I'd like the jungle more and more.

Much later, when I saw how many problems people have with capitalism, I was grateful for my previous experiences in trade, because I had no real problems with entrepreneurship. I was like a fish in water. The real change in my professional life only came later, when I opened my own bureau and employed several collaborators. Only then did I fully realise the old times were irretrievably gone... But back to Studio Shape.

Jaromír Hník and his melody boys

Jaromír Hník, my classmate from elementary school, established and led Studio Shape, directing work at large international exhibitions. His group brought together a number of capable people. The basic team was composed of three people with clearly divided tasks: Jaromír Hník took care of trade, production, and representation, Jirka Černý was in charge of the technical side of things – lights, sound, projections, computers, information systems –, and I managed the design and architecture.

We did many commissions around the world, our clients were almost exclusively Western companies. I enjoy reminiscing about several interesting commissions, many of which were also huge challenge because virtually everything was a problem in the Czechoslovak Socialist Republic. One of the really nice ones was a project at the Tsarevets Castle, where we used strange light and sound installations to tell the castle's history, bound for many centuries to the fate of Bulgaria. I recently got a call from Jaromír – apparently the Bulgarians are still very happy with our work twenty-five years later and would like to invite us to come and see that everything is still operational.

I have to say our great results were mostly down to the extent to which both Jaromír and Jirka insisted on technical excellency, ruthlessly demanding the best, chiefly of themselves. Compared to me, the trench fighter, these were generals of an excellently organised army on the frontlines.

For Art Centrum, Studio Shape was the goose that laid golden eggs. The chiefs knew that if they let us work, they'd barely have to do anything themselves. And since we had verified that whatever we didn't do ourselves would probably end in disaster, we left them only petty administration, and 40% of the profits.

Jaromír Hník
(2016)

For seven years, this was my link to Jaromír Hník, Míša Brix, Tomáš Paul, Kurt Gebauer, Jirka Černý, the fantastically talented architect and draughtsman Luboš Jíra, and dozens – no, hundreds – of others.

I should mention, even briefly, the writer and screenwriter Petr Hořejš. As an anti-socialist, he was persecuted by the regime, so he wrote under a nom de plume – 'Hora'. After the revolution, he made his name with a popular book series titled Toulky českou minulostí (Rambles Through Czech History). I have to say the brainstorming sessions that included Petr were pure joy. He's a very well-read and entertaining guy, always full of understanding for a mad idea.

Thanks to this work, our lives within the confines of socialist greyness were freer but also quite schizophrenic: we lived in socialism, but we worked in a functioning market economy. In any case, it was a huge experience and one that made us a lot more prepared for capitalism when it burst into our lands following 1989. As is the custom in the Czech Republic, many were convinced we could only have done this "dream job" at the cost of cooperating with the secret police – I will happily present them with my negative lustration certificate.

When I left the SIAL Nursery, Hubáček told me I was leaving the opera (i.e. real architecture) for operettas (i.e. exhibitions). What I learned, however, is that operettas are often much harder on one than opera.

Expo 86

The legendary Expo 86, the theme of which was transportation, took place in Vancouver, on the Canadian west coast. It was also to celebrate one hundred years since the completion of the trans-Canadian railway. Jaromír arranged that Studio Shape was invited to participate in the competition for the themed pavilion of the History of Transport, financed by a large oil corporation and installed in a century-old heating plant: The Roundhouse.

This was no easy match – we found ourselves competing with several dozen of the most renowned teams in the USA, Canada, and England. It was a competition of two rounds with a six-week break between them. I think our success was considerably aided by the fact that once we handed in our proposal for the first round, we kept working hard even though we didn't know whether we'd advance to the second round. We were awfully relieved when they called us to say we had. Very few times in my life have I felt joy like I felt when we ended up winning it outright.

Naturally, this couldn't have happened without a great idea. Creative brainstorming was done in a team comprising Jaromír Hník, Petr Hořejš, Jirka Černý, and myself. We decided that we'd display the most famous technological exhibits from around the world on the ground, while above them, in the air, there would be something like a dream theatre.

A hundred years on, we realised the machines of mad inventors, on which actors from the Na provázku Theatre sailed above the heads of the awestruck spectators. The result was a combination of reality, hyperbole, theatre, and outright madness, which the audience accepted with enormous enthusiasm – they were willing to wait in line for several hours!

Expo 86 was a big undertaking, its budget set at around seven billion dollars, led by manager Jimmy Pattison – he became a good friend of ours. The local government of British Columbia trusted him with this important position because he was famous for never losing money on anything. After his long working day, Jimmy would often come to our pavilion, climb atop one of our machines and jaunt around while doing his paperwork. He'd pedal and pedal, rabidly shouting into his telephone, which looked more like a walkie-talkie back then.

Jimmy Pattison and Expo Ernie, Vancouver (1986)

Roundhouse exterior, Vancouver (1986)

Jimmy Pattison and Whale-Fucking Bay

We left the unions at home, so the Czech workers were almost on forced labour. They worked from seven in the morning to ten at night for five dollars a day – their food, accommodation, and Czech wages were already covered. To increase comfort and lower costs, we had our own cook.

Jimmy, who was pretty severe with everyone, took an interest at the time: "How much do you pay them? Five bucks an hour?

And I said: "A day! Plus food, a bed, and their wages running up back home."

"Fuck me, that can't be. Just under two hundred a month?"

"Really, Jimmy, they like it. I keep telling them they're the best in the world."

"Well, they probably are," he said. "How did you talk them into it?"

"I'll tell you a grand Czech secret," I said. "I promised them I'd show them the bay where the whales go to fuck, and I'll make good on that promise. They'll be the only ones in Czechoslovakia. They're looking forward to it so much. That's part of the reason they've been slaving away for three months."

When the pavilion was nearly finished, Jimmy came around and handed out invitations to his yacht to the workers.

The men stood on the peer dressed in their Sunday best. An enormous luxury yacht arrived – back then, Jimmy had about three billion dollars, which is quite a lot even in American terms. They were welcomed by a whole crew dressed in white – steward, captain, engineer, and three secretaries. They also had a synthesiser that could play like any instrument. Jimmy sang and the three secretaries formed a choir. This was their celebration of labour for a group of socialist workers. Jimmy said he really liked how they worked, and that he'd like to thank them. And because thanks should be personal, apparently, he'd take them all on a three-hour cruise on the sea. And he'd even sing along.

One of the workers came up to me and asked: "Hey, Martin, is this a capitalist?"

"A classic capitalist," I retorted.

"And do they all sing like this?"

"Don't be stupid," I said. "He only sings for you, because you're the best in the world!"

"The comrades won't believe this," he said. I suggested we make some photographs so the comrades would believe him.

Jimmy's secretaries were like multi-coloured flowers in a garden: black, white, and Asian. This was part of his democratic worldview. In short, Jimmy was someone who fits right in with that New York City airport joke – a policeman asks a passenger: "Father's name?"

"I have no father!"

"Mother's name?"

"I have no mother!"

"So, who are you?"

"I'm a self-made man!"

It would also be polite to mention the exhibition was extraordinarily successful. I was asked to present it to an audience of several thousand. We screened many beautiful pictures: romantic shots of Kurt Gebauer's swiftly sculpted reliefs or Vláďa Jeník's old and rusty models: a twenty-wing airplane, a railway powered by the wind, or an emergency suit for women to use in the event of a ship sinking.

Authentic silent films about inventions and inventors were also part of the exhibition: these blokes would lecture on their inventions inside an airplane motor blown up to twenty-four times its size, fitted with a golden railing, padded with red plush, and featuring a curtain drawn by Míra Jiránek. He painted the nose of an automobile, personified by a nude girl whose flight across the sky symbolises the triumph of power and speed. It looked a little like an Austro-Hungarian imperial brothel and I enjoyed it immensely. Jaromír Hník could put together the best of the best. The music for the film was composed by Michael Kocáb.

It was a hell of a lot of work. I had two tasks: to make sure that the English would lend us a precise and functional replica of the most famous steam locomotive in the world – "The Rocket", and to figure out and oversee the correct placement of this unique machine at the Roundhouse. Stevenson, who built it, was a similar whizz to

Gustav Eiffel, who built a steel tower in Paris in 1890. He's my adopted great-grandfather and my favourite person among builders, right after Hubáček.

The Portable Engine and the Aboriginal Canadian on the Roof

The engine driver from the museum in London was a slim older gentleman with a piercing gaze. He carried a briefcase containing a white single-use overall made of paper. He'd slip it on over his suit, so he was always ready. A reminder: this was the time of the Cold War, the Iron Curtain, and Czechoslovakia, with its Slovak president, Dr Gustav Husák, was considered one of the worst world tyrannies.

I flew from Canada to London with a passport full of stamps, and I was immediately accosted by a serious black officer from immigration asking for the reason of my visit. "To borrow the Rocket locomotive and take it to Canada for the world exhibition."

He stared at me in disbelief: "You're trying to tell me that you, a Czech, will take our famous Rocket to Canada, and you just want me to stand idly by?"

When I explained the situation, he burst out laughing. "My kids are going to shit themselves laughing when I tell them." And he let me go.

The portable engine, with its hellish power, was a key exhibit for us. For those who have no idea what I'm talking about – it's basically a precursor of the tractor. A huge steam engine on wheels which doesn't move on the strength of its motor, so it had to be dragged onto the field. It was a kind, strong, universal machine. A little stupid, but just as people do, it made up for its stupidity in strength.

I was to decide which one we'd take, and unfortunately, I chose with emotion, not reason. I opted for the largest, and two days later, it was in Vancouver. But it was so awfully big and heavy that the poor thing collapsed into a canal. It was a huge cock-up and, of course, I caught a lot of shit for it: "You're a total idiot and you've gone and fucked it up for all of us."

It caused me so much grief that I got depressed, thinking of my poor wife Johanka going mad in our flat in Malá Strana while I was going mad in Canada. It broke me, so I climbed atop the roof of our skyscraper and estimated how long I'd take to fly down, and where on the ground I'd burst apart.

God knows where he came from, but an Aboriginal Canadian was sat there. He started talking to me in this strange English. He asked me what my plan was, and I said I intended to jump off because life is an absolute bitch and I'd fucked everything up and thrown a number of people into slavery. And he started talking about all manner of things – about the animals he knew in the forest and how he is the last of a great lineage and how everyone had already died of measles or starvation.

We talked and talked, and I suddenly said to myself: "Nothing doing, I'll go downstairs, have a shot, faint, and that'll be it for the day." And I realised what a coward I was. "So, what – I chose a large portable engine, it fell through the basement, they'll lift her out and everything'll be alright. Part of the steel structure is fucked, but the world isn't about to collapse." In the end, we opened the exhibition and people stood in line for hours. Even though I occasionally suffered, I enjoyed all the phases of the preparation immensely.

So, we gradually became experts at the grandest world Expos and everyone was asking about our next big hit. But I told Jaromír: "You know it from the Bible. Seven years of plenty have passed, and I'm moving on. From operettas back to the opera. Thanks to you, my friend, I've even got decent money to do it!"

M. R.
(1994)

Nora Geislerová with Arnošt
(1994)

The Revolutionary Years (1986–1998)

—

The autumn of 1986 was the peak of the tragedy with my first wife, Johanka, of whom you'll hear more later; and I was also establishing a new company, DA Studio – 'DA' because we did both design and architecture. Everyone said:

"You've gone mad! You can't stick your neck out like this, you have to be discreet. Buy a villa and live off the money you made in Canada!" It's true that opening a private company at a time when doing business was a crime, rewarded with a pretty hefty prison sentence, was mad. But it was also a brave act.

I just went ahead and had a stamp made, and because no administrative box and no legal norm existed for this form of work, we had to be freelancing artists. And since visual artists were a no-go, we became co-authors of exhibition scenarios – in short, literary men. But little work came for us, and the money from Vancouver gradually disappeared. We were in the red for the first year and a half. Bravely, I covered our losses.

DA Studio began working with the arrival of Markéta Cajthamlová, Lev Lauermann, and their friends Tom Prouza, Jára Zima, and later Standa Fiala. Because we were going through Art Centrum, we liaised with an Austrian studio and also called in Honza Mleziva as coordinator, who was able to pull the right strings and secure the possibility of travelling to the West for work, a big problem back then.

Wages still exceeded income, but I was accounting for that. The situation improved slowly. We started doing international competitions and everything was on the right track. But then, a mid-life crisis struck me, and by the time Jirka Němeček snapped me out of it, the revolution had begun and I felt a new stage of life was starting. I was forty-five, and missing a lot of skills...

Three Stories with the Bolsheviks

Before the ringing of the keys ushered in the revolution, a number of great and small conflicts with the dying regime took place, and I wouldn't be me, the old rabble-rouser, if I hadn't fed the fire. For all the cuts I left on the butt of the Bolsheviks, let me name three at least.

It was 28 October 1988, and there was another fight with the police on Old Town Square. After the protest, I went to Maxov without getting changed. On that day, everyone at the summer house in the Jizera Mountains would meet by the huge fire that Jára Horník always made. Sausages on the fire, drinking, and everyone in a good mood.

When I arrived, they started laughing at me – I was dirty. But revolution is like work – you need special clothes, and if you work well, dirt is a distinction. "Martin, you're a grown man, stop acting like some idiot. Bolshevism will be here for another three generations." These people were certainly no fans of Bolshevism – they were just trying to draw me back to reality.

But I got terribly pissed off and said: "You know what, if Bolshevism is still here in the year 2000, I owe each of you a bottle of whisky. And if not, you'll each pitch in and buy me a few crates. Proper whisky too – my favourite is Cardhu single-malt from the river Spey."

So, we bet on it: me against twenty-seven people. We spent a long time getting drunk after that, because they all made good on their promise, even though they brought it to me bit by bit, acting as though they'd ripped it out of their children's or grandchildren's mouths. As we drank through it gradually, everyone took great joy in it.

In 1988, we had a financial review of the studio, and because I knew we had a number of problems, I strengthened myself with the 'alcohol with a human face' – Stará myslivecká, or Myslivec, also known as Czech whisky. The reason it was called 'booze with a human face' was that the label presented a hunter, his nose and cheeks red from drinking. Lev Lauermann rightly criticised me for my disorderly management of the office, which threw me off.

I ran out of the office and jumped on the subway, where I found a discarded edition of Rudé právo – The Red Truth, the communist party newspaper. Gripped by rage, I twisted it into a speaking trumpet and paraded through the car screaming "Death to Bolshevism!" The policeman

who was sat there – probably a decent fellow – pretended nothing was happening. Everyone else exchanged looks and grimaces, which provoked me to scream even louder.

When I got out on Malostranská, they were already waiting for me. I felt the alcohol spreading through my body, my legs getting stiff, and I thought: "Now you've finally fucked it. Lev is right – you're terrible." But my emergency mechanisms kicked in after all. They were dragging me to that booth in the middle of the platform when I told them:

"Comrades, bear in mind I'm just drafting a villa for comrade Štrougal and I'm in a bit of a rush." Štrougal was the prime minister at the time.

They exchanged silent glances and then dragged me to the drinking fountain. They put my head in the water and shouted: "Now get up, you fucking piece of shit, and stop your shouting!" Thankfully, it ended there – on that occasion, at least.

Story number three is called: "Can a decent architect build in SANOPS[4] for the children of the central committee?" The answer is YES, though I don't know if it's quite kosher. A great bloke, Dr Standa Kusý, came to me, and he said: "You do these nice things for kids, joyful and colourful. I work in a clinic for deaf children nearby, in Smíchov. Make me a building where the children won't be afraid of the doctors. Where they'll be happy, and they'll know nothing bad awaits them."

So, we sat down and drafted a building with loads of toys, a butterfly flying across the surgery beating its wings, and a padded swing to sit on. The excellent painter Aleš Lamr worked on it with us, among other people. First, we put together the interiors, but when I looked at the project, I was overcome by terror and I redrew the whole thing in a few days.

This was some nerve – back then, I was Mr Nobody. Nobody here was interested in a successful exhibition in Canada, and except Máj, I had no significant projects to my name. Thankfully, the project received the necessary blessing and construction could start.

When I arrived at the site, the concrete entry gate was not only crooked in all kinds of directions, it was also badly sheathed. I said: "You can build your Bolshevik buildings however you want, but when I'm here, you'll build properly! Now take it down and sheathe it correctly!" The site manager came over and admitted that it was a disgrace.

Four days later, it was done in concrete once again. A little better but still crooked. I was livid: "You must've gone mad! Do you really want to piss me off?"

"Watch out you don't piss us off," they replied. So, I came back by car in the evening, put a rope around the pillar, and tore it down.

When they came 'round in the morning, the gate was on the ground. They wanted to report me to the police.

"Feel free," I said. "But bear in mind they'll drag it through Radio Free Europe."

Their highest-ranking boss came and said: "Comrades, the architect here is right. It wasn't well built, comrades. And your brigade of socialist labour should be ashamed of itself."

Opening of the children's eye clinic (1986)

Lev Lauerman, Markéta Cajthamlová, Johanka, and me as a waiter at the opening of the children's eye clinic (1986)

Opening of the children's eye clinic (1986)

4 A state-of-the-art hospital for exclusive use by Communist party members

So, it came to pass that the third time round, the comrades built it properly. Of course, they thought I was a total lunatic. How could some crooked gate anger anyone living in late socialism? The hospital opened and one arch-Bolshevik, an art critic, wrote: "It remains a significant question why our comrades selected as obvious an anti-socialist as comrade Rajniš. Why should he preside over such a prestigious project, a centre for their children? There should be a meticulous examination by the comrades in the committee of the Architecture Union."

I told Standa Kusý: "Now for bravado... We'll do what the Bolshevik kids have here but in a normal hospital. All children are equal, aren't they? Or are the red kids better?" So we built the same in a hospital in Lužiny.

The building was drawn up by Alena Šrámková, but victories can also be bitter, especially under socialism. Even though the children and their mothers loved it there, the nurses had no love for our beautiful surgery. They protested: the children are unruly, it's too colourful, and the kids come into the consulting room all sweaty. These nurses, royal bitches that they were, treated our hospital like stepmothers – I think it was closed down after just a few years, while the department at SANOPS still survives, though in a derelict state. Sad, isn't it?

I asked myself whether I wasn't sucking up to the communists by working for them, and I found two answers. First, it was necessary to get the project approved so that 'average' children would have the same opportunities. Second, I remembered how pissed off I had felt as a child when I was treated differently because of my parents. I said to myself: "You're not going to treat a deaf communist child differently just because you don't like his daddy, mummy, or both!"

This was my Solomon's answer, but I felt a little like the New York rabbi who found a thick wallet on the street during sabbath and began contemplating the conditions which create a miracle. And then, he suddenly realised that the miracle was that the sabbath was all around him, but around the wallet, it was Tuesday, so he could calmly put it in his pocket...

Golden Eggs for Vlado Milunić

We were doing well, and our business annoyed a number of people. People like Vlado Milunić or Honza Línek, who mostly worked on old people's homes, reproached us for being so full of money that the lard was running down our chins.

Once, after the revolution, Vlado came to me and said: "Martin, tell me, how do you do capitalism?"

"I'll give you one piece of advice, Vlado. You always have to watch your cashflow."

"What's that?"

"That's how the money flows through your company."

"Fine, I can do that."

So, I continued: "You always have to have at least 40% of that money in the bank, otherwise the company will go bust once in a while."

And he says: "But where do I get that money?"

"Yeah, if you had lard running down your chin like I do, you could just scrape it off." His grimacing was awful, but in the end, he started laughing.

Vlado is mad, but very skilful too. Once I gave him a "golden egg". It went like this: Shortly before the revolution, Jaromír Hník told us that the Bulgarians wanted us to build a museum of Todor Živkov for a lot of money.

I told him: "I just won't build a museum for that Bolshevik swine. Sorry. You're my friend, but I want nothing to do with this."

"Recommend someone, then," he said.

"Milunić, Línek, they're good," I replied.

A few days later, Milunić calls me in shock: "Martin, you passed us a golden egg!"

"What golden egg?"

"Živkov!"

"That's no golden egg for me – for me, he's a Bolshevik whore."

And he says: "With permission, my dear, fuck that. I'm from the Balkans, both my parents were partisans, revolutionaries, and communists."

I replied: "Vlado, enjoy it. I'm not doing it, but I have nothing against you doing it."

Then the revolution arrived and the entire brilliant project went up in smoke before even the first fees had been paid. I'm not saying this with spiteful joy. But one has to be careful – where revolution stirs in the land, it's no idyll...

The Unfortunately Velvet Revolution

Remembering the revolution now, I have to say that after twenty-five years of experience, I regret it wasn't more forceful. See, for example, the story of the deputy principal who so tortured me and whom I met as a hunched up old man on Národní třída, surviving only as a wreck one cannot even punish. When I see the communists giving themselves airs, and that son-of-a-bitch Putin, what I witness daily is the fifth column watching and waiting for a weakness – it all seems truly absurd.

When I return from my travels and land at the Václav Havel Airport, I'm never in a great mood. I just never really look forward to returning to our little Czech valley. Why? When 54% of us vote for the monster sitting at the Castle not five hundred feet from my beautiful nest in Úvoz, and when I look at the little houses people are building all around Prague, and when I see the hundreds of hectares planted with shitty Smurf houses (and rapeseed), I have to say to myself: "Damn you all to hell!" All of it will be there for another three generations. And I'm supposed to live in this country? It's as if you had pissed in my bed and wished me good night.

Among other things, the Bolsheviks stole dozens of buildings I could've built. They took away the opportunity to learn languages by staying abroad, they robbed me of my naturally equal position in the field of architecture, one that wouldn't be smeared by human and political filth and compromise. They destroyed my family – my grandmas, my aunt, my dad, my mum... It's fair for me to tell it like it is, isn't it? The regime should not be allowed to just quietly fizzle out!

I saw Germans who stayed in the Sudetenland who were afraid of saying even a word in German. When they couldn't say it in Czech, they simply gestured, like Frau Posselt. She was a German who didn't leave during the 1945 expulsion, and she was a shop assistant at the local general store. Her behaviour at least reflected the guilt she felt for the past.

But I registered no such penitence from the Bolsheviks. Quite the contrary – the arrogant bullshit they constantly let out! They serve as a fifth column in the Czech lands, acting in sympathy with the regenerating imperial Bolshevik-nationalist Russian regime, and there is no doubt in my mind that they would build concentration camps again without a moment's hesitation. They certainly have their lists ready, and I'm sure many of my friends are in leading positions.

Even though democracy is often quite powerless, what's great about it is that if we say NO in sufficient numbers, the entire political class can vacate the field. And this stinking, sweet-and-sour brine the whole country is wading about in is the reason I don't like coming back here and why I always get depressed when I do. But two or three days later, I pull myself together and ask myself: "Who are you?" And I answer: "A right-wing anarchist who can't afford to be diffident, defeatist, and depressive! That's no course of action! – So, get over it!"

Protests and the Warm Grenade in the National Gallery

You know what they say: when a horse is on its last legs, that's when it kicks the hardest. But those kicks, thank God, were a little off target. With a large group of friends, we attended practically all the protests. For example, Palach Week – that was really something! The police would throw all manner of disgusting stuff at us, such as tear gas, but we were armed with gloves, hats, and wet cloth over our mouths.

Meanwhile, in the studio, we were designing interiors for the National Gallery. The work was led by Míra Masák and the team included Alena Šrámková, Emil Přikryl, and many others.

Once, I was in a rush to get to a coordination meeting with a deputy director of the National Gallery. The meeting was on Old Town Square, but a great battle with the police started on Jungmannova, where I managed to catch a burning tear-gas grenade in flight and throw it back into the OT-64. They jumped down like fleas out of a coat, cursing terribly and chasing us around Národní třída with their batons. I picked up a burnt-out grenade, still warm, but I suddenly realised I should get to the meeting – I'd completely forgotten about it in the furore of battle.

Grimy all over with the warm grenade in my pocket, I arrived at the National Gallery. Johny Eisler was there, and the old buffers present had something to say about my appearance, of course. That pissed me off, so I pulled the grenade out: "I'm a revolutionary, so kindly dispense with this nonsense. Until we finish up the revolution properly, this work won't be worth shit anyway!"

After a moment, Alena Šrámková's exclamation interrupted the stunned silence: "The young one's right, damnit!" And that was that.

17 November 1989

At the time, we were designing the furniture for the Technical Library in České Budějovice for the A-8000 studio, run by Střítecký and Krupauer. On the day before the crucial protest on November 17th, we were working our asses off – we were due to hand in a load of drawings.

Jára Zima came in: "A warrior against the Bolsheviks like you, and you won't go to the protest?"

"Go to hell, Jára. We've got a deadline – it's noses against the grindstone until Tuesday. It's tight enough as it is. Besides, this protest won't be anything wild..."

But Jára insisted, "You have to be there!"

So, we went to Albertov, then up to the Slavín cemetery and onto the embankment. We turned onto Národní třída and I was in the front rows.

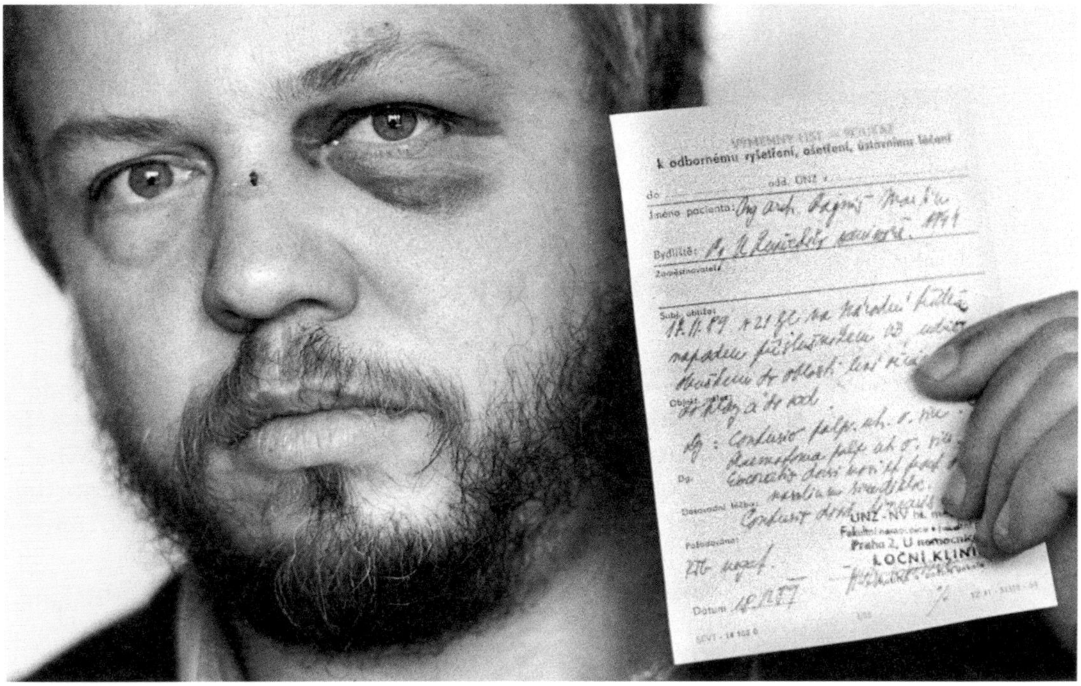

Protest on Národní třída, Prague (November 17th, 1989)

Hit in the face on Národní třída (November 17th, 1989)

Beautiful girls gazing admiringly at myself and V. Havel (1989)

Suddenly, I sensed it was getting juicy. We stopped in front of Máj and sat down. Facing us was the famous police squadron. I glimpsed Tom Prouza near the language school and then the action started.

They chased us into a cloister, and I was staring right at this poor beggar with a baton, so I got hit in the face – I ended up with a broken nose and a mild concussion. My eye was swollen, but I managed to manoeuvre my way through Ostrovní, Legion Bridge, and Kampa, all the way to bed. My head hurt like hell in the morning, but I decided I had to work. So, I went to the office, where Pavel Štecha was photographing some models.

Jana Němečková was there too, and, by coincidence, so was Jirka Němeček, my doctor and friend, who said: "Chop chop, we're off to the hospital." Off we went to the Na Františku hospital. As they were filling in the report, the nurse said: "This was probably in the bathroom, right? You slipped and hit your head on something..."

But I retorted:

"Not at all. I was assaulted by a rabid policeman."

And they warned me: "Sir, they won't be happy about that at your work."

"Work? That's just me! I'm a private company," I argued.

"Okay, we'll write it in if you insist."

We came back to the office and Pavel Štecha said: "We have to take a picture of the eye. But you look like you've been in a bar fight – take the doctor's report and show it to the camera." Pavel was a master of his craft and this photograph raised me up to celestial heights. When – less than a year later – I took my students on our first trip to Berlin, I was hung up in the Museum of Dissent at the Czech Point, among the other dissidents. The students roared with laughter: "So you're a worthy dissident, something like a Czech Sakharov, right?"

DESIGN. DA ARCHITECTURE.
D.A. STUDIO.
XAVERIOVA 3
CS-150 00 PRAHA 5
CZECHOSLOVAKIA
TEL. 02/54 86 68

Almost a Politician

I spent a few weeks doing politics too. This was how it went: we occupied the Union of Architects and established the OFA – the Civic Forum of Architects, an extension of Občanské fórum (Civic Forum), the political movement of the revolution. Míra Masák called a few days after the revolution: "Václav wants an architect to lead the ministry of the interior. A few people have already told me to fuck off, so I thought of you. Vašek agrees. You'll be minister of the interior!"

"Míra, have you gone mad? How many policemen would I be commanding?"

"Forty-five thousand. You've got some experience with the police, haven't you? You'll be great."

I panicked. "Are you crazy? I can't do that!" But he pushed and pushed until I agreed: "Great times demand great acts and great sacrifices. If you'll be my deputy, I'll take it." I felt droplets of sweat running down my neck, over my back, and down to my bum. It was a lot to take in and my nerves were shot. Thankfully, four hours later, Míra Masák called again: "Well that's a load off my mind, and yours too – they found some squirt from the People's Party who'll do it – Sacher." Once again, I'd escaped just in time. Míra later admitted he was also immensely relieved.

I was thrown into the water and I had to learn to swim. As quickly as I could muster, I learned to do business from Jaromír Hník, and the way I worked with money was trial and error – which of course meant I'd occasionally drown quite a lot of money somewhere. Even though trouble certainly made no effort to avoid us, we usually got pretty lucky.

But then there was this highly unpleasant episode: we had some cash in our company cash box, and following a general consensus, we had agreed to leave it as a reserve. Imagine our surprise when we found it was gone.

This was in 1991, when a manager of ours – together with some other lads of a similar ilk – decided to establish a new company, and for capital, each of them would "withdraw" money from their current jobs during the holiday season. A fantastic way of securing working capital, isn't it? They knew our justice system was a total shambles and what's more, they had all the documentation – with that, it would be easy to claim that part of the money was in fact theirs and thus transfer the affair from criminal law to civil law. I was mad with rage.

And now, I'll tell you a fairy-tale: There was once a bandit called Honza. And my message for that smart-ass is: "Dear Honza, go fuck yourself! You robbed your friends and one day, the earth will be heavy on your grave!"

A conversation I later had with the smart-ass Honza really did me in. In true-to-form arrogance, he said: "Forget ever seeing that money again. Let me put it this way: bribing the public prosecutor will be about a hundred thousand, plus another hundred and fifty for the lawyer, so if you recall your lawsuit, I'll give you the two hundred and fifty thousand. It'll be less work for me, and you won't have the million and a half, but you'll have the two hundred and fifty thousand at least. Better than getting shot in the foot, right?"

Of course, I got pissed off. "You fucking whore, do you think I'll accept a filthy mafia agreement like that? I'll get you into a striped uniform one day!"

With my colleagues from the DA Studio, from left to right: Jaroslav Zima, Tomáš Prouza, M.R., Stanislav Fiala (early 1990s)

DA Studio business card (early 1990s)

M.R. as an orderly entrepreneur (early 1990s)

Stamp of the Czech Chamber of Architects ("authorised architect") (1990)

And the nimble entrepreneur told me: "It seems you still look at the world with the eyes of a realist. See you later!" The tougher the times, the more important it is to play fair, and the worst thief is one who steals from his friends...

The Chamber of Architects

Most people thought I'd do great in capitalism – I was trained for it, so I'd simply raise the anchor, chase the galley slaves below decks, and sail out to sea with my golden ribbons fluttering about in the ocean air. But it was a little more complicated than that. For a long time, conditions here were uncertain, with bureaucratic procedures taking up loads of time. To ensure that not just anyone could wipe their asses with architects – as had happened before – we established the Civic Forum of Architects. Nobody can reproach us for wanting to become a respected profession.

At meetings, we'd discuss the problem of how you are to make a young hen if there's no mother hen, no cock, and no egg – simply put, no one to fuck it and no one to lay it. Thirty of us were sat in the Malá Strana Palace back then, and we agreed we'd lay the first thirty eggs. And we immediately agreed that the other twenty-nine would vote on each of us to determine whether they could become one of the golden eggs and receive the chamber's round stamp. The situation certainly did not lack historical irony, but as Uncle Lenin used to say: "When you cut down a forest, splinters will fly." I didn't push to get to the table, so my registration number is 00028. The revolution imprinted in us a humble and helpful spirit.

Revolution in the Czech lands is a complex, never-ending bureaucracy – there's memoranda, analyses, appeals, declarations, and for us anarchists, that's boring. There were a number of things with which none of us had had any experience, so we learned as we went. Once, they came to see me from the Chamber, asking how they calculate architects' fees abroad. They dealt with it following my instructions, and my own office later wrote invoices for a nice few million based on the Chamber's fee system. It's not a bad thing when the revolution lets its children make a little money.

Ten years after the revolution, my life couldn't be better. I was earning decent money and I learnt to deal with "long money" without being scared of it. I met a number of people returning from emigration, and developers started contacting me too. I married a wife who gave me energy and courage and who could appreciate the charm of the newly created social standing that money put us in. I was suddenly also a father to the three children whom Lubka brought into our marriage, and perhaps it was also due to them that I felt I really had to go at it hard. The twins squawked day after day, from six a.m. to midnight, and I wasn't built for that at all – but since I worked a lot and I was away often, it was bearable.

And big commissions started coming. I always had a clear idea on how they should be executed, which gave me strength in the meetings. Back then, I was able to answer even treacherous questions on the spot, so I worked pretty fast.

When the Iron Curtain fell, various characters began appearing, and they wanted to develop property here. I realised our country was not ready at all – the authorities, planning materials, and everything else...

Then I remembered a Radio Free Europe broadcast in the days of the revolution. It was about a family of beavers somewhere in Canada, who – as there was no water around – lived for several beaver generations in a very un-beaverly way: on dry land. So, the observers performed an experiment with this beaver family: they took them several thousand kilometres away to true beaver territory with trees and water and everything, just to see how the beavers would react. To their enormous surprise, within two years, they started building dams and doing everything else that proper beavers do. Their instincts were not lost! And the people on Radio Free Europe said:

"Friends, for people, free entrepreneurship is as natural as dam-building is to beavers." So, I stuck with that...

I was never taken aback by commercial success. True, it cost me a lot of money to keep DA Studio in business. Everyone moaned about how poor we were, but it takes a while before something really gets moving and starts making money.

And then interesting things started happening: The Austrian company Plan und Bau approached us with a number of commissions, and we started working on them with gusto. But our darling was the developer Moje Lenardson, whom I knew from Máj. He was a tall Swede, a friend and collaborator of Ole Norlin. He married a Czech woman, but he worked for Ingvar Kamprad and his company, Ikano, which owns Ikea.

We made a nice number of buildings with them, including a large house, Wenceslas Square 32–34, on land worth 220 million crowns. We also built a house recently nominated for the Mies van de Rohe Prize, next to the Congress Centre in Prague 4 – Martin Kloda worked on that a lot. It was a normal rental admin building, but the funny part was that in terms of economy (construction costs versus profits), we became the best in the country. It was unique: reasonable architecture and big money were suddenly not in opposition but instead walked hand in hand.

I'll allow myself a few more words on economy: the way you build is that first, there's a property developer. He buys the land, puts together an idea of what should be on it, hires an architect who draws it up, then receives the appropriate paperwork and builds it, and when it's done, the developer tries to sell or rent it.

When renting houses, the "rendita" (assumed revenue) is an important economic indicator. It is measured by the percentage of yearly income against all the developer's expenses. In Vienna, for example, it was around 7% at the time, which was considered a huge success. We achieved a rendita of an unbelievable 14.15% of the developer's outlay.

It was as if the hen had laid us not one but two golden eggs every day.

When this sum was published, the phones really started ringing. I became the goose that laid the golden eggs, sent to scratch around in Canada for a while, so that I could return to lay a few at home.

Smíchov (1990–2005)

—

In Smíchov, a south-west district of Prague, the Velvet Revolution came along with a revolution in urbanism. It followed that the architect Prager had spent ten years drafting a new Smíchov, but what had come of it was truly bizarre. At least a few elements illustrate my point: for example, his tunnel was to exit Strahov hill straight into the heart of Smíchov, demolishing pretty buildings like the Women's Homes. Houses built on huge legs would tower above the city, with people living only on and above the fifteenth floor – not the only "big hit" these buildings offered!

Following the revolution, the politicians changed, and the people expected to finally be able to participate in the meetings which determined the future of their own neighbourhoods. The ODS party could feel this. Their representative, Eva Kalhousová, said something like: "You're young, you're not communists, and if you've got so much to say about how shit Prager's plans are, draw us your idea of Smíchov!" Yes, back then, I could still talk to politicians –they acted like fairly normal people.

So, we said to ourselves: What's the most important thing about the city? That it's full of people wanting to meet. People need to have the opportunity to share their troubles and joys; see others in action. In the streets, cafés, and pubs, we witness every day the fantastic theatre of life which makes the city a habitable structure.

Working at the DA Studio (1990s)

Old Smíchov (1990)

One of the first models of the regeneration of Smíchov, DA Studio (1992)

That's what we tried hard to achieve in Smíchov. For people to live good lives in the city, it has to have normal things: streets that are just the right width, houses that are just about the right size – an older one here, a new one there, shops, cinemas, cafés, wine bars, but also post offices and dry cleaners – in short, services – and parks. All these places create a need to meet, make contact, and feel good.

We gave this to the councillors of Prague 5 and the Office of the Main Architect, and they said, "Draw it!"

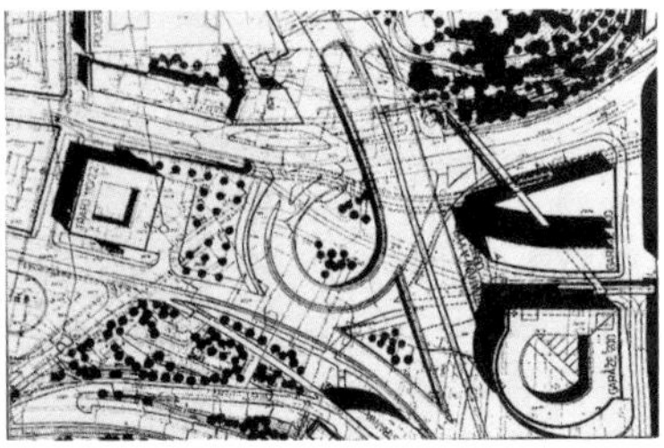

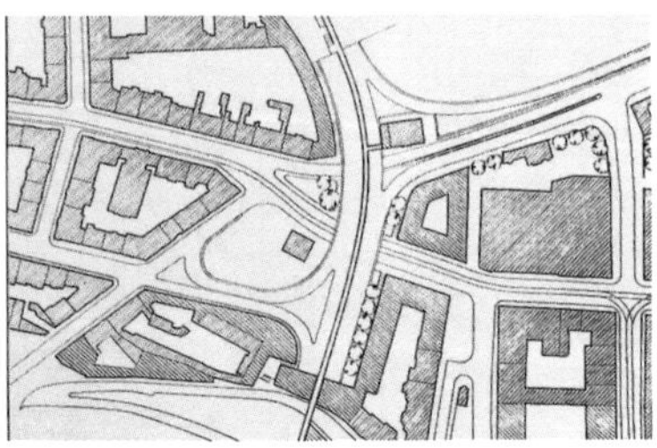

We were full of zeal, of course, and we all had the same thing on our minds: "We'll finally build a normal part of town!" After the long communist period in which everything was abnormal and illogical, "normality" was a crucial quality. Our work was also beginning to achieve normal parameters.

Before 1989, what we did was more or less semi-illegal, but now we finally had professional status – we became a private limited company, just like millions of architects around the world. This is another terribly important thing about the revolution: me, my friends, and many other people could finally do their more-or-less normal job under more-or-less normal conditions.

But how do you build a normal city? Certainly not like Prager. Reflections on the structure of a city are similar to what a man looks for in a woman. Does he want a skinny or a curvy one? Temperamental, or a quiet soul? In any case, we had a vision of a city filled with the things that belong in a city. We were already thinking about the metropolitan part of Prague – twenty-five years on, we worked on some of these things with our friend Roman Koucký, who completed Prague's metropolitan plan.

Working on the Smíchov project, we first made a precise diagram showing how many good buildings Prager would have needlessly demolished, and conversely, how few we wanted to tear down. We drew a very dramatic tunnel for Smíchov – Tom Prouza and Jára Zima raised their noses from the drawing boards (we didn't have computers back then) and shouted: "Martin, it'll go from tunnel to tunnel, what do you say?"

I replied, "Gentlemen, what an idea." The tunnel was aimed like a cannon at the heart of Smíchov, and we hid it under the hill.

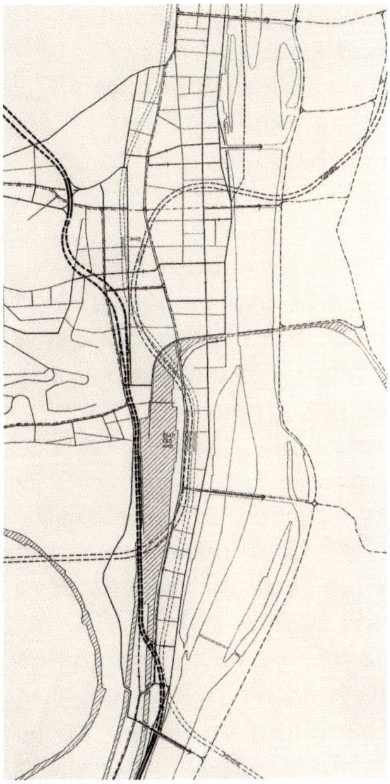

Some architects from the DA Studio were part of the society of Golden Eagles (Zlatí orli), young men who donned black clothes and neckties with the elegance of first-republic intellectuals, grabbed a funeral wreath and a coffin, and made their way over to the exhibition where Prager was presenting his plans. They bowed, put the coffin and wreath down and left without a word, which made our position on the plans more than clear.

I wasn't there, but I know it really shook Prager to his core. He wasn't used to positions other than his own. Nobody had ever disagreed with him. He'd been working hard on a project for fifteen years, then when he presents it, he gets a coffin – terrible! Even though I had always deeply disagreed with Prager, I felt a bit sorry for him.

Naturally, the meetings were awfully tough. Billions of Czech crowns would run through this, so it was the municipal investor who had the strongest position, and to them, I was a strange character. They received some information on me and were apparently a little terrified that I was quite good friends with Vašek Havel and Míra Masák and I already had Máj to my name. On top of that, I could twist my way out of any tricky situation.

I stood up in front of them and said in a slightly shaky voice: "Gentlemen," (there were no ladies present), "get used to one thing: you'll be hearing the names Prouza, Zima, Cajthamlová, and Rajniš very often from now on. We want to do everything differently – your tunnel, which is to kill Smíchov, will be deflected and sunk into the hill, in the words of my colleague Prouza, 'from tunnel to tunnel'."

A sketch of the southern mouth of the Strahov tunnel, GAMA studio (1988)

A study of the regeneration of Smíchov; a sketch of the southern mouth of the Strahov tunnel, DA Studio (December 1990)

A study of the regeneration of Smíchov; transport scheme, option A (December 1990)

They went pale. This was a billion-crown investment, they had implementation projects, filing cabinets full of folders with positive statements, so for them, I was the very incarnation of the devil. But I was confident, and they realised that Prague 5 had a similar opinion, as did ODS, and even the Castle – from a distance – so it dawned on them that things were getting tough and they redid it. Not quite how we had imagined, but we saved a chunk of Smíchov none the less. If they had gotten their way, there would be cars everywhere today, and no space for people. It wasn't that common then, but after Blanka was built, driving through tunnels became a Prague phenomenon.

We handed in the plans, I vaguely remember there being some back-and-forth over the fees (you can't avoid that in this country), and we slowly started projecting and building. Some of the projects were better than others, but even today, we're quite proud of them.

Not much happened for some time, but then the elegant and super-smart Evžen Stein entered our lives. He wasn't an architect, but his sharp eye saw more than any of us did. What's more, he knew the paths taken by big money from the international financial market (in our case, Vienna) and was a great organiser.

Evžen had a good friend in Vienna, a certain Dr Glatzel, who took part in the huge developments on Ring Strasse, so he knew big capital and a hundred million dollars was no great sum for him. These two gentlemen owned a number of companies that had contracts to buy extensive estates in Smíchov, like the land under the crumbling factory, once known as Ringhoferovka. We architects call it "brownfield land", because it's all rusty. So, Stein and Glatzel established twelve, maybe fifteen joint-stock companies – one for each building to split the risks.

Evžen came in one day and said: "The UBM (Union-Baumaterialien-Gesellschaft from Austria) wants to turn the centre you drew into a part of town." We didn't know each other much back then, but we were soon on first-name terms, as is common among those of us with an Anglo-American outlook. He looked at me searchingly and asked: "Will you do it?" I agreed without hesitating. Back then, I didn't think about whether I could take the hellish money and the tough relationships that come with it, so we did it.

It was meeting after meeting, but suddenly we were stuck – the Austrians wanted someone who would represent them well and I still looked like a wild animal out of a zoo. They weren't used to it, so the meetings died down. About a year later, Evžen calls me again: "The Austrians found partners in Belgium who did fifteen versions and they scrapped all of them, so I said, 'the only one who can save them is Rajniš and the DA Studio'." We answered, "Let's get to it then, shall we?"

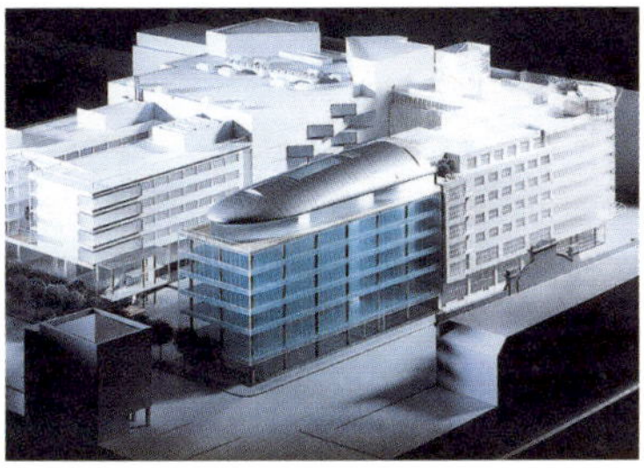

Then the hard work really started. It was an eternal debate between David and Goliath and we had to slog away like motor mice. For three months, me and Tom Prouza dithered between Prague and Vienna – we would hop in the car at half five off to Vienna, a rough meeting at nine with half the conference room covered in little drawings, then hop back in the car and get to the office.

When we kept showering them with possibilities with unfading strength – and it got to about a hundred and forty possibilities – they finally relented: "Which of these would you recommend, professor?" I selected the version that stands there today. A little square, streets, twenty-two houses… I'll admit I was happy. What's more, I wasn't scared of Goliath and I shot him straight with a relatively high fee for the standards of the time. After some negotiation, we came to an agreement. The DA Studio was gradually becoming a mid-sized studio – we had thirty employees working on several other projects.

When we came to drawing up the contract, a comical situation arose. At the time, you see, the Chamber's fee system ended with creditable costs of up to a billion crowns – a peak you couldn't climb in Czech conditions. But when we were calculating the costs for Smíchov, it was twenty-two buildings, each for a hundred or two hundred million, and we got to three and a half billion. I took a pencil and a French curve and simply extended the line to four billion.

Evžen Stein and Karl Glatzel (1991)

Models of the centre of Smíchov (1990s)

Madness ensued. They screamed at me, but I was calm – I knew they wanted to work it out. So, we closed the deal. But it was obvious that the key would be getting the sweet "yes" from all the appropriate authorities, a process which is called "engineering".

So, I turned to Evžen.

"What'll your fee be?" I asked.

His demand was five times the normal asking price, but nobody else would have been able to do it, so we shook hands. We got to work making Smíchov happen and the civil engineer hyenas began yapping at our ankles immediately – they felt a chance and immediately set astronomical fees. It drove me mad back then, but I have to laugh now...

Treat Me Like Your President

One of my strangest meetings involved a group of Frenchmen who decided – again with Glatzel and Stein – to build Nový Smíchov; New Smíchov, a shopping mall. I suppose the French learn from the crib onwards to scorn everyone, even one another... I enjoyed the arrogance we know from Jean Gabin and Alain Delon to the full.

The head of the Czech division of Carrefour – a gigantic company – would look at me and say something like: "Professor, we have two hundred and seventy of the units we're developing here. The gross cashflow of Carrefour is considerably higher than the budget of your entire country, so kindly treat me as if I were your president."

If my president Václav Havel were to say such things to my face, I would probably reply, "Go fuck yourself, Vašek, I'm not doing it."

The climax of our contract meetings took place at the Gellert hotel in Budapest, truly a beautiful structure, enormous marble columns with classical capitals growing right out of the pool. Then they dragged us straight to a brothel and without lingering on small talk – like only the French can – they sat two naked girls on each of our laps and thrust a contract into our hands; concerning a sum considerably lower than what we'd been squabbling over for weeks.

Aerial views of the transformation of Smíchov (early 1990s)

I turned to Tom Prouza with what must've been a desperate look on my face: "What are we going to do?"

He replied: "Just sign it so we can finally get out of here." Yes, the world that operates in large sums of cash is not a jolly place, but one learns all sorts of things. And after all, why should I – a bourgeois boy – complain that the world is going down the same path trod by my grannies and granddads.

I think Smíchov turned out pretty well – at least part of what we aimed for came through. From Plzeňská to the south are the twenty-two houses we built, and we certainly didn't want to make them all the same – our dream was to attract other architects to create a diverse mixture of contemporary Czech architecture.

Experience, you see, tells us that a diverse block housing a diverse population – which also ages differently – is much more viable. And if there's a bad building here and there, it can be demolished in a hundred years and replaced by a better one – Prague has gone through this process of positive selection numerous times. Only after a number of waves of this can the process of centuries of selection tower over the individual architects, developers, investors, city halls – everyone. Prague is a beautiful example of what a shame it would be not to continue like this. So, that's exactly what we aimed for.

Since I had gotten used to standing in front of Máj listening to things like "What idiot built this?", we were very careful that this large mall called Nový Smíchov wore a pretty dress, surrounded by smaller buildings to cover its enormous back, with smaller brothers and sisters facing the street. That went well too. I think that even though Nový Smíchov is twelve times bigger than Máj, its entry into the urban structure is much softer, more gradual.

Even though I really love Máj and have immense respect for Johny and Míra, I tried to find a way of inserting a large mall in a city as beautiful as Prague without it sticking out or attracting too much attention. After all, there are other, more important things – beautiful residential houses, churches, concert halls, libraries... At any rate, today Smíchov lives a normal life and people seem the same walking through it as they do through Malá Strana. It is simply part of the beautiful city of Prague.

I believe – and I'm certainly not alone – that proper urbanism and proper family houses are architecture's most crucial goals. And what's more, in a city like Prague, the responsibility doubles. Prague has a certain rhythm which it is not worth interrupting. A city like that isn't built in blocks, but in individual houses. You might get to go wild on all kinds of horseplay (which is not to say I don't like doing that), but this is the grunt, like my grandmother used to say – the family farm; the essence; the core. The grunt of every city. So please, try looking at Smíchov from this perspective.

As concerns my part in this huge undertaking, I was more in charge of things fitting together, in there being funds to work with and chairs to sit on. I sketched some of the houses, but if I'm being fair, I have to say a considerable part of the work was done by my DA Studio partners.

The Call of the Wild

As I've suggested, running with the French wolves expedited my feelings. Like Jack London's White Fang, I suddenly felt the call of the wild. I yearned for freedom.

It was my preparation for 'jumping off the tiger'. I was fifty-four –in the Middle Ages, we'd have been long gone at that age, but now we're at the height of our powers – so I repeated Hubáček's flowery sentence about the bows and the violins, mentioned early on in this book, to my partners, and told them that they would have to play on without me henceforth.

Few things make me as happy as a friend ascending to higher rungs than I ever dared climb. It's pure happiness. It is an incommunicable pleasure to feel how the art named architecture crosses on strange paths from body to body, mind to mind, between men and women... This must bring each of us joy! It is exactly what happened with the DA Studio – they made it!

I had a compulsion to keep a place there for myself just in case, which is probably normal: before escaping to the prairie, the animal leaves the gate to its den a little open so it can return for some warmth when the weather outside becomes unwelcoming. But my DA colleagues said to me, quite logically: "Without you, your share is worth nothing, so you'll have to make a choice!" I accepted that: I heeded the call of the wild and left. After I returned, I began again somewhere else...

How I Became a Professor (1994–1999)

—

The fact that I could make some money came as no great surprise. But that I'd become a professor – !?

In this respect, I was in total agreement with my father. Dad came to my graduation in the Carolinum when he was already an old man, and we had lunch together in his beloved Rotisserie, where he gave me a gold watch and said: "I'm enormously happy that you are a professor. But tell me, honestly – what kind of country is this where someone like you can be a university professor?" It was simple: students came to me from UMPRUM and wanted me to apply for the position of director of the Architecture One studio.

There are four architecture studios at UMPRUM and One is the best. It leads the way. The idea that I could be a professor there is comparable to a ballet dancing hippo or a whale teaching long-distance running in the desert. It was an absurd vision. As a sworn enemy of the communists, I had many adversaries in the field, which is part of the reason my projects had never even made it into Architekt magazine. And that such a guy should be appointed a professor of an arts institution? The way the revolution stormed through all such institutions after 1989 was truly comical.

On that late spring day in 1990 when the selection procedure for the A1 director began, I was in an awful rush: we'd won a commission from the French for a building next to the Four Seasons (which we ended up not building). I raced to the contest the students had pushed me into and I took a large folio to fit our entire portfolio, held closed with a strap. Only when I arrived did I discover the others had as little as two A4 pages...

The panel was headed by Karel Hubáček, who smiled at me the entire time. It was hugely encouraging, so I really got into it. Afterwards, Hubáček came out and said: "Čudla, you won it."

"That's impossible, boss," I said.

"Of course! It's simple – you were the best."

Hubáček wouldn't have said anything like that if he didn't really believe it. It was a joyous feeling.

I soon received a visit from the rector: "What do you think about getting together with Jakub Cigler? He wanted to do design and architecture with Bořek Šípek, but Šípek is more interested in design and Jakub architecture, so why don't you two do it together?" I went to Malostranská kavárna with Jakub, and we shook hands on it.

I have to say that not even a straw was ever broken between me and Jakub – we didn't argue, we didn't blame each other, quite the contrary: we supported and praised each other. Our families were friendly too – we used to travel together to a little house in a village called Deià, on the south-west coast of Mallorca. Me and Jakub complemented each other: he's tidy, extremely hard-working, enormously gifted graphically and in a number of other respects. In short, working with him is a joy.

I insisted we wouldn't play professor and assistant – I wanted an equal partnership. We came to the studio as two architects, and after six years, Jakub left as a senior lecturer and I a professor, but we always acted as equals, and in order not to confuse the students, we tried to give them our opinions on their projects together.

I admit I was a little horrified with the students at first. Everything was painted black, they wore t-shirts with skeletons, skulls, and crossbones, and their projects involved spikes jutting out of buildings – tough guys. Don't forget that back then, I was a decent boy who wore a shirt and jumper in marine blue. But things moved on.

The head of A1 before me was a communist, but I can't say a bad word against him – quite the opposite. He took care of the studio, he selected great people and gave them excellent tasks, so it happened that we soon found a way to each other, even though he was a leftist and I was a rightist (and an anarchist to boot). But we both had so much respect for craft and architecture that it didn't bother us. He treated both me and the students most correctly. His name was Professor Zdeněk Kuna.

The first thing me and Jakub decided was that the students needed to get to know the world around them, so we'd take them travelling. The year was 1990, so it was no surprise that 60% of the students had never been to the West. First, we went to Slovakia, then Austria and Germany. One of the things we wanted to show them was just how cheap a ten-day trip could be. Jakub took some money from his office, I from mine, and fifteen people departed in three cars stashed up to the roof with students and food.

It was beautiful. In Slovakia, we slept for free in my wife Lubka's uncle's garden. We had a picnic in the centre of Vienna. The students were awfully shy, and because I wanted them to have authentic experiences, I established the question of money: who does what for how much and why. Sometimes some scouts would take care of us and let us sleep in their gym, other times, when we couldn't find cheap accommodation, we'd go to Šumava for the night and then right back to Austria. Just like I was used to. And I suddenly felt we were starting to understand each other.

I think we developed a really nice relationship and I now take a very honest joy in the fact that many of them are now absolute professionals, some of the best colleagues one can have in this country.

Facade of the building of the Academy of Art, Architecture and Design in Prague
(1882)

With Jakub Cígler and students of the A1 Studio
(1995)

With Jakub Cigler on the Vltava
(2000)

We also tried at all costs to have equal numbers of boys and girls – like in life. Nobody should give a fuck about the idea that women have different brains for which spatial concepts are too complex: it's not true at all.

First, I demanded a proper contract from UMPRUM, one that would establish all my responsibilities and freedoms: to exhibit final works once every six months and to select good people during the entrance exams once a year. I felt a huge appetite to share with these boys and girls things which I had so laboriously discovered on my own: things I loved, but also things I hated.

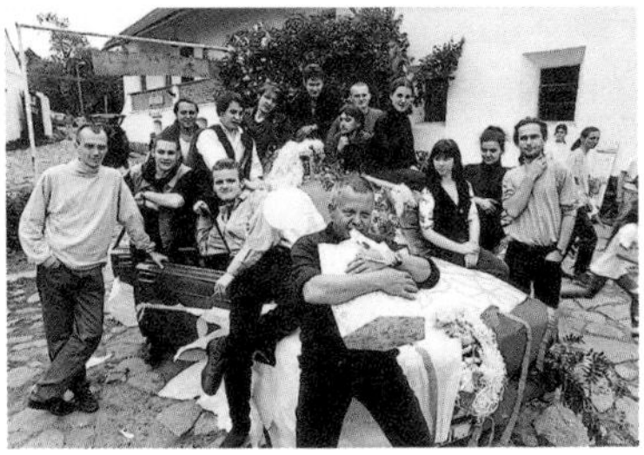

I was also hell-bent as a teacher to avoid waffling on about nothing; to avoid being a bore. I don't really feel like I taught architecture. Why should I? I don't know what architecture is anyway.

Entrance Exams

The toughest thing about being a professor was deciding on the admittance of candidates. The entrance exams lasted for five days and we had fifty to seventy applicants every year, of whom I could accept, at most, three. I begged: "Five, at least!"

I would take two to three, sometimes four, and when I later got the impression that someone was not up to the heights we were aiming for in the studio (the heavens began right above us, you see), I had to be tough and expel someone, which was simply not done at UMPRUM. To be honest, I have never really known how you recognise talent. Definitely not based on grades. I have to admit I felt more inclined toward those with lousy grades.

Traditionally, at least half of the studio would take part in the entrance exams. We kept coming up with outlandish methods of telling who was good. I liked giving them questions they couldn't prepare for, because they definitely didn't teach them anything like that in high school. I'd drag them to the window and ask them which building they'd demolish in Malá Strana, or how you can tell that an egg is hard-boiled.

We went so far that once, we blind-folded them, let them into Jakub's pitch-black basement, and asked them to make a map of the space based on touch. We even invited a psychologist, but it was still an awful feeling when we had to pick three or four chosen ones out of seventy people.

After five days, I was completely exhausted and deeply depressed – I was scared the geniuses had slipped through my fingers, that I hadn't recognised the golden nuggets of talent in those pimply youths and terrified young ladies, that those rough diamonds had been irretrievably carried away by the river...

I kept repeating that I'm no Miraculous Virgin, and when I say no, it doesn't mean a lifelong "no". It simply means that I and their talent, at this particular moment, in this composition, did not line up. And what's more, the probability of it being my mistake was almost the same as it being theirs. Despite all this, they cried...

The students were about fifty-fifty in gender, and I was glad when girls got in, because then the talent too was balanced.

My 50th birthday celebration (1994)

The christening of the first year group of the A1 Studio, Mrač (1995)

Vážený pan
doc. Ing. arch. MARTIN RAJNIŠ
Podle § 15a zákona č. 172/1990 Sb., o vysokých školách, ve znění zákona č. 216/1993 Sb., kterým se mění a doplňuje zákon č. 172/1990 Sb., o vysokých školách,
Vás jmenuji
s účinností od 1. prosince 1993
PROFESOREM
pro obor
ARCHITEKTURA

Unfortunately, Václav Havel's signature on my professor's diploma has faded a little (1993)

The Burying of the Amateur

At the beginning of the year, it always seemed that the students were stupid and it would all be for nothing. But when I started getting to know them, we always came to an agreement. Not just me and Jakub, but the students too. For the select few who were admitted, what followed was the admission ritual, always quite wild. It usually took place on the plains of the Ore Mountains, where one of the students had a cabin. The girls would receive a porn mag and had to describe in detail what was taking place, several people had their heads shaved, and everything ended with the burying of the Amateur, who was laid to rest in a realistic – cardboard – coffin.

The Amateur was a naked pink being which we carried like a true deceased. It was all so realistic I once got a call from the Rectorate: "Professor, those lunatics of yours killed and buried some poor sod up north. The police in Ústí nad Labem has an

eyewitness. Why didn't you stop a ritual murder? This way you're an accomplice!"

I tried to explain to the police that it was just a joke, but they started investigating anyway. They called me three days later: "We dug him out and you were right."

Yes, those were a good seven years together in Architecture One, and we're still friends today. What's interesting is that those few students with particularly bad grades in high school are now the most capable and successful architects.

How Do You Teach Architecture?

I stand behind what I said about schools. They're terrible institutions that do more to ruin young people than anything else. Even though I took on the role of the professor, I still have great doubts about the teaching of architecture. How can I teach something if I don't precisely know what it is? And I suspect barely anyone knows it. Is it something that flows out of people, imprinting itself into the world around them through construction technologies? Or is it something else?

Architecture is doubtless multi-layered and polymorphous, which is also why it's so hard to define. And as for my teaching: I didn't actually teach them anything – I just egged them on. The most I could do was come up with a task and give them my time. That's all. 99% of the work was them and only 1% Rajniš.

And so, the only way to teach architecture is to travel. When travelling, relationships play a crucial role: between the students; the students with me; my position towards them; all of us together with certain events in the external world... All this is a narrative that's hard to describe, one that's created of its own accord.

I always tried to get my students to understand another point of view. Not only did we travel the world together, looking and talking, but I also arranged some student exchanges between studios, like between us and Bořek Šípek's. At the Technical University, the studios are not conceived as closed groups, whereas with Emil Přikryl at the Academy, they only accepted students who already had a bachelor's degree, so it was actually a master's programme. Our optimal model of operation was only being born back then, and so I found myself at the beginning of revolutionary changes.

Later, considering departure after seven years, I opted for the approach they used in ancient Athens – the students received black and white marbles and were told to decide anonymously: white – I should stay, or black – get out. I only found whites in the box, which made me happy, of course, but in the end I left anyway.

I had begun to feel burnt out, a phenomenon known at all good universities. There is an interesting institutional precaution against it: after four years of teaching, you keep getting your salary, but you have to leave the school for a "sabbatical" year. It is even required that you go abroad to soak up new impulses. I opted for a sabbatical de luxe: after seven years, I left for a proper long time.

New Delhi
M. Kloda, J. Cigler, A. Lapka, J. Hofman, B. Škopová, M. Topič, J. Nedvěd, L. Zemen, M. Rajniš, A. Pražák, J. Klubal, P. Kocych, J. Slezák, S. Kocychová, K. Benoniová, Z. Málková, R. Vávra
(1994)

Devprayag
A. Keil, M. Kloda, M. Hakl, A. Lapka, Z. Málková, Juraj, J. Hofman, A. Pražák, M. Rajniš, M. Doskočil, A. Voverka, J. Nedvěd, J. Cigler, L. Zemen, R. Vávra, M. Topič
(1994)

A while back, we had our last A1 studio meeting, attended by about thirty people – all friends! It was truly wonderful. And most of them are real whizzes too, attested to by the selection at the Generace+ exhibition, which presented work by architects in three categories: 30+, 40+, and 50+. The fifty best architects from around the country were selected. Twenty-two of those were either my colleagues at SIAL or the DA Studio, or my students. It made me very happy to see the work had borne fruit.

What's more, my theory about accepting kids with bad grades showed itself to be effective. They were people of my blood type – high school simply wasn't a good fit for them. They didn't believe they could succeed, just like I didn't believe at first that I had the qualifications to teach.

Of course, I fumbled about at first, learning as I went. Then I became a senior lecturer, but I kept teaching just the same way as before, and finally, my professorial lecture about the instant demise of Czech architecture was so successful I got a score of 17:1, which is excellent, apparently. Only when my title was officially confirmed by Václav Havel did I believe it.

Travelling with the Students (1994–1997)

—

Like I said, me and Jakub Cigler always shared the conviction that travelling is the best school for everything. It also develops what the Americans call "team spirit". So, we started travelling.

We discovered the term "outward bound". It is a sailor term, to describe when a sailing boat leaves the shore during low tide and cannot return because the wind takes hold of it and chases it out onto the open sea. During World War II, a naval captain couldn't make sense of the fact that in shipwrecks, it is not the youngest and strongest who survive, but weathered old sea dogs. Their survival, you see, was down to state of mind. In a critical situation, everything depends on whether one does not give in to fear and hopelessness: once you're on the sea, you have to sail!

I remember reading this article with Jakub: Full of excitement above Cala Deià Bay in the Mediterranean Sea, we immediately started planning hellishly dangerous trips. There were extreme suggestions, like walking through a minefield in Yugoslavia – suggestions dismissed following our wives' intervention, agreeing that we'd start with something light and romantic: crossing the crest of the Carpathian Mountains and the polonyna (grassy mountain meadows) of Carpathian Ruthenia.

Taking the train to Carpathian Ruthenia
(1993)

Carpathian Ruthenia with the A1 Studio
(1993)

Carpathian Ruthenia

My dad wrote this of the region: *"Before I concluded my university life, I realised an old dream of mine: to see Carpathian Ruthenia; Czechoslovak Canada, as we called the easternmost corner of the republic. Today, it is Zakarpattia Oblastů; the westernmost region of Ukraine – after the war, we magnanimously gave it away to the Soviet Union. Why do I speak of Canada? It is the promised land of tramps – mountains, forests, and virgin nature."*

When travelling to Carpathian Ruthenia, our initial assignment was somewhat mysterious: meet in the morning at the central train station, depart in an unknown direction. Length of journey, eight days; food cannot be resupplied; drink can. After spending the day on a train, we found out the bus which was supposed to take us to the start of the hike was out of order – there was no money for fuel. So, for eleven dollars, we found a bus, a driver, and diesel, and we took a few local people along who were going in our direction. We got a map – a top secret document over there – for two dollars from a soldier and off we went to Volovec. On we climbed, up and up in the autumn wind, towards the peaks of the Carpathian Mountains.

We walked for a week, but ooof – my knees started creaking like mad, so I had to announce our descent. After a day's journey, we arrived in the valley, where we found a sorrowful band of lumberjacks.

They were sat around the fire cursing, so I asked them: "Why are you so pissed off?"

"No one's buying any wood! They don't have money, so they steal some in the forest and we're fucked."

"Do you know what charcoal is? Imagine a black paper bag with flames drawn on it, full of charcoal. Believe it or not, rich Czechs will come over here in their shiny cars, wiling to pay up to three dollars for a little bag like that."

"Out of the question," maintained the resolutely depressive lumberjacks. "Three dollars will buy you a whole truckload of wood."

"Fuck your truckload of wood!" I insisted. "I'm talking about charcoal. You know how you make that? Easy: you dig a hole, bring in a stack of wood, throw it on the ground and set it alight from two or three sides until it starts smoking. You watch over it, and after about a week, it stops smoking and you've got charcoal. Then all you need is the bags. And you can bring it into town on a horse. A company truck comes through and you sell it to them!"

They were good blokes – they even treated us to some moonshine. The poor know that they should share. But wait, there's a great ending to this story: six years later, Jakub was walking through the same valley, and he found the very same lumberjacks making wooden coal! They were no longer cursing. But back to our descent.

We went down the valley, and the forest path gradually became a battered gravel road. We met a tractor bouncing along, pulling a trailer full of women. I waved, he stopped, the women helped me up and I finally let my creaking knees rest. The women on the deck asked me where I was from.

"I'm Czech – from Prague."

And one of them says: "We're very fond of Czechs." Another starts rummaging between her tits and hands me a meatball, lukewarm from her womanly warmth: "Since you're Czech, have some meat."

We continued in this warm-hearted atmosphere all the way to the village pub in the valley. I arranged food and drink for everyone – we had golubchiky: rice and meat with this excellent sauce, all baked in a cabbage leaf. They made five large baking tins and the vodka flowed. Once it was all done, I told the innkeeper I'd pay, and he tells me: "But it'll be expensive – three dollars..."

We arrived at the train station in Mukachevo the next morning. It must be said the locals don't like Ukrainians very much, and Russians even less so. The express train from Moscow arrived, and imagine our surprise – it was ten minutes early. "Great, they've got fast trains," we thought. Nonsense! The train was 23 hours and 50 minutes delayed! And what's more, they wanted ten dollars from each of us.

We didn't want to pay that much, but we needed to get back to civilisation, so a heated bargaining session ensued. We tried everything: we cursed at the guard, told him it was robbery, threatened that the Czech police would take them away in handcuffs, but nothing phased them. Whatever we said, they repeated the same answer: "A kto eto skazal?" – And who said that?

Petr Kolář was one of the students – today, he is among our best architects – and he finally overcame them. When they said their twentieth "A kto eto skazal?", he screamed "Lenin eto skazal!" That really did them in. From that point on, they were on the defensive, and when we got to the central train station in Prague, they even brought us the equivalent of 230 dollars in Czech crowns, saying they'd "get it out of those fucking Russians somehow." Well, that was a life lesson too...

On the night express train back from Carpathian Ruthenia, we encountered two tanned, unshaven mountain-climbers who were on their way from the Garhwal Himalayas in India. Me and Jakub immediately decided that would be our next trip. Every Tom, Dick, and Harry might go there today, but for the amateur explorer in 1994, it was pretty much the edge of the world.

Petr Kolář: Lenin eto skazal!, Mukachevo (1993)

With my students in India (1994)

With the A1 Studio in the Himalayas, Kedarmath base camp
Bottom row from left to right: A. Pražák, M. Rajniš, M. Šimek, top row from left to right: J. Hofman, J. Nedvěd, M. Doskočil, K. Amblerová, M. Steinbachová, B. Novotný, P. Kolář, M. Hakl, R. Kalmár, O. Hrozinka, M. Topič, M. Kloda, F. Šlapal, L. Zemen, J. Soukup, A. Keil
(1994)

With the A1 Studio in a pub in Smíchov, Prague
Bottom row from left to right: A. Pražák, M. Rajniš, M. Šimek, top row from left to right: J. Hofman, J. Nedvěd, M. Doskočil, K. Amblerová, M. Steinbachová, B. Novotný, P. Kolář, M. Hakl, R. Kalmár, O. Hrozinka, M. Topič, M. Kloda, F. Šlapal, L. Zemen, J. Soukup, A. Keil
(2016)

We took two of Jakub's friends with us – a doctor and a bloke who'd been to the Himalayas about twenty times, so he knew what we could expect. We managed to make it very cheap: including flights, food, and accommodation, five weeks in India only cost us 120 dollars a head. Rom Vávra also made a documentary film about this journey, which features – among other things – me singing with a wandering Indian minstrel who was also called Rajniš.

Being a Sahib is Beautiful

We got onto the track and ascended slowly in order to acclimatise to the altitude. The guys we hired extremely cheaply (seventy crowns a day) to carry our luggage were given the film equipment and medicine while we carried our personal belongings, with only two exceptions: me and Pavel Štech, as the only two grey-heads, had personal carriers.

It was as if the marvellous 19th century had returned: every morning, the carrier would scratch my tent, shake off the hoar frost, and bring in a tray with hot coffee, then while I ritually drank the delicious liquid, he'd collapse and pack the tent and bag in a flash. I felt awkward at first, but a friend who knew how it went enlightened me: "They're used to it, and if you suddenly start changing the rules, you'll only confuse them." I stuck to this advice throughout my stay in India, and I'm glad I did.

The Garhwal Himalayas were completely bare at the time, so we only met about twelve Westerners during the month. We travelled to the main source of the Ganges in a rented bus, but believe me when I say that going to the mountains after the wet season is a pretty terrifying experience. The driver has a helper, equipped with a whistle, and every turn is taken about ten times: they go back and forth, and all the while half of the back wheels are off the road, dangling above a chasm of several hundred metres. Getting off and walking would make no sense either, because this situation repeats every one hundred metres. It took us eight hours to get to a camp that was 120 kilometres away – and of that, the last 30 took us six hours.

The Ganges has three sources, and the main one – where everyone goes – is called Kedarnath. The eponymous mountain is about seven thousand metres above sea level and a number of lakes stretch out under it. We had our main camp near one of the lakes from which the Ganges flowed, but we were headed for the lake of dreams: Masartal.

We climbed over the glacier in thick snow and descended through a long, long valley, to enter an authentic village with houses carved from wood. We had to leap over fissures in the ice without much to keep us safe. We couldn't resist this kind of scenery, so ended up taking the so-called 'bath of the Bengal tiger' – we stripped naked and delved into the cold (but not terribly cold) bubbly Indian waters.

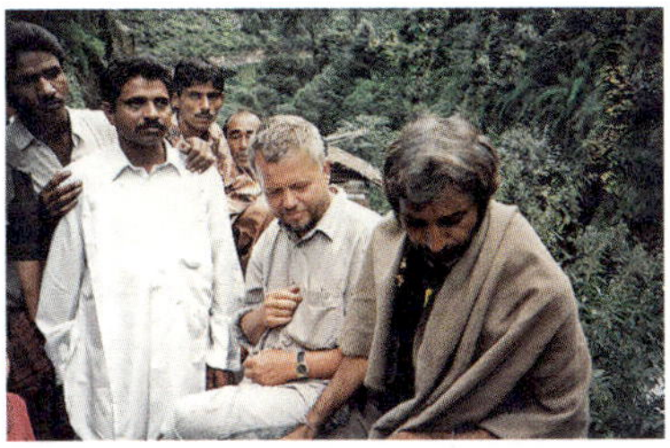

It was soon revealed how prudent it had been to bring a doctor along. A few of us developed high fevers, and soon, everyone except me and the doctor were sick. They couldn't stand up, so in order not to leave them there, we tied their feet up under the horses' bellies and took them away like corpses.

We rafted down the last few dozens of kilometres of the mountainous part of the Ganges, all the way to the holy city of Rishikesh, where the Beatles had tried to find enlightenment. We jumped off our rafts and delved one final time into the cloudy waters of the holy Ganges. I'll admit the Garhwal Himalayas have a special place in my heart.

Professional Suicide Bubbling Up

The key question is: "Why is the ringmaster – a little over fifty and at the height of his strength – committing what could easily be considered as professional suicide? Why is he leaving a studio that's doing well, that has a lot of commissions and therefore money and fame? Where is he going in this moment? Isn't he a bit mad? Might it be a midlife crisis?" It all seems suspiciously similar to one of Graham Greene's most famous novels: A Burnt-Out Case.

The Garhwal Himalayas (1994)

I mentioned that I had given out the black and white marbles in school. They gave me all whites,

but I still felt bad, as if the road along which I was dragging my body was fogging over. I asked myself: "What are these houses we're doing anyway?"

At the time I was also endlessly bogged down with managerial tasks: meetings, contracts, money, human resources, and so on. If I happened to have some time left over to draw, it was at nights and weekends. Was this what I wanted? Was this the peak I'd been scrambling towards my entire life? Not that the houses were bad – just that my goal was suddenly out of focus.

Exaggerating a bit, you could say my sights were set to shoot around the corner, and I suddenly felt the need to step back and take a look from the other side. Not as a constructor, an office boss, an architect, a professor, but as an ordinary person – which, first, I had to become again.

I realised I really needed freedom, nature, and other such everyday things, and I really didn't want to have each day planned out (often for months in advance) and always be thinking about what I could and couldn't say. These thoughts and feelings finally forced me to stop everything and leave the office. The boys knew something like this was coming – we kept having the same conversation for a year and a half. I planned my departure around the fifty-third year of my life.

Big Travel Plans

Some payments came in, and I started doing things that in retrospective seem naïve, even comical at times. But I assume that in twenty years, when I remember that I was dictating my memoirs, I'll have a similar feeling.

What was certainly naïve was the idea that in order to relax, in order to learn something and break away, I'd have to make a detailed travel plan – us architects, you see, are used to planning. I drew a map of the Earth and established all the places I'd visit: where I'd sail, where I'd travel on land, and where I'd fly. I worked it all out into a plan of several years – such nonsense! If you're travelling in order to change, you can't make plans!

The charm of travelling is not in planning, but in letting oneself be carried away by the situation.

Tumultuously, spontaneously. A little like slow-motion footage of a grenade exploding.

The first prelude to my travels was a trip to Iceland, a country I'm immensely fond of – I've visited four times, I think. It was also a kind of farewell to the office, and it was a good choice. The way I planned it was that I forced some students onto my friends who were going at the same time in their jeeps, and they distributed the students around the black volcanic desert, Ódáðahraun.

Do you know how you get to Iceland? Easy: through Denmark, Norway, and the Faroe Islands. You leave Prague at the beginning of the weekend, you drive to Copenhagen and jump on the night ferry to Oslo, where you sleep like a baby. After a good breakfast of sweet pastries, you start slowly rising up into the forests – snow appears, gradually. You keep going up to Jostedalsbreen – the biggest glacier in continental Europe; the beauty of all beauties. There is up to four metres of snow there, and you can also see glaciers and mountains stretching out to infinity. You go down, and suddenly there's bellflowers, and deer jumping around. You go up – snow again.

And it continues like that. It's indescribably beautiful: as playful as Smetana's Vltava and as

Iceland
A. Thiel Lhotáková, R. Kalmár, M. Steinbachová
(1997)

Iceland, Vatnajökul glacier
J. Cigler, M. Steinbachová, R. Kalmár, L. Zemen
(1997)

Iceland with the A1 Studio
J. Soukup, M. Steinbachová, A. Thiel Lhotáková
(1997)

Iceland
From left to right: L. Zemen, I. Hrabincová, J. Soukup, R. Kalmár, A.Thiel Lhotáková, M. Rajniš, M. Steinbachová, M. Lehečková, J. Nedvěd, M. Barták, S. Měšťanová, K. Amblerová, K. Slušný
(1997)

wild as a snow-storm. If you were to mix a snow-storm, rocks, sun, sky and glaciers, a bit of sea, and fjords in the rhythm of Vltava, you'd get these mountains. A miracle.

Lost Keys? Minesweeper!

I travelled by jeep with Kamil. We were to meet the students before lunch on Tuesday in Bergen, about eighteen hundred kilometres from Prague. Then we had a ship to catch, the Norona, which would go to Iceland via the Faroe Islands.

We arrived in Bergen on Monday evening, and that's where it happened: Kamil was brushing his teeth, and as he jumped around, his car keys rattled out of his pocket. But this posh car couldn't be unlocked or started any other way. All our things, of course, were inside, so I immediately started coming up with frantic ideas: they'd send us the code from Japan and we'd have a new key cut. Or I'd pay for a helicopter to pick the keys up – all fantastic scenarios. But suddenly, as if by a miracle, a group of paramedics appeared with a metal detector and fished the keys out of the moss.

So, through the Faroe Islands, the Norona arrived at the deep and beautiful fjord Seyðisfjörður, littered with a few houses. Four jeeps full of students arrived, whom we dropped off at the edge of a desert half the size of Moravia, while the rest of us continued along the Herðubreið tuya – a type of volcano which looks like a cake with a hole in the middle, because it erupted under a glacier.

We arrived at one of the two bases where we had arranged accommodation for our somewhat more sensitive women and children. I immediately got scolded: "Martin, that's too much! Leaving those kids at the edge of the desert..." I tried to calm them down, but they started wailing: "You have to save them, otherwise they'll get lost and freeze to death!" They laid into me for two hours, until I got the guys to jump in the jeeps and go save the students. It took us two and a half hours over that little strip of wild desert.

We get there and everyone was happily snoring in their tents! They welcomed us grumpily: "What are you doing here? We thought we'd finally be rid of you!" I explained that we'd been sent out by our weeping women, and they laughed at me: "We thought you were tougher than that. It seems the women can do whatever they want with you."

Hot Baths on the Glacier

Iceland is a fairy-tale country. You're walking along a glacier, and suddenly, there's a huge cave. You go on, you can't see the end, and there's suddenly a river, hot as a steam bath. You strip naked, put a hat on your head to catch the drops that fall on you, and you swim under the glacier in hot water, submerged in the dark-blue depths – an incredible, indescribably blissful feeling. Occasionally, of course, a chunk of glacier the size of a table plummets into the water, so an inattentive person will be out of luck.

They warned me: "Martin, don't be crazy, don't swim there!" But I would not rob myself of this somewhat dangerous nirvana for anything in the world. I could speak about Iceland forever, so I'll just add two more brief stories.

In Iceland, there's this lido appended to the wall of a geothermal power station, which spits out really hot water full of some super healthy additives. These minerals can cure everything: from syphilis to psoriasis. But they also eat at watches and rings. So, there's a kind of deposit area, but wait – there are no lockers, just mighty long shelves. You come in with your credit cards, wallet, gold watch, wedding ring, diamond buttons, and you lay them all out, one next to another. Nobody looks after it, and it still never happens that someone 'mistakes' someone else's Rolex for their own...

There's also a prison where they let the inmates out for the weekend. It's like a job: you're only locked up on weekdays. It used to be the only prison in all of Iceland, and when no one's inside, they fly a white flag. I went past this prison five times, and every time, the flag was there. Is there no crime in Iceland?

One thing's for sure: it's proper expensive there. When I met the students after three weeks, I was so happy they were all alright that I invited the whole group for a beer. One beer was about five hundred crowns then, so the bill ran up to over thirty thousand. You can imagine how entertained everyone was that "Uncle Scrooge" had laid his own trap...

Miss Rybová's Hot Slit

On the northeast coast of Iceland lies the Mývatn lake. On our way there, we decided to stop by a volcano. We were snaking around these little volcanoes when suddenly a car stops next to us, a girl comes out, and says to us in Czech: "You know about it?"

I replied intuitively: "Sure." I had no idea what she was talking about, of course.

And she says: "The hot slit is a well-kept secret here in Iceland."

So I declared without hesitating: "I've been looking for it for some time, but I guess my directions aren't that good."

"Well then I'll show you!"

Her name was Rybová and she'd lived in Iceland with her father for over twenty years. She led us over a lava field and suddenly the earth opened up before us. A wooden ladder led down into the depths. Rybová says: "And now you have to get naked." I wasn't that fat back then, so I agreed. We climbed down and observed an incredible phenomenon: as far as the eye could see, there was a fissure in the ground full of crystal-clear water, of about forty-two degrees Celsius. Light flooded in through various openings; you could see over twenty metres into the deep; from this perfect illusion of a fairy tale, only the elves were missing.

I later called this magical spot "Miss Rybová's hot slit", and when I led the other members of the expedition back there, they nearly lost their minds. That's what I call the 'real' Iceland.

As we departed, observing Iceland slowly disappear in the haze of the North Sea, the girls cried, and even we men grew misty-eyed.

That was the last trip I took with my students, and boy was it worth it. When we returned to the Czech Republic after six weeks, I organised a good-bye party at the cabin. My friend, the photographer Pavel Štěcha, may God's eternal glory rest upon him, said: "You'll stand here in your hat and you won't move a muscle. Everyone around you will jump, I'll shoot it on a long exposure and they'll be like stretched-out ghosts of your friends." He also photographed Arnošt, playing with a stick as if it were the most important thing in the world.

Running Wild; Journeys (1997–2003)

—

Then, we really got going: we started repairing a ship, which took almost a year, and I bought a Land Rover Defender 110, with its perfect wheelbase of a hundred and ten inches and a Maggiolina tent on the roof. It also has additional heating by Eberspächer, a winch so you can get out of any jam quickly, and even hood scoops to let air in. Though I'm not a big car guy, the Grouch – as I call him – is my beloved.

Me by a glacier in the fjord, Svalbard (1998)

Kačenka Amblerová by the Lofoten, Norway (1998)

Kačenka on a ferry near Narvik (1998)

Mája – the ship – and Grouch were now our bases, and in order to get my somewhat weakened bodily casing in order, I wanted to take a training trip north in the autumn. I convinced my student, Kačenka, to be my sparring partner. I'd be sad all on my own, and she was mighty tough.

Svalbard with Kačenka

We were rising up the Svenjuftjutysjakä river to a vast uninhabited region in the high mountains of Sarek. It was pouring down in the valley, but three hundred metres above us, there was snow. During an intense snowstorm, we waded through snow up to our knees, up and up through the snowdrifts, and suddenly, we stopped in amazement: the sky lit up as if some intergalactic spaceship were landing. The clouds broke, the sun shone, and a ray was reflected from the surface of the lake right in our direction, passing through the mists and creating an image I never saw again in my life. I thought: "The light bulb in your head has finally switched on, my dear..."

We had curious companions for the ascent – a herd of wild reindeer with their young and mates. You'd think that a journey like that would make you feel dejected, but nothing of it. I was jolly, and suddenly, out of nowhere, a song started sounding persistently from the depths of my soul:

"Three drummers walked home gaily from the war, the youngest with a red rose in his teeth..."

And suddenly, I felt the icebergs of big architecture and big business, of regional planning maps and other trappings of my past life breaking away from me and drifting into the mist. Though frozen, my body felt pink, light, and happy. It had finally returned to its true territory, and the reindeer seemed to smile at me in encouragement.

Then we travelled far above the arctic circle to Tromsø, a really pretty wooden town with the northern-most university in the world. From Tromsø, we flew to Svalbard, only eight hundred kilometres from the North Pole.

Immediately after landing, we went to arrange a boat rental, and they offered us two versions of protective polar wear: the cheap one, also known

as "wet", which means that if you fall into the water, you don't stay dry. And the expensive one, "dry", which is watertight like a diving suit.

Always the gentlemen, I took the dry one for the lady and the wet one for myself, not suspecting that I hadn't helped Kačenka at all. When we were landing, it was she who had to leap into the water while I steered.

"And a walkie-talkie?" they asked. It was another small fortune, so I said we'd make do without one. But I couldn't help but ask: "What if we get stuck somewhere?"

"Don't worry, we'll find you within a month," was the answer.

And as if that weren't enough, there was another problem with the bear rifle. I told them: "But I don't want to shoot bears!"

"Only three weeks ago, a bear ate a fifteen-year-old girl."

And Kačenka replied quickly: "We want the rifle, of course!"

On the boat, I told her: "You only know me as the Prof, but here, we're on the sea, and though this is only an inflatable boat, I'm the captain and I'm responsible for you, so whatever I say goes."

When we were about half a kilometre from the shore, I heard a strange hissing noise. It turned out that I had unfortunately punctured the dinghy with the sights on the rifle. Not a massive hole, but we were losing air.

"We'll go straight to the shore, patch it up, see how it behaves and –"

Kačenka looked at me sideways and said: "Are you always this scared in open waters?"

"Okay then, let's keep going. Won't that be great – you'll swim for two days and me, in the wet suit, I'd say I'd have about ten minutes."

I tried to patch up the dinghy in the water, but the wind picked up and waves beat at the bandages, so they wouldn't hold. After several long hours in the boat – deflated like a condom – we finally made it to shore, and I have to admit I was fairly relieved. Even for me, a sailor with dozens

Me on Madre de Dios, the upper tributary of the Amazon (2001)

Aleš Voverka and I in the silver mines inside the Cero Rico mountain at an altitude of over 5000 m MSL, Bolivia (2001)

of years of experience, the idea of sinking to the bottom of the sea in an inflatable dinghy amidst the icebergs was a little wild.

Despite this somewhat dramatic event, I have to say that Svalbard is amazing. Mouths, eyes, and fins belonging to walruses and seals constantly pop out of the water, and there's not a single person in sight. The beaches are covered in dry wood coming in from Siberia. These beautiful, whitened, battered pieces of wood probably still remember Uncle Lenin.

We were about two and a half thousand kilometres north of the arctic circle. Svalbard, you see, is further north than Greenland or Iceland, somewhere on the level of Novaya Zemlya or Franz Josef Land, so in July, there's light all night, but the wind is freezing. Like I said, Kačenka is an adventurous gal, so she went swimming in her "dry outfit".

The sea is about two degrees Celsius. You can withstand two or three minutes at the most before dying from hypothermia. But as if on purpose, Kačenka managed to poke a hole in her suit, so the Arctic Ocean reached up to her breasts inside the once-dry diving suit when she got out. We took out the warming part of the suit, while I jabbed three logs into the ground, filled the space between them with smaller chunks of wood, and drizzled some petrol onto the windward side. Of course I had to listen to her lecture on how a Scout would never do this as long as he lived, but I thought to myself: "Fuck the Scouts – as long as it burns."

And really, a miracle happened. A long flame appeared, stretching up along the five-metre logs, and we spent about five hours drying the suit. Of course we made sure it didn't catch fire, as it was awfully expensive, and while the animals watched us from afar, I found a huge old blue whale vertebra that now adorns my cabin in the mountains.

This training trip to Svalbard, which marked beginning of my journey of freedom, was unforgettable. It'll probably sound naïve, but everything started going easier, faster. As if I had

switched to maximum capacity without getting tired. I felt a calm, a wakefulness, and inner strength. This was one of many powerful strong moments at which I thought: "Thank God I went travelling." The moment in the rain and snow among the reindeer, with the melody of Three Drummers in my head, was very, very important for me.

The Caucasus with Kačenka and Martinka

Travelling east of our lands is always rough – in many respects. With Kačenka and her friend Martinka Lehečková, we spent the entire day rattling along in the Grouch over some Caucasian road that was so battered you couldn't cover more than ten kilometres an hour. Grouch got stuck up to the windows in some places – the Soviet Union, what can I say!

Towards the evening, we set up camp on this tiny clearing up in the hills. I went to take a leak near a stream, and when I returned to base, there were about eight guys in camouflage gear and one in a suit, all carrying AK-47s. "We're fucked – it's a Bolshevik-nationalist commando unit" – that was what went through my head. They considered us Western spies, of course.

From my stays in Russia, I knew that the only way to deal with similar authorities was from a position of power, so I started shouting my head off about how my friend, the Czech president, is a personal friend of their president – at the time, it was Shevardnadze. I behaved with the utmost disdain, and the result soon manifested itself: their tone let up a bit. I kept roaring – as far as my Russian would let me – that I'd get them sent to prison and make sure they were beaten up every day.

Then their tone changed completely. They informed us that we were in a highly dangerous area and we'd have to go down to the valley with them immediately. The one in the suit had a bit of the limp, so the others used their AK-47s to suggest that I should make space for him in the car. Kačenka also had much to say about that. I decided we wouldn't sit in a car with such riffraff,

so in the end, the Suit limped in front of the car and I put on the high beam.

To my horror, it started drizzling and I felt mud, which is a catastrophe for poor Grouch. The slope on each side was about forty degrees and I had my ass clenched with the fear of falling off. But we made it.

This was followed by a three-hour interrogation during which I repeated my strategy and the girls toughened up too – they were more cheeky, confident, and aggressive by the minute, so they ended up letting us go at about five in the morning. After all, they weren't sure if we didn't really have connections.

For the traveller, the lesson here is that modesty and decency is in order until the other side is holding a machine gun. You just can't show thugs fear. As Lubka used to say: "Fear is no kind of agenda."

Ship Across the Atlantic

I remember another truly exceptional moment during my travels. Me and Kačenka were sailing across the Atlantic. We took turns at the helm, twice a day for four hours a day, and believe me, it wasn't easy – the strain was comparable to fast cycling along a rocky road. And what's more, you never know what the ship will do when the waves get bigger.

The night at sea has a powerful magic – in the dark, every breaker sparks up at the peak with luminescent plankton, so there's a long shining groove behind the ship, and above you there are stars you can never see on dry land. You steer and steer, and if you do it dutifully, after about two weeks, you feel something strange – your mind and body become part of the sea and completely adapt to the activity of steering. You become a brother, sister, and cousin to the flying fish which gush from the bow, you're one of the clouds sitting on the throne of the sky – all this embraces you and draws you in.

All these things, one after another and then all together, cause something to switch in one's brain. Levels of stress decrease significantly, energy

increases, emotions are arranged, and the ones that swim to the surface are predominantly positive.

But I have to admit that Kačenka played an important part in bringing me closer to nature. If someone foolishly thinks that as a young architect, she learned more from me, it's really the opposite – I understood many important things thanks to her.

With Aleš in South America

Another key moment in my travels took place during a three-month journey across South America. But first, I have to say a few words about Aleš Voverka.

We were introduced by Jakub Cigler, whom he knew from the maternity ward – they both fathered a considerable number of offspring. Today, Aleš is one of my best friends, and if I were to confess everything I like about him, I'd go off on a rant. He has a lot of qualities that most people lack, so to me, he became a model worth following.

Paja brava – a symbol of natural architecture, Altiplano, Bolivia (2001)

For example, we may be rising up a hellishly steep mountain slope with a guide. My only concern would be to get to the tent and lick my wounds, but Aleš would immediately attend to the guide: does he have enough food and drink, is he in any pain... I have seen a number of private art collections, often of very famed artists. Aleš – this guy with three years of hotel school – beats them all easily with his.

On one occasion in China, he liked a coin. There was no paper around, so he scribbled the proposed sums first onto his own body, and later also onto the saleswoman's body. He haggled the price down to where no one else would dream of going, but what's important is that they were both laughing their heads off the entire time. My friends – this is supreme economics in practice.

So with this fantastic Aleš, we burst into Bolivia, climbing onto the high plane between the two shoulders of the cordilleras – it rises from Lake Titicaca to an altitude of 4500 metres, all the way to the Atacama Desert. We rented a jeep with an Indian and off we went, crossing the largest salt flat in the world, Salar de Uyuni, with its fantastic island – Isla del Pescado.

In the centre, to the south of the salt planes, an enormous bowl-shaped valley opened up before us. All the way to the horizon, there were millions of growing circles about a metre in diameter. Our Indian pointed to the plants, repeating the words "paja brava". I felt immediately that I had seen the plant of my life, and all of a sudden, the secret of architecture was laid out before me, solved...

Paja Brava

Paja brava is in fact a little sphere made up of individual branches that take an awfully long time to grow – about a centimetre a month. When the sphere grows to a diameter of one metre, the plant is a hundred years old. I realised that this was exactly the structure I was searching for. It's composed of small, simple pieces, and though each one is different, there's a similarity too. It's unbelievably modest but also very resistant.

It can adapt to surges in the terrain, to rocks – it can grow over anything.

Paja brava managed to create a perfect universe: it has its order and system, its tactics and strategies, even a plan, and yet it does not lack freedom and independence. It isn't tied down by detailed rules and it harmonises beautifully with anything that approaches it. I saw it with the utmost clarity, right in front of my eyes: an image of the architecture of the future.

In this little sphere, the world's most beautiful invention lay in front of me, and I thought: "Boy, here you are, five thousand metres above sea level, with your head spinning with an altitude sickness you haven't been able to drown with tequila (that's what they called their spirits so the Westerners would understand) or dance away with the native women, and the solution to all the pains of your soul has suddenly revealed itself to you." I finally knew I'd made it to the edge of the world in which I was trapped, like an architectonic creature surrounded by loads of shiny bullshit. This little plant took me in, and since then, my heart lightens whenever I think about it.

All of Latin America is fantastic, but Bolivia is special. Mean neighbours bit off chunks of its territory from all sides, but it's still a huge country where every bus journey takes several hours. It also became the world champion of staging revolutions.

Our first steps went in the direction of the Cerro Rico mountain, a silver mine which made Spain a world power for three centuries. They ate through the silver like termites, killing seven million people in the process.

Me and Aleš soon found out that if you buy presents, the locals will let you down into the mine – a mine that is considerably higher than Mont Blanc. We did get a helmet and a carbide lamp, but there was nothing to pump the air in. Scattered around the entrance were wooden huts – they looked like they belonged in Jiří Trnka's puppet film, Song of the Prairie – that sold dynamite. No copies, real dynamite signed Dynamit-Nobile. The people there chew coca leaves and drink 96% alcohol.

Aleš Voverka and I, photo from the peak, Pisco, Peru
(2001)

The peak of Pisco mountain (5650 m MSL), Cordillera Blanca, Huascaran area, Peru
(2001)

When I asked why they drink pure alcohol, I got a laconic reply: "If you want to dig pure metal, you have to drink pure alcohol." Coca, cigarettes, alcohol, fuses, and dynamite – all ideal goods for a Central European anarchist. Oh how I wish there were stands selling dynamite at democratic prices on Wenceslas Square. Then the Lord at the Castle would see how things are...

The Amazon River

Probably all travellers dream about the upper tributaries of the Amazon. We took the road from Cuzco, the old capital city of the Inca Empire. There were travel agencies offering expensive trips lasting a few days, but me and Aleš decided we'd go for two weeks without spending more than five hundred dollars. We did.

We met a local, an indigenous man called Fidelio (which means loyal). He promised he'd be our guide and he stuck us straight on a bus that spent seven hours rattling up the hairpin bends to the Cordilleras and then another six going back down.

An amazing view – on an area of only a few hundred kilometres, you find all kinds of environments: up high on the grassy plains, it's cold, then there are more plants, trees, then you're in an enclave of screaming parrots, and only at the very bottom do you find the first village with a pub. Of course it's the only road going over the mountains to the lowlands where the Amazon flows. The bus stopped there, so the next morning, we were off – hitchhiking.

When it rains, mighty, wild rivers rumble down from the mountains like in the Himalayas. Some Indian was lying about on the shore with some canoes next to him, so I asked him whether he could take us the fifty metres to the other side of the river. He agreed and asked for eighty dollars. "Are you crazy? Five dollars and not a cent more," we haggled. He shook his head, lie down in his hammock, and fell asleep.

Fidel explained to us immediately that the prices here are a little different. Before they shot most of the merchants with machine guns, prices were determined by coca paste, so it was normal to make a few thousand dollars in an afternoon. They won't even get up for five dollars. "But there's no more coca smuggling, is there?" I asked naively.

"No, but they still can't get used to it," Fidelio replied.

Coca paste is basically a semi-finished product: the leaves are ground, shredded, and mixed with some gunk. The green paste is then processed by a cocaine and heroine factory, where it's then shipped out by small planes that don't even land. They have these buckets with an amazingly long loop, and since the plane with the hooks flies slowly, they hang one or two buckets onto the hooks on the ground – the people on the plane simply pull these up and throw down a bag of money. And repeat. Everyone there manages this landing-less transaction fantastically well...

Following Aleš's crucial instructions, Fidelio arranged another boatman, so we could soon jump into a small pirogue with a powerful motor. The current there is very strong, so if you're going against it, it has to be full steam ahead, which increases fuel consumption. That's why everyone has a good supply on board. Up by the Amazon, the price of petrol is multiplied by four.

Aleš was disappointed by the jungle and I had to agree with him to an extent – you trudge along for ages, then you're in a sunny spot for a moment and back into the darkness. And what's more, there's mosquitos spreading malaria everywhere. It's much better from the boat. The parts of the river we passed still had gigantic trees growing along the shore – these had been felled a long time ago further downstream.

Our visit to the funeral of a local chief was a strange experience. Fidelio took us. To our great surprise, what lay on the table was not the deceased, but his stuffed clothing – that's what they used in the ritual. The Indians accepted us as a matter of course – if an Indian came to our

village to a grandfather's funeral, I'm not sure the bereaved wouldn't tell him to fuck off...

Nocturnal crocodile observation was another sensational experience. It's pitch black and you climb into the mud. It reaches up to your chest, and if you're lucky, after several hours, you glimpse two shining crocodile eyes in the distance – some adrenaline rush. There are very few crocodiles there, though, because the Indians gobble up whatever they can find – monkeys, parrots, crocodiles...

We rushed downstream. After covering about four hundred kilometres in four days, the Indian at the helm suddenly slowed down and said: "If you don't give me three times what we agreed on, I'm turning around and we're going back!" Aleš screamed like an ox: "Take us to shore immediately, we're getting off!"

Our extortionist was not expecting that. Fidel put on a tearful expression, mumbling: "Boss, that'll be the end of us, we'll die here! There's nothing here, just the jungle and wild animals." But Aleš insisted, so we alighted. I was calm because I knew him well enough. "There's a military base down the river. We can fly back from there," Aleš informed us. I retorted: "All good, but there's not exactly loads of boats going through here." Aleš replied calmly – it would figure itself out.

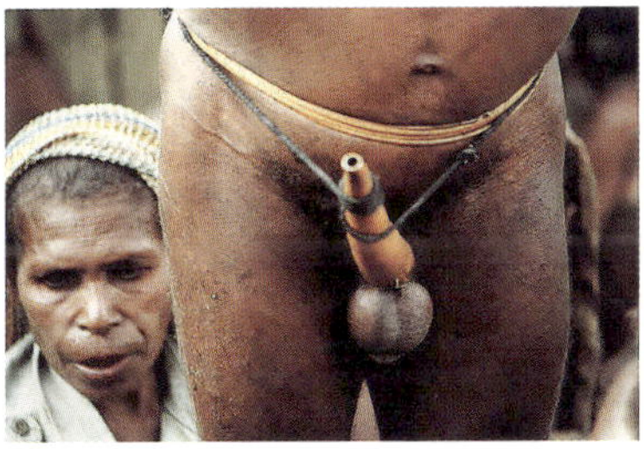

And so it was: miraculously, a slow Indian boat came farting by half an hour later. Fidel started whimpering again – they wouldn't take us, they only take machine guns and soldiers. But we called them over by waving our clothes, Aleš arranged fantastic conditions, and we were off downstream.

It was about four in the afternoon when we saw our original Indian-extortionist with some white man waving at us – now they surprised us. The white man was a prospector who spoke both Spanish and English, and he started telling us it was all a terrible mistake, that we had misunderstood him, and that he needed the money for his journey up the river because he's got a pregnant wife and blah blah blah.

So Aleš arranged for new conditions: he would pay his wages every day. We set up camp on an island and Aleš unpacked our treasure – seventy-percent slivovice distilled by our friend Aleš Lapka's dad, hence its moniker: lapkovice. It couldn't end any other way – the prospector drank like a fish and could do nothing but lie on the ground flapping and vomiting. In short, it became apparent they were not built for alcohol of this quality.

We got up the river without a problem, the Indian got paid, and I'll never forget what he told us at the end of our journey: "I thought the worst to bargain with are the Jews, but now I know it's the Czechs!"

This was the trace of entrepreneurial craft we left behind.

New Guinea

I can't leave out a fantastic trip to the western part of New Guinea, where tribes who were discovered only a few decades ago live. We owe this extraordinary journey to Bára and Lukáš, who took us on in order to fill the extremely expensive planes and split the costs.

This country is so remote and dangerous it couldn't be colonised. The English used to keep statistics on how many soldiers out of a thousand died in various dangerous places. In New Zealand and Australia, the count was two or three people a year, while in

A warrior from the Asmat tribe, New Guinea
(2001)

Examining the process of attaching the kotek, New Guinea
(2001)

The gentleman's protection is known as a kotek, New Guinea
(2001)

New Guinea, it was seven hundred and fifty – worse than a lost war. There are five kinds of malaria there, so our vaccination cards were filled up from top to bottom.

Applying these medications, however, is no easy feat – some antimalarials have to be taken three weeks before departure and two weeks after re-entry, and the worst is that some of the pills influence your mind – you can even go crazy. One medication, Lariam, has had a number of victims: many psychiatric wards have a small, isolated Lariam department full of travellers who went mad and never got it back together. I felt weird too, but – thank God – it passed after two days.

To get to know tribes that were similar to those I saw on Zdeněk Burian's illustrations and read about in Eduard Štorch's books, to see them with my own eyes – it was fantastic. Every tribe, no matter how small, has its own language, so people living twenty-five kilometres from each other can't understand a word the other is saying. Not even their greetings are the same.

This is because every valley is a world unto itself, where people have lived for twenty to thirty thousand years without migrating even a few kilometres. There was no trade, but there were wars, and if you lost, you were eaten. To get to places where virtually no one had ever gone before was one of the most incredible encounters I had during my travels.

The western part of New Guinea is administered by Indonesia. They call it Irian Jaya. Indonesia is a huge country with millions of islands and a population of three hundred million. It's seven thousand kilometres long and fifteen hundred wide. New Guinea is virtually on the equator, so it rains often, it's awfully humid and hot, there's mud, insects, and walking through the jungle is truly hellish.

The first expedition to cross New Guinea only did so a few years ago – it took almost a year and was only really made possible by helicopters dropping supplies. After struggling through the jungle myself, anyone who can withstand it has my

A mummified chief, New Guinea (2001)

An Asmat warrior in formal dress, New Guinea (2001)

undying admiration. How did we get there? Bára Šlapetová and Luky Rittstein travel there often, so they know how things work.

In 2001, they invited me and Kačenka to go with them and we were very excited. We couldn't do it without them, of course. It was an expensive trip, thousands of dollars flew by like nothing, so we had to save money wherever we could. After two long days of flying, we landed in Jakarta, arrived at quite an expensive shanty completely dead, and then dragged ourselves back to the airport the next day.

But then: imagine you spend an hour flying above the jungle, you land in the centre of the island in the city of Vamena, and completely naked people are walking about the airport, wearing only a little gourd on their knobs. Some of them have something like a silver tie around their necks – only the chiefs have the right to wear this pendant made of tiny sea shells.

All the men wear the gourd, primarily to protect themselves when making their way through the jungle. But it also has another purpose: its size doesn't depend on knob size, but on the size of the things its owner needs to transport. You might add a chicken and tie the gourd to your body. When you're naked, you can't carry anything in your hands – that's where you hold your bow and arrow...

Because there are no roads there, they use small planes. These can't carry more than eight hundred kilo, so everyone including the pilot has to be weighed before take-off. You can imagine how they looked at my fat belly...

You can't get by on New Guinea without a guide. We were lucky to have this great fellow that Luky and Bára had met during their previous journeys. At the beginning of our pilgrimage, we encountered a mountain tribe. A teacher-missionary lived with them too. When he saw us, he gave them the day off, because an expedition visit is the greatest event they have, and it only happens once or twice a year.

The local children there are very curious – when I stepped aside to take a leak, I was attentively

observed by eighty little boys and girls, who helped me along immensely with their hand gestures. Our guide knew the people of the tribe well, and he brought them a live seventy-kilo pig as a gift. He also had a theory – very attractive to me – that the white man won't fall ill if he eats well and does not exert himself too much. A very nice attitude towards the traveller…

Every tribe has its own mountain peak, its own hillock, or its own valley, and each of them speaks a different language. Kačenka and Bára caused a sensation – everyone gathered around them in mute amazement. They both had long blonde hair and the natives didn't consider them human beings at all.

They even let them sleep where women were strictly forbidden from entering: with the religious artefacts, weapons, and sacred relics. Only men are allowed – at most, women can hand them food through the window. The women there are about two heads shorter than ours, and their black hair is like a wild thicket.

You need to realise that the locals have lived on this impassable, very sparsely populated territory

Lukáš Rittstein, Kačenka, Bára Šlapetová and Martin + the pilot, guide, and cook before the flight (2001)

My adoption by the Asmat tribe, New Guinea (2001)

Lukáš, me, Bára, Kačenka with the indigenous people, New Guinea (2001)

Kačenka and an Asmat warrior, adoption by the Asmat tribe, New Guinea (2001)

for thirty thousand years without interruption. To avoid malaria wiping them out, the statistics say population density has to be under 0.18 human beings per square kilometre. In practice, this means you spend hours trekking through the jungle, then you arrive at a village with two or three houses, and the next village is another half-day's march.

So, it happened that each miniature population developed an entirely unique language. There are thousands. The languages spoken in New Guinea form a fifth of all registered languages around the globe. It's as if Řevnice had one language, Dobřichovice another, and Černošice a third. And they couldn't understand a word the other said. No writing system developed, so the languages will presumably perish. In short, it was an expedition into the Paleolithic age along with all it entails, and it was an immensely profound experience.

A Conversation Among the Korowai in the Middle of the Jungle

Once, a storm came in the middle of the night and woke me, giving me the opportunity to witness a fireside conversation between several men of the Korowai tribe. Since I occasionally lecture myself, I notice how people communicate.

Of course, I couldn't understand a single word, but I could recognise how they gave each other space, how they considered what was uttered, and how – following careful consideration – they answer slowly and thoroughly in a series of extended sentences which evidently require a rich vocabulary and a virtuosic command of syntax.

Suddenly, it seemed as though I were listening to two English lords, detailing some trick in the game of cricket in the club and treating each other with some ceremony. This conversation in the middle of the jungle, deep in the interior in the heart of the Pacific completely upended my idea of the spiritual character and verbal capacity of the local people.

Independently of this, I later read an article about the now-extinct inhabitants of Tierra del Fuego. Turns out they had over thirty thousand words in active usage! I remembered that we commonly use around three to five thousand words, and if memory serves me right, Karel Čapek runs up to about fifteen thousand and Hemingway about twenty thousand.

But that would mean that these "naked hicks" – seen from our perspective – have an active vocabulary 50% bigger than the Nobel laureate for literature! I thus realised that the human species does not develop into cleverness from stupidity, but from one form of cleverness to another.

It's a tragedy that these people or their children, when they are given something revolutionary (to them) by our civilisation, be it a mirror, a metal fish hook, or a razor, abandon their complex and difficult world and start scorning it. And so, thanks to us, these fantastic civilisations are fucked…

The local people are direct and their behaviour has its rules. In one village, for instance, there was an unbelievably pissed-off man – his wife had run away and slept with whoever was available on her way. He was on her trail in order to make right the sexual relationships in his vicinity, and the others warned us: "Cower down and look at the ground! If you look at him, he'll get pissed off and you're dead!"

The early phases of the construction of a Korowai treehouse, New Guinea (2001)

A Korowai man in his home, New Guinea (2001)

Lukáš Rittstein and our guide visiting a Korowai house, New Guinea (2001)

The Asmat People

We also visited the Asmat tribe, who live on the shore of the Arafura Sea. According to an old legend, the tribe was started by Finirupin. He was alone in the world, and he was sad. Then the forest animals caught him and kept him in a cage, where he almost died of sorrow, until one morning, a sea eagle landed next to the cage. He chewed through his prison, a tortoise took him on her back, and so he sailed out to sea with the eagle and the tortoise. They landed on a small island with plenty of food where everything seemed to be drenched by the sun, but he was still sad, so he began carving statues from the trunks the sea washed up.

Then, he discovered fire, he made a drum, and one night, he decided to drum by the fire. And suddenly, the statues came to life and became members of his tribe. He sculpted his fellow tribesmen and drummed them to life, and the eagle and the tortoise became their friends. This is how the Asmat tribe was born, the tribe which later adopted us. They have a theory, you see: either adopt you, or eat you. We were lucky they chose the first option.

When a Man Dies

The Asmat have various rituals. For instance, they believe that when a man dies, his soul searches for a way back into the body. And since this is not an easy process, the soul is awfully pissed off and wreaks havoc: it kills people and animals and generally wrongs everyone it can. And so that the spirit of the dead man cannot gain control of his wife, they cover her in a layer of mud so he can't recognise her. And in case he recognises her and finds her anyway, they cut off the tips of her fingers so that the ex-husband knows she can no longer do anything for him. I saw women who were widowed twice in this way...

In the meantime, the men build beautiful statues that can take up the whole room, depicting warriors, canoes with oarsmen, fish, turtles, birds... Then they organise festivities, where they cut the statues into slices and throw them into the swamp around the village. The desperate soul of the dead

warrior then slithers into them, and through these bits of statues, enters the first new-born. The circle is thus closed and peace finally arrives.

The Asmat do not live in families, but all together as a tribe, divided into male and female houses. In the beautifully decorated, spacious male houses, every man has his little own little fire. The women bring food and firewood, but they cannot go inside.

Every woman has her own hut where she lives with the children. Sometimes, there are multiple women living together. As far as I've understood it, the men are quite inconstant, but the children belong to the mother. The village is controlled by the women.

Our tribal names were derived from our feet: they called me Warrior's Print and Kačenka Big Foot – the size of her feet became an absolute sensation. The Asmat walk barefoot. Some of them have even developed opposable big toes, so they can pick up branches from the ground with their feet.

Over those thirty thousand years, they've become extremely diverse visually – they come in various sizes and with differently formed heads, noses, teeth, hands – everything. The most beautiful thing about them, however, is that they laugh incessantly. I think they're happy – they have their wives, children, little houses... They're amazingly skilful and admirable people.

I have two university degrees and decades of experience in the architectural community, but I'll admit I'd find it pretty difficult to decide, say, where we should build a new village. Their urbanism is no simple thing. There has to be a river full of fish and sago palms. And some of the trees have to be old and full of worms so they can be felled – the Asmat could kill over those worms...

Much more than elsewhere, natural selection is alive and well with the Asmat people: three quarters of new-borns die before the age of one, but those who survive are well-equipped. Medically, you can see terrible things there: huge festering wounds, leprosy, various pseudo-arthroses and unnatural growths...

This is a very competitive environment for missionaries – Catholics and Protestants compete for influence and you can see it everywhere. Each denomination has its own airline, and of course, they despise each other. An agnostic like me thinks they'd do best to get out and let them live their own way.

On the other hand, I know they are often cast into an environment with certain levels of civilisation, like in Papua New Guinea, which was administered by Australia. When jungle people come to civilisation without having grown up in it, they're helpless and easy to manipulate. Anyone can take advantage of them, and it is often the missionaries who can help them and protect them from the most trivial commercial tricks.

Their civilisation, however, is amazing. Take their sculpture, their knowledge of nature and animals. Their constructions from natural materials are a chapter unto themselves. They make very complicated structures that would make engineers' heads spin. They use what are known as 'semisolid joints'. We use them too, but they are often at risk of deformation when moving.

The Asmat people resolve this problem through the use of liana vines which allow them a certain amount of leeway. Their estimates are so good that the structures in the treetops can even survive heavy storms. The semisolid joints move and turn lightly and the structure has the necessary static force to deal with haphazard forces like horizontal wind or high loads.

In other words, the Asmat are masters! At construction, urbanism, hunting, in the complex world of symbols and fantasies. And in art, especially in sculpture, they achieve results comparable to the best in the world – sometimes even surpassing them.

Before our journey to Guinea, me and Kačenka had a long conversation. The crux of it was this: "Are we not contributing to the destruction of this world by going there on a trip?" We weren't

sure about the answer, but we couldn't resist the idea of experiencing the Stone Age. The reality far exceeded our expectations.

When we thought about the same problem after our return, we arrived at the joyless conclusion that these old civilisations are probably beyond saving. One small yet representative example: a tree grows in the forest which, when it rots a little, smells wonderful. Arab sheiks are willing to pay a fortune for a kilogram of this tree – they use it to heat their posh tents on an open fire. So, prospectors plunder the jungle, mollifying the indigenous people with a few worthless knick-knacks.

The world of the indigenous tribes, which can produce none of the doubtful conveniences of our consumer civilisation, thus slowly falls apart. What's more, their bodies are intolerant to alcohol. Alcohol consumption devastates them and many human hyenas make use of it.

Unfortunately, it is often the missionaries who accelerate this disintegration. They go there with idealistic goals, of course, but the results are often catastrophic... These beautiful and pure human beings live on the lowest rung of social hierarchy and are unprepared for the tricks of our "wonderful" civilisation. We were born into it, so we know how to live in it. They, on the other hand, are tabula rasa, and they fall down to the very bottom of society. It's a tragedy, and unfortunately, I'm not at all sure whether we can still do anything about it...

The way back was also very adventurous, though in a completely different way. The screens at the airport were showing some awfully boring film shot in New York. The director had a static shot of the smoking Twin Towers, which were in ruins. The story was written in such an unlikely way that the Twin Towers had collapsed... "Those Americans must have gone completely crazy..." Unfortunately, within a few minutes, I understood that it wasn't just another bad catastrophe blockbuster, but a fact.

To Please an Unknown Traveller...

Every airport in the world was in shambles, but we finally managed to fly through Bali to Jakarta. We

were a mess, so we went to a hotel with AC and without mosquitoes to clean ourselves up.

"Girls, do you have any cash?"

"Not a dime, Martin," came the answer. "You always have the money, don't you?"

I went to several ATMs, but no cigar. I later found that my credit card had expired.

We paid for the hotel with the last of our money, and since we didn't have even a dollar for the remainder of the journey, Bára suggested we could go get some cash at the embassy. This was a completely absurd situation to me, that after decades of being comfortable, I didn't have enough money. I just wasn't used to it and it really threw me off. I tried to send Bára there, but she protested: "You've gone mad! They'd kick me right out, but they won't leave the Professor in the lurch." So, I went to visit the lion's den.

On the road with the boys, Mali
(2008)

A Bedouin-style kaftan and turban come in handy in Mali
(2008)

Turban, Mali
(2008)

High Atlas, Morocco, with Luboš Loibl
(2013)

Some inferior official told me to fuck right off, but this was our last hope, so I insisted: "I want to speak to the ambassador!" After a quick exchange, I was told the ambassador would see me in half an hour. They brought me a perfectly chilled Pilsner Urquell and the situation was immediately more cheerful. Half an hour later, I was led in to see the ambassador, and I couldn't believe my eyes.

First, I have to go back ten years: It was just before Christmas and I was in Moscow, at Sheremetyevo 2, where a plane broke down and it seemed like we'd have to spend Christmas Eve there. Next to me, in a huddle of desperate people, stood this bearded, reasonable-looking man, and he said, "I'm fucked. I have kids at home and no money on me."

So, I told him: "My friend, I can lend you some. The only flight now is to Vienna, and then we'll find a way to Prague." I bought us both tickets to Vienna where we made straight for the pub. He was extraordinarily decent.

"Jesus, how can I repay you?"

"We're travellers, it happens. Today, me; tomorrow, you."

We made it to Prague and he was all about getting me the money the very next day. "You know what," I said. "Think of it as Santa Claus on a plane. Don't worry about it. Maybe one day I'll need you..."

Now, he was the Czech ambassador to Jakarta. "That's great, welcome! What can I do for you? Come on, let's eat something good." He gave us enough money for the way back, we had some beers and reminisced. So, dear children, a good deed done for an unknown traveller can come in very, very handy.

Travels with Luboš

When the construction of the Venice Biennale started, a student of architecture and my good friend, Luboš Loibl, suddenly appeared. Since then, we have made several trips, ranging from Greece to Singapore.

Luboš can do a number of useful things, particularly those that I can't do, such as repairing complex technical equipment or converting currencies in the heat of temperamental negotiations. What I admire most about him, however, is that he understands women, a gift that was unfortunately not bestowed upon me.

This fantastic travel partner is a miller's son from the Bohemian-Moravian Highlands. He had to drive a tractor and a combine harvester as a child – hence his technical skills. We both detest the Christmas madness, so we usually set out in mid-December and return mid-January. We've been to several places repeatedly, so we're well known there – like the guardians of the Sahara in Morocco.

One New Year's Eve, we were camped out by a river similar to Punkva – occasionally emerging from the sand before delving back into it – and we suddenly saw lights approaching. It was the same policemen that had checked on us last year and the year before that. They remembered us well. The lieutenant rushed towards me, asking boisterously:

"You have wine?"

So, we took out a box, distributed the wine, and he sent out his soldiers to get some firewood from the thorny bushes. Soon, we had a fire going and were drinking together... Yes, I could get used to those New Year's Eves in the Sahara!

China and Japan with Kačenka and Aleš

When me, Rock – that's architect Roman Koucký, director of planning in Prague –, and Patrik Hoffmann took a short twenty-four-day trip around the world, we stopped off in Shanghai.

China is a fantastically interesting country, so it wasn't difficult to convince Aleš and Kačenka to go there. As always, Kačenka needed to be back in a flash, but Aleš and I continued to Japan. China is huge, there's an incredible number of people there, and every bit of it has its own unique elements, so that you feel like you've been to loads of different countries. We experienced all kinds of things: Aleš, for instance, competed with the local labourer women in carrying bricks on their backs – and, unlike them, he nearly collapsed. And he's fit – quite the sportsman!

With Luboš Loidl on Inle Lake, Burma (2015/2016)

High Atlas, Morocco, with Luboš Loibl (2013)

With Aleš on a raft on the river Li Jiang. The Chinese admire my Buddhist bodily proportions (2004)

On my way through China (2004)

One unforgettable experience was chasing our plane in the city of Chien, where the terracotta army is buried. We mistook the take-off by an hour, so we buried the taxi driver in cash to get us there in time. I'll probably never see again what that man did in the forty kilometres or so to the airport through a completely gridlocked city. We went through overgrown fields, sidewalks, down flights of steps – but we made it!

When we talk about travelling, I can't fail to mention that Chinese technical miracle, the maglev (magnetic levitation) train, which achieves speeds of almost 500 kilometres an hour. The journey from the centre of Shanghai to the airport – about 70 kilometres – takes twelve minutes! It's so fast it spends half the journey speeding up and the other half decelerating.

When you look at those beautiful Chinese paintings on long rolls of handmade paper, with amazingly virtuosic portrayals of rivers, mountains, blossoming almond trees, and birds, you can't help but feel it's a little exaggerated. Surely, it can't look that way! All the same, we visited a landscape that looks exactly like that. There are rocky towers hundreds of metres tall, with rainforest garlands hanging off them and the river Li Jiang with its bamboo rafts flowing beneath them.

There's one other great thing about China: I never felt as good when stripping down to my swimming trunks – the Chinese love chubby people. My Buddha-like body even garnered appreciative smiles from young girls. In Southeast Asia, it is simply an advantage to be fat; and also if you've got a bit of a beard...

I mentioned the Buddha. If I feel close to any religion, it's Buddhism. The reasons are obvious: it is not really a religion, more of a search for a path. And it also has no institution – no church, no chapel: in short, no hierarchy. And as for architecture: how can we compare our work to any Zen Buddhist temple in Kyoto! It's rare that you see anything so simple, so unpretentious, and yet so cleverly planned.

Me and Aleš didn't want to go to an overpriced hotel in Tokyo, so we laid down to sleep in a park on the seashore, covering ourselves with huge banana leaves. Early in the morning, we went to a gigantic market, where we savoured cheap but fantastic sushi, caviar, and fresh oysters. What a breakfast! The Japanese even gave us discounts, because for them, we were a little like 'good luck' bears.

On the way back, we flew for hours and hours over Siberia, where there's no civilisation – only meandering rivers. Seeing this view, one realises that sooner or later, the world will probably have to make sure the Russians let in those nations currently crammed into Asia. But an old traveller cannot help but gaze wondrously at this enormous expanse of land, as yet unspoiled by human hands.

What I experienced during my travels brought about an essential change somewhere deep down in my brain, where thoughts are not yet thoughts but only forerunners of thoughts, and based on their merits, thoughts finally hatch. A number of things suddenly seemed to fall into place: I found out I could lecture, I enjoyed taking part in film shootings, I was able to do a project a week, and what I had once spent three months on could suddenly be finished in five days.

I discovered unsuspected abilities within myself: my mind's eye could suddenly see projects in 3D, in colour, with lights, shadows, and mirroring. All this and several other things strengthened my conviction that going travelling was the best idea I'd had in decades. I even think my behaviour changed: I slowly started speaking in a more pleasant, comprehensible, and kind language. The reward was that the people around me began responding better – though I'm not saying there's no room for improvement... In short, it transpired that I probably desperately needed a time out and a step back.

Counting it up, I spent five years travelling altogether (1998–2003). But I never stopped working completely, and you could also say that

when I was working, I had never quite stopped travelling. The only difference was that when I left the bureau, I'd spent forty weeks in a year travelling instead of the usual ten.

The journeys are a kind of peel. The important thing is what happens inside your brain and body, and especially your soul. My soul suddenly calmed down. It started talking to me, even flirting, which never used to happen. Simply put, it stopped being sad. To this day, I can feel how fantastic this decision was...

How, Oh How To Understand Women...

—

I keep putting it off, but I'll have to get into it. I should probably say something about women. Believe me – though I'm a big talker, this topic is not an easy one for me at all. Unlike my dad, you see, I never knew how to handle women. I didn't get enough cuddling as an only child, because tenderness was simply not cultivated in our family – it was considered inferior: "The lower classes cuddle and caress each other." But we, we were the elite. I found the following in my father's diary:

"We considered emotional aloofness a part of culture and we looked with pity upon those who hyperbolically threw around not only words and gestures, but also emotions. To us, they were primitives. Perhaps it had to do with style, perhaps it was just fashion, applied both in life and in some artistic disciplines. Dispassionateness, restraint, deliberateness, calm, and elegance – these were our principles for communicating with the outside world. But that doesn't change anything about the fact that I enjoyed looking at pretty, slim creatures, undressing them with my eyes – after all, I still do that today."

Getting into bed with my parents, for instance, was absolutely out of the question. If I had stroked my mother's cheek, she'd probably jump back as if she had been bitten. It seemed really strange to me that both my mother and aunt Milena not only addressed their mother in the respectful "Vy" form (like the French "vous") – they spoke to each other in the same way.

Nobody cuddled anyone in our home. That was that. For them, that was a carnal manifestation of the lower classes. My dad was brought up to believe that some things not only aren't done in the family – they aren't even spoken of. But he liked girls, and even in his later years, he could attract them much more skilfully than I.

The only exception was beautiful aunt Milena. Though we led rather intellectual debates, she embodied animality and didn't bother to hide it much. She was probably also a champion at sex. There were even stories of her entanglement with Julius Fučík, the communist journalist who was executed by the Nazis in 1943. One time, she mentioned that Fučík was a terrible communist – but a wonderful lover...

Milena simply liked beautiful men – her SS ex-husband was also quite the stunner. Today, I think perhaps I should have given everyone more love. Or at least tried! But I didn't know how to go about it...

The being I felt emotionally closest to, and whom I cuddled the most as a child, was Judita, the boxer dog. I only learned about physical contact with humans much later, but I'll probably struggle with it till my days are through. Only my second wife Lubka, who was very passionate (as Slovak women usually are), simply would not allow any shyness on my part.

It later got a bit out of hand, and my Slovak wife and her three children let the money flow – they had the expenditure of an F-16 fighter crew, about three and a half million a year, and I ended up becoming the biggest cuckold in the country...

Johanka in the Dolomites
(1985)

In Gran Sasso
(1985)

In the Žemlička's car, Italy
(1985)

Dáša and Honza Žemlička, excellent friends to me and Johanka, whom I continue meeting today, often in the most varied places around the world
(1984)

Viktorka and Mirek Jiránek
(2005)

I was still completely undeveloped as a teenager, and as I recently found out, the girls used to call me Plaváček – a character from a children's story

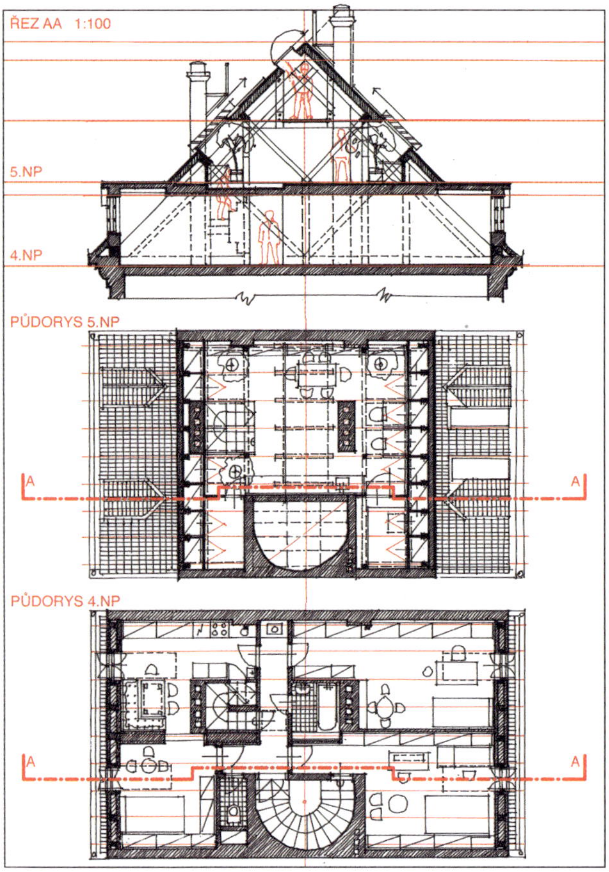

who was left to float down the river in a basket and brought up by a fisherman; a sweet, kind boy; the opposite of a tough guy – and made bets on which one of them would fuck me. No-one succeeded. But that didn't stop me from imagining girls at all times.

They'd come to me before I went to sleep, and through manipulating my member, I would quickly bring about enormous eruptions of semen. My developed schoolmates paraded in front of my eyes – I did not dare speak to them, let alone touch them, because I thought women were strange beings and one had to come up with something madly sophisticated to get them. To connect desire with intelligence, with vigour and sex. Only I didn't know how to do it.

I did not search for inspiration in literature, nor did I allow the firm hand of an older lady to lead me to the fountains of knowledge. I looked like a twelve-year-old boy, so it's no surprise that I was a laughing stock to my female classmates who were already grown women in high school. It took a lot of effort and money for me to get into anyone's pants. It brought about such extreme arousal that I had to pretend to have spilled water on myself to mask that my pants were leaking like custard out of an éclair. The suffering of a young, inexperienced only child – Plaváček.

But still, none of the crucial results materialised. One summer, I managed to lure one classmate out to a concrete pipe I inhabited for the holidays. She was a patient girl from quite a decent intellectual family. She climbed into the pipe with me and let me fondle and cuddle her. And I hadn't washed for several days at that point! It seems I had attained a certain dexterity and she was quite enjoying it, but I didn't know exactly what I had to do. How was I to lead this game to a successful ending?

I couldn't ask the boys from school for advice – they'd been around the block, so if I admitted my absolute underdevelopment, I'd be treated like a dirty dog. My father was also a no-go – we never spoke a single word about sex. My mum was from a good family, so I couldn't tell her either. And my aunt or my grandmas? Forget it! So, I suffered like a horse.

Finally, in a wine bar, the older sister of one of my classmates suddenly started tickling my belly and then moved lower. We drank a lot and she dragged me off to her lair. She was about twenty-five and it probably seemed wonderfully entertaining to her. Hallelujah, praise be to her! But it didn't continue and I had to achieve further results by my own means.

In the end, I learned how to do it pretty well. I remember that a chap recently won the Czech championships in masturbation – I think in my time, I would've been quite his match. Just to set the record straight, though, I eventually learned how to copulate, only that it took me longer than the other boys.

Studio, U Lužického semináře 10, Prague
(1992)

The façade of the house in
U Lužického semináře no. 10, Prague
(2016)

The seasonal hop-picking jobs organised by our school were also linked to sexual experiences. We didn't want to uproot hops for three crowns eighty per sack – even if you ripped as fast as you could, you couldn't do a sack in less than forty-five minutes and your fingers were bloody anyway. So, we arranged for work in a hop drying room in Hořesedly.

This was a long barn with a chimney jutting out of it – what you'd call an oast house in England. Coke was used for heating and the hops were thrown onto huge sifters. We had twenty-four-hour shifts – a day of work followed by a day off. The furnace warmed the water used in the ladies' washroom, which provoked not only our sexual curiosity, but also my entrepreneurial spirit.

Me and my friend Standa carved a discreet hole into the wall and we'd let the boys look through in exchange for beer. We saw all the females, including the teachers – a thing of beauty. We regularly had up to fifteen boys, so business was booming and we had a surplus of beers – we couldn't drink them fast enough. Our bliss culminated, we felt like we were on top of the world, and we dared to do more and more.

Until one time, one friend bought some cigars, got carried away, and flicked off the ashes onto the ladies below him. They looked up and saw us – clamour and scampering ensued. He also fled recklessly, so recklessly that he slammed his head into a rafter and blacked out. He had to go to the hospital with what turned out to be a severe concussion. This was a right mess, they found our sexual burrow and I had to work hard to pretend I wasn't even there at all... Such were the sexually motivated sins of my early youth.

Johanka

Unfortunately, I never achieved that most natural thing in the world, to form a good couple with a woman. Although when I met Johanka, that beautiful, kind, playful, and extremely diligent creature, I cheered with enthusiasm. We were introduced at the technical school by our mutual friend Jarmila Otčenášková, who was helping Johanka out. Even then, she had problems which I –

in my naiveté – considered resolvable. But even the great president Masaryk, when his wife went mad, said it was stronger than him.

Johanka was suffering from the early stages of schizophrenia. It gradually got worse until it ended in tragedy. She had a sad fate and I still feel unspeakable sorrow about it to this day. I'll probably never get rid of the feeling that I failed, that I could have done something better, differently… We lived together for fifteen years, and in the end, it was she who asked for a divorce.

But although this story has an unhappy ending, I have to say we lived a nice life for years. Johanka was actually the perfect woman. Hardworking, she never said a mean word to me – and boy did she have reason to! She came from a terribly interesting family with four brothers. Her maiden name was Jiránková, and her eldest brother Vláďa was the famous author of the children's show Bob a Bobek, as well as numerous other animated films and thousands of fantastic jokes. Vláďa was slowly drinking himself to death.

The Jiránek's parents made children regularly and throughout their lives – her youngest brother, Mirek, was ten years her junior, while the eldest Vláďa was ten years her senior. Mirek and his wife, Viktoria Ban from Russia, are my friends to this day. Mirek is not only a very good painter, but also a good person. He's talented, but he isn't pushy in any way.

At one point, Mirek and Viki were living with us on Kampa, above the Čertovka canal, where – together with the Jiránek boys and my friend Stano Slušný, possessed by a passion for construction – we built another storey and a half for a studio above our flat. We built this strange gallery: you could go out through a dormer and observe the panorama of Prague from the Castle to the National Theatre, which me and Míra would do often. We'd sit up there, sip our drinks, and philosophise about life.

We'd all meet at the elder Jiráneks' place, a small farm in Hlínoviště pod Bezdězem. It was awfully

My Slovak wife Lubka Šťastná (1995)

With Lubka and the twins in the Alps (1994)

Lubka, Kamil, Blanka Plzenská, Marek, Lucie, Fero Komoráš (my secretary), Tom Plzenský, and me with Arnošt, cabin, Christmas (1996)

romantic when the whole big family gathered there. Everyone loved the mother, who ruled with a firm hand. She had no exceptional education, but there was an almost shamanic force of deep reasoning and also great talent, which manifested itself in different ways in all five of her children.

Father Jiránek was a sworn "perpetualist". Whenever Johanka – who, remember, had a university education in physics! – tried to explain to him why you can't make a perpetual motion machine, he would raise up his index finger and thunder prophetically: "You will wipe the floor with your hair in front of mine, when it's running in a shop window on Wenceslas Square!"

The Jiráneks had me down as a freak. When I was tasked with drafting a chicken coop, I counted up how much work I'd spend on it, what the value of the structure would be, and how this would project onto the price of one egg, which would thus grow far above the level of a commonly available consumer egg.

Today, I'm surprised they didn't tell me to fuck off. They commented haughtily: "He didn't grow up in the country, so he doesn't know what fresh eggs are. He's a little backward, but he's Johanka's husband, so we'll be nice to him."

Johanka's health was quite the fateful package. In addition to her schizophrenia, she was infertile after a botched appendix operation, which depressed her terribly. A combination of this sorrow, the rough drinking which the Jiráneks have in their genes, and the sense of abandonment stemming from my frequent business trips caused her psychological state to deteriorate gradually but deeply. I've never experienced anything worse. When an episode comes on, the loving person becomes a foreign, contemptuous being, trying to drag those closest to it down into the depths of its curse...

When her condition got so bad that she'd run off and wander around parks all night, and even sometimes pulled a knife on me, she had to be

hospitalised in a secure psychiatric ward. Her doctor told me: "If you don't cut yourself off, you'll go mad. You have to realise this is transmissible and contagious. It's easy to destroy your psyche, and practically irreversible." In the end, she didn't even want to be with her family. She died in isolation.

I could never quite get rid of this sadness, and remembering it is awfully hard. It is a small consolation that Johanka's family, her brothers and friends, did not lose all love for me. They never told me I was a coward for leaving her at the mercy of fate. The thing is – they couldn't find a way to help her either...

Lubka: "Fear is Not a Programme!"

I mentioned my friend Stano Slušný – a cameraman and passionate builder. Entirely by coincidence, I came into the sights of his wife Lubka. I was like an abandoned trading ship which had suddenly been sighted on the horizon of Bratislava, where Stano introduced me with the words "This is the famous Martin Rajniš."

When Lubka found out I had just received a juicy fee in dollars, I suddenly transformed in her eyes from a trading ship to a gold-loaded galleon and she instantly understood that she and her three children – Kamil and twins Marek and Lucie – had found a chance to anchor down very comfortably. She left Stano, and within two years, I was hitched. We went to Florence and Lago di Garda for our honeymoon, and to give it that proper Italian zest, Lubka tasked me with buying erotic toys...

While Johanka wore her hair short and was more of a boyish type, Lubka looked like Maid Marian from Robin Hood. Her ginger hair flew about her face and she dazzled everyone with a broad range of expressions, chatter, and tricks... She was immensely adept at controlling men and situations and could do this with great prowess, joy, and elegance.

The alpha and omega of her life, however, were her children, and she was willing to do anything for their security for their security. She saw to it that

Kačenka Amblerová, Svalbard (1998)

Sunset on the Lipno Reservoir with Kačenka (2016)

Kačenka sailing on Lipno (2016)

they were bound only to her. She did so elegantly, but without any compromises.

In the eyes of Bratislava's sophisticated dissident society, she was a gold-digger, but I have to say she did me a lot of good. If I have at least a pinch of courage, it's thanks to her. I used to be afraid often, but Lubka taught me how to fight fear.

I remember once, sat in my cabin having breakfast, I was green with terror. It was the day I was supposed to hand in a competition project for the Technical Services of the City of Linz, for which we had already claimed a considerable part of the advance. Lubka asked:

"Martinko, what are you doing?"

I answered that my teeth were chattering with fear. She put her chest out, stretched her neck out, and replied:

"You know what? Stop shivering."

The words "stop shivering" contained so much derision it chilled me. And she continued:

"Fear is no kind of agenda for a man."

Since then, with her help, I – quite a fearful son from a middle-class family – started slowly getting rid of my fear. I guess you can't eradicate fear completely – I'm still afraid of heights, for instance. But when Aleš Voverka chased me out into the rain and mist to climb some ladders and look at the most beautiful Peruvian city, I overcame my fear and started to climb. Suddenly, the mist spread, the sun came out, and I realised I was on a practically vertical wall, three hundred metres above the ground – as if I were climbing the Empire State Building! My fingers curled up with fear; I was completely paralysed. Aleš screamed at me:

"Shout something, shout 'fucking cunt'! Swear! It helps."

So, from then on, I'd scream: "Nasrat!" (Fuck this!), grab hold of the next rung with one hand, and repeat. Thankfully, the mist grew thick again and I made it to the top.

So, whatever you might say about Lubka, I can't deny that she helped me manage my fear. Strong, wild, courageous women can inspire you. Lubka kept chasing me into various brave stunts, while teaching me that you have to take care of your welfare. I looked on in fascination as she kneaded her fate right in front of my eyes, shaping events to her advantage.

But I can't say I feel like a victim. In a nutshell, Lubinka knew what she wanted and knew how to choose. She did cost me a lot of money, but what ultimately cost me most in my life was my own stupidity...

However, Lubka was no fan of my passion: adventurous and rough travel. With her, it had to be the best hotels, villas, cars... Still, we went to Iceland, Scandinavia, or Mallorca where I rented a beautiful stone house with a pool and ten bedrooms, all in a village which had once hosted George Sand and Franz Liszt as well as The Beatles.

At the time, I was shouldering the full weight of the bureau, the school, the apartment, the cabin, Bratislava, two cars, several properties, and long holidays for my large family. I was working all the time (but I enjoyed doing it) while Lubka had absolute freedom, which she enjoyed accordingly.

To manage it all, she recommended her friend Fero Komoráš as a secretary (Lubka took great care that I didn't have some young secretary under my nose). I'd recently gotten off the tiger's back and stopped making big money, but our expenses kept going up. One day, Fero told me he couldn't keep looking on: "Hasn't it crossed your mind that you financed the publication of the poetry collection of that gentleman from Canada? Why do you think Lubka no longer goes on holiday with you?"

True, that pissed me off a little. Perhaps it was also due to our marriage/non-marriage: the family lived in Bratislava, while I lived in Prague, and we only saw each other on vacations and holidays. She stretched the divorce that I had asked for out over many years, so that I had to change lawyers several times and our ten-year marriage only officially ended in 2002. My weak neck just couldn't keep clear of those huge horns. Yes, Slovak girls are a handful...

Kačenka

In 1997, we accepted one of those students with bad grades in high school into the A1 Studio. She was a twenty-year-old, blond, defiant, strong-headed mule – Kamila Amblerová. Kamča to most, Kačenka for me and a few others close to her. She was a strong individual with a sharp judgement and tongue. We took the students to Iceland in the summer, and it was there that I noticed Kačenka wasn't made from sugar.

At the time, I was starting to break loose from my chains and I was looking for a travelling buddy, so I convinced her to take a "trial trip" north with me – I was looking to get into shape there. She resisted at first, but then it probably started to seem like a great enterprise. So it happened that, surrounded by steam rising from the blowholes of whales, we became close.

Kačenka's father had wished for a son, Artur, and before he got one, he had given his daughter a strictly boyish education. She was incredibly well-built and resistant – ideal attributes for a traveller. I never heard her say she was cold, she was hungry, or that she wanted to go to a hotel and fill her belly. Quite the opposite. With raised eyebrows, she mocked my concern for her: "You want sweet little me to go stay in the sweet little house?" At the time, I was almost fifty-five – at that age, you get a little creaky and need a bit of comfort once in a while.

Travelling with Kačenka was fantastic. She charmed me not only with her youth and beauty, but also with her view of life and nature and her enormous capacity to sense even the most subtle shades of Nature. She allowed me to let nature affect me, teaching me to see and feel it in an entirely new way. She just had a knack for making a trip a juicy affair. She has a sense of mystery, she's drawn to unreachable places, she can make quick decisions, and if needs be, improvise – in short, she lent great spirit to our trips.

I also gradually realised that Kačenka is among the top architects I know, like Johny Eisler, Emil Přikryl, or Mirko Baum from Germany, all of whom were

taken into architecture's loving embrace. They have a gift from on high.

Me and Kačenka lived together for over three years, but from the very beginning, I realised it wasn't forever – that we weren't heading for the classic happily-ever-after, and that our relationship would end one day. Every hour with Kačenka I managed to snatch back from fate had – and has – unspeakable value to me, and I'm happy that we remained friends after it ended.

When I look back, I have to observe that I'm probably completely useless to women. I rarely get out of the shell of my work. I'm a mule of a medieval craftsman with almost no private life. Everything important to me happens at work, so I understand that life with me is sad for a woman. And believe me – I'm not proud of it in the least. I have an attraction to my work which is written in the stars, and my relationship with architecture is so strong it impoverishes my relationships with women.

But I want to say that in general, I look to women with great admiration and, especially, hope. I'm convinced that our future is in their hands. Women are much more intelligent and suited to life, and soon, they'll march up and say: "Well, gentlemen, that's the end of your games, step away from the table. You've messed things up just about enough!"

The Mystery of Architecture

—

I agonised for a long time over how I'd write about my greatest love, architecture, without sounding like a textbook. Then, I remembered Surely You're Joking, Mr. Feynman! by the American physicist and Nobel laureate Dick Feynman. He came up with this great theory. The way he tells the story is that he was once in a pub and someone was spinning a plate on a stick. The plate kept spinning and tilting, which captured Feynman's attention, so he did the maths and explained the phenomenon.

His explanation of this illustrious discovery goes something like this: "... so I applied it to physics and got the Nobel Prize." I wish I could put it that simply! I'll save a more detailed treatise on architecture for a completely different book...

I went into architecture thinking it would be an amazing experience. I wasn't wrong. I'm even finding it more and more fun. Simply put, it's exactly what I was meant to do in life.

I've mentioned that me and my dad didn't see eye to eye on nearly everything. So, it's something of a surprise that it was he who told me: "Become an architect!" How many times now have I confessed how much my father helped me? It turns out he understood me more than I could've ever imagined.

At the beginning of my career as an architect, especially at SIAL, I suffered terribly. Compared to the others, I felt stupid. I had a feeling that I was no good at this stuff, that everyone else was faster and brighter, they all had juicier ideas. How could they not be better, seeing as they were the elite of an entire generation of architects! But they were all polite – they didn't make a show of my insufficiency and slowness. They could do it at twenty-five, and I slowly shuffled forward to be at the same point at fifty-five.

I'm a slow-moving machine – the sloth of architecture. And I need time and freedom for my work, which was the main reason for letting myself off the leash, as I've mentioned. But the devil took hold of that chain and now there's nothing to catch and tie me up with – I'd call my inner feeling, "chainlessness".

I've already said I'm slow as a sloth, and I'm not alone: architecture is the same. It's based on very gradual development, while today's world is changing at breakneck speeds. It's sad that we architects are perceived – and there's some truth in it – as the bearers of civilisation, and that civilisation is no longer viewed positively. Previously, it helped people and tamed nature. Today, it devastates nature.

Symbols and myths have lost their power, so instead of the mystery of cathedrals or churches, we draw what we need from the internet. The world stopped being an "aesthetic theatre" and artistic styles are no longer unifying principles of lifestyle, making our civilisation all the more plebeian. However, at least we are finally accepting the fluctuating balance between order and chaos.

I'm convinced that without imagination, without a naturalness, all rules are questionable. Ask yourself: Was architecture ever natural? I think it usually was.

Let's take a Baroque village in south Bohemia. It wasn't designed by an architect. The buildings there were erected by a closed community that lived in one place for generations. They all knew each other, and what's more, most of them knew their way around construction. Unlike us, they knew very well how important it is to choose the right spot. They didn't have a plan, no cursory surveys, just a few sticks in the ground. If a farmer built a house that didn't fit in, nobody in the pub would speak to him. Local materials were used, the houses resembled each other like leaves on a tree, and the result was more than pleasant – in their homogeneity, the villages felt natural, like, say, a forest.

So, it happened that in a village where some of the villagers would have been illiterate, better houses were built than we build today. Extensive planning, you see, destroys our capacity to adapt, to incorporate chance and any innate juiciness...

I know we can't look into the past too much, but couldn't we try to go back, at least in some respects? I feel like the crisis in contemporary architecture is mostly down to our inability as architects to offer people something they like at first sight, something they love and form an attachment to.

I'm also more and more convinced that the essence of architecture is not in functionality (like heating or lamps), but in profundity of experience, in magic. When I love someone, that's magic. When I'm talking to my dog while we play, we're connected, and that's magic. We've had this in our genes for millions of years.

After the lamentable decades of the 20th century – lamentable for other reasons too, not just architecture – we simply have to man up and present architecture that will speak to the depths of people's souls! It will be their friend, their lifelong lover, their intimate corner to hide in, a place where they can lower the anchor on their life.

Such architecture will be good for birth and death, in good times and bad. It just has to arrive. And now, my key message: without good and generally popular architecture, society can never experience satisfaction!

Of course, I know a nostalgic view of the past won't be enough. We need a new, contemporary architecture, and I insist on one simple thing: when we don't know how to continue, let's not shy away from finding inspiration in nature. Nature, after all, is a design studio that has been in business for millions of years. Its labs are spaced out throughout the universe, using the method of trial and error to ceaselessly experiment and provide amazing results.

Can you imagine a situation where you're standing in front of a grown tree and people stand around grumbling: "We've never seen such a repulsive and arrogant design. Which idiot drew this?"

Nature is our cradle and our grave, we arise from nature and return to nature.

So, I decided I'd try to do things based on nature, using natural materials like wood, stone, or glass (only occasionally complementing them with a piece of concrete), and searching for structures similar to those in nature. Just like us humans, it would be a combination of a well thought-out concept with a pinch of chaos – because why wouldn't we build houses that are the same as we are?

For me, this resolves all the fierce debates about the essence and future of architecture. It's so simple: structures need to be comprehensible even to people like Marie!

Marie was a simple woman that used to take care of our household. I'd go show her a project and ask for her opinion. Usually, she'd clasp her hands together and start lamenting:

"Jesus, Martin, what's this? Where's the chimney?"

And I'd reply: "Marie, they don't make chimneys that much anymore."

"And it doesn't have white walls, a red roof, and eaves!"

I was always sad, but I have to admit Marie was right. I was confused and over-educated! You see, it takes one an awfully long time to realise that things should be ordinary and simple. Complications are nothing but a distraction from the essence!

It's really beautiful to have creative freedom. To sit down with a sheet of paper, draw something, think about it, and then say: "We'll build it this way!" It has to be cheap enough that we can build it even without a particular client. This is how dozens of our projects were born: I drew them completely freely and only some of them were realised.

I work best at the cabin: in the pleasant winter season, I sit down by the fireplace, the wood crackles, the wind howls, the dog snores in his bed, and I start constructing. I start with, say, a piece of wood or stone, and I go back to my childhood, when I connected bits of Meccano with bolts. Suddenly, it's as if my mind sparks, and I feel I've found the right idea. Like when an animal is born – it's ugly at first, but just the fact that it saw the light of the world is a miracle. It's the same with architecture.

Portrait of M.R., Vladimír Vlna (2012)

For the visual component of this book, I selected a number of photographs and sketches to document some of my most important projects. Since we're more fertile than rabbits in Australia, choosing them were tough decisions. I hope it's a selection of our best realisations and projects. You'll find some pieces from the first half of my life, before I broke loose from the chain, so to speak, but also a lot of work from later on.

My Third and Fourth Lives (2003–2034)

—

Despite all the positive effects my journeys doubtless had, I had this question in my mind for a long time: was this break, this withdrawal from the system, complete lunacy, or my only option? Whatever the answer, when I got back from my travels, it was the 21st century and I had finally caught my breath. Over the twelve years of my professional life that followed, I did more work than ever before. What I call my third life began; after childhood and adulthood, when one acquires property and creates lasting value, then comes the third life. By then, one should be on top of things, learning to look calmly and composedly towards death. When the Twin Towers collapsed, I lost some money, but hey – that happens sometimes. That was part of the reason that, following my return, I didn't just want to draw houses, I wanted to build them too. And I was really looking forward to it.

My good friend, the well-known photographer Pavel Štecha, was supposed to go to Latin America with us, but then told us he was withdrawing because of some awful back pain. When we got back, he was lying at home, diagnosed with bone cancer in his spine – the doctors had given him a few months at best.

I really loved Pavel. We often visited each other at our cabins, and sail together too, so I rushed over there as soon as I found out.

"What can I do for you, Pavel?"

"You know what? I'll give my house in Černošice to my children, but you could draw me a vejminek." A vejminek (or výměnek), known in German as "Altenteil", is a form of remainder interest wherein (usually) the young farmer builds a house for his parents to spend the rest of their lives in when he takes over the farm. We chose a beautiful spot on Pavel's estate and then we talked for a long time.

I drew a sketch, we dimensioned it, and that's exactly how the house stands today. Pavel insisted on wood and it occurred to me to do it like they do in America and Canada. They call the method "two by four", because the profile of the boards is two by four inches. The little house had two modules for the living room, i.e. just under six metres, and one module for each bedroom, and the rest were small rooms. We turned one of them into a sauna – Pavel had a huge yearning for one. In short, a simple little box with a view of the distant horizon and a huge shaded southern terrace.

Later, I was astonished at the number of magazines that wanted to print pictures of it, and the number of interviews we gave about this structure...

Pavel once told me that the house kept him alive for another five years. The opportunity to help a friend by building a simple house really moved my life along. I suddenly saw things with completely different eyes, and this was when my career in wood began; I was fifty-eight years old, and this was my new beginning.

Štecha's house became famous, and like an actor who was so great in one particular comic role that nobody cast him for anything else ever after, I started to build one wooden house after another.

The Wood Period

The offers started coming in, so I started a company and gave it a poetic name: HRA – Hoffmann Rajniš Architects ("hra" means game in Czech). We built these awfully simple and cheap houses, and gradually, we started doing something like construction sets. We attracted some attention with our post office atop Mount Sněžka, the highest mountain in the Czech Republic. Foreigners always consider it bizarre, which is quite unwarranted given that it has been there since the Austro-Hungarian period at least.

Around 2005, Patrik Hoffmann and I broke up – on bad terms, a first for me. He evidently hadn't heard know the stories of my childhood, so he didn't realise what a risk he was exposing himself to. But despite all the bad blood between us, I want to say that Patrik Hoffman is not a bad architect. He just has something strange in his soul...

With Pavel Štecha in the Krkonoše mountains (winter 1988)

On the Venice lagoon with David Kubík (2012)

Then one time, Emil Přikryl invited me to be an external examiner on David Kubík's thesis. It was a nice project with fantastic visualisations, so I told him: "Look, my dear Kubík, how would you like to work with us?" He agreed. Pavla Pokorná joined us at the same time: always nice, kind, and an extremely important member of the team. Without her, we would have perished in confusion and ruin long ago. And so, together with my old friend Martin Kloda and some others, we started building houses.

We went slowly at first, but then it really took off. We received more and more commissions and started to look for a new name. Via E-MRAK, we arrived at the current name – Huť architektury. Why huť – "guild"? In medieval times, it was guilds who built, say, a cathedral. I even worked with one such guild in Cologne once, repairing the cathedral, and I liked it a lot. So, I became the guild master in a small guild in Malá Strana, right under the Prague Castle, an area I truly cherish. For some seven years now, we've made our home in a house owned by the Cigler family – a house with gorgeous

Neighbours by the café, split Martin (both left and right) (2013)

The Huť architektury office in Úvoz Street, Prague (2016)

Huť architektury in the studio, from left to right: Pavla Pokorná, Martin Rajniš, Tom Kosnar, David Kubík (2016)

"Zeman is not my president" (2013–2018)

views of the Charles Bridge Tower, Petřín Hill, and the Strahov Monastery.

I feel great there, and I also realise increasingly that without a proper local pub, life seems desperately insane. Every bit of the city is only really anchored down when it has its own pub. Until recently, ours was U zavěšenýho kafe (Suspended Coffee). Kuba Krejčí and his wife Helena did a great job running it. You'd find them there almost every night, and what's more, you could always talk to them about anything. It's thanks to them that I know the names of my neighbours and their dogs. By the way, the ""suspended coffee" is a great tradition from Naples: those who had money paid a coffee forward for the poor – leaving it "suspendedsuspended" or "hanging" for someone in need. I left a good few hanging there myself...

Towers (Bára I, Bára II, Máminka, Doubravka)

I hope the kind reader will remember my friend Aleš Voverka, who joined me in my struggle through the jungle. Well, Aleš has a Bed and Breakfast called U Čápa (At the Crane), with a slope and ski lift to go with it. One time, he told me: "Martin, I want to build that round tower you drew, whatever it takes." But before we go any further, I have to tell you about my towers and their fates.

Me, Honza Mach, and some friends finished an angular experimental tower on my estate, which during the German times was called Scholzberg after the Scholz family. I kept the name out of reverence. Soon after that, the city of Chrudim called – they'd like a tower too. So, we started coming up with towers and drawing them.

In the end, we came up with several options: three-sided, round like a cylinder (we liked this one best), and square. Chrudim chose the three-sided one, which worked like a stack of drying wood. Its inception is quite interesting: when we were in Japan with Aleš, I dragged him to the former capital city of Kyoto, which I really love because of its old wooden houses – they're like balm for the soul. We came back with the Shinkansen train – originally, back in the '30s, these were called dangan ressha, literally "bullet trains". That was where I pulled out a notebook and sketched the three-sided tower – like a stack of wood. We later added it to the other plans in the competition, and fate would have it that we won.

We called the tower Bára. Thanks to novelist Božena Němcová, Divá Bára brings up a sense of a dangerous destiny for most Czech people: it is the name of a short story about a courageous young woman, Bára, whom the villagers believe to be the descendant of a wild woman or a witch.

Believe it or not, four days after the tower was finished, a tornado came – unheard of in these parts – and destroyed everything in its path. It broke metal poles like chopsticks, threw around eighteen-wheelers like children's toys, and picked up roofs and entire attics, spreading them around the village. It didn't spare Bára either: it took off the top, relocated it by a few dozen metres, and ripped the bottom to bits. When everything was over, the remaining third of Bára stood sadly on a pile of shattered planks.

I'll tell you one thing, being the author of a collapsed structure was very tough for my childish soul to swallow. I went over there right away, and I wore a suit, because it was obvious they would be all over me like wasps. I was right – the TV journalists were on their way. "Mister architect, sir, where did you make a mistake?" Reporters are trained to destroy you, to make you into a thief – or, even better, a scoundrel, a bonehead, and so on.

I explained that I hadn't made a mistake. They should have done some research on the facts and valid regulations: in accordance with the guidelines, our tower was built to withstand wind, which, in our parts, should only blow at speeds of up to 130km/h. When a tornado arrives, of the kind we associate with America, it turns every place it visits into a picture of destruction, however solid the buildings are. And, when it's 230 instead of 130km/h, the forces upon the structure aren't merely doubled – they grow quadratically, following the formula S = C.S.X.V2, where S is the force

Team Venice in the Prague studio,
from left to right: P. Pokorná, D. Kubík, I. Fialová, M. Rajniš, V. Kopecký J. Tichá, D. Pavlišta, M. Kloda, V. Pešek
(2010)

Team Venice on the beach
(2010)

Team Venice relocating to the boat exhibition
(2010)

Vašek Horecký mirroring into infinity
(2010)

generated by the wind and V is its velocity. It gets a little complicated with extra coefficients...

But thankfully, our client, Zdeněk Vodvárka (who's nicknamed Lord of the Forest because he is the director of the city forest authority) had the structure insured, an unusually orderly step in Bohemia, and very good thinking too. The insurance company didn't balk, but paid out, and the local ODS politicians who were in power at the time decided that Bára was to be built again.

But the social democrats started blubbering: "That crazy Rajniš befuddled us all, why don't you use the money to build benches or renovate the park!" The deputy mayor (now mayor), said: "Let's be strong like our ancestors. When the National Theatre burnt down, they built themselves a new one. We'll build a new Bára!" But he set us an awful task: "This time, it won't be built to the guidelines, but built to withstand winds of over two hundred kilometres per hour."

A few clever gentlemen advised us, and in the end, we made the same structure, but with four times the strength, and called it Bára II. Ten years later, Bára II stands proud. My old friends Tom Plzenský and Martin Kloda also undoubtedly deserve undying credit for it – they came up with a fantastic anchoring mechanism.

Building Bára II, I met brave people who can stand their ground and who are willing to risk their career to help you prove that something is possible. I have to say that building towers is a thing of beauty. We've already built twelve, and several more are in various phases of development.

We came up with the names following the alphabet: our choices for the post office on Sněžka all began with the letter A, all the next towers started with B, and now we're at D – preparing a Triffid, Doubravka. The latest finished tower, Máminka (Mummy), on Krušná hora near Hudlice, is named after the investor's mother.

The Venice Pavilion

In the meantime, fate began to show its kinder side, as we won the competition for the Czech pavilion at the Venice Biennale. It was as if we had been invited to a royal banquet, and that doesn't happen all that often – at least not to me.

By the way, the Czech and Slovak Pavilion in Venice is very nice. But as usual, there wasn't much money, so I started jetting about and finding more. You see, we decided we'd do these huge models at a scale of 1:6, a size that can't fit inside a normal room. I went around my friends, trying to convince them to buy the models first and only exhibit them later. Aleš was the first to agree, followed by other friends, and later some rich people I didn't really know. This was during the crisis, so I had to make quite an effort to secure the cash. Prague ended up giving us half a million, so we managed to put the exhibition in Venice together. The results were fantastic.

Anyone who entered and inhaled the air in our pavilion would comment: "Hmm, what a beautiful woody smell." How could it not be, seeing as the hostesses continually sprayed twenty litres of concentrated pine tree essential oil into the air. This was a tip from Jaromír Hník, experienced exhibition matador and a friend of ours. Two famous art theorists, Irena Fialová and Jana Tichá, also helped with the exhibition. Without their ideas, reputation, and renown, probably nobody would even have talked to us.

The way we built the pavilion was a little like the times me and the boys would travel around the world without any money. We cooked our own food and in place of expensive hotels, we slept in the pavilion illegally, or sometimes – if the mosquitoes allowed – on the roof. We also used an old expo trick: we covered the long walls with mirrors from floor to ceiling, reflecting to infinity, so we suddenly had the grandest pavilion in all of Venice. I was glad the exhibition was such a success, but what made me happiest were compliments from Aleš and Kačenka, who both came to Venice to see it.

In the end, Bahrain won the competition for the best pavilion. It wasn't bad, but I should mention that their budget for an exhibition about a third of the size of ours was more than forty times greater. Years ago, when we did the History of Transport exhibition in Montreal (which I discussed earlier), my fee alone was considerably higher than the entire budget for the Czechoslovak pavilion in Venice.

But making do with minimal resources is part of the craft. You start learning this on the street and it takes a lot of work. I find it really perverse, though, that a state with a budget of one trillion crowns cannot provide adequate funding for an event of such scale and importance which represents it around the world. Well, whatever, they can go fuck themselves...

Model builders at the Expo, factory in Chrastava
from left to right :D. kubík, J. Jirásko, T. Zdvihal, V. Hybler, M. Rajniš, Š. Brabec, J. Mach, V. Jemelka, D. Pavlišta, D. Baudis
(2010)

Model of Bára, Chrastava
from left to right: D. Pavlišta, T. Zdvihal
(2010)

Dinner in Venice
D. Kubík, M. Rajniš, V. Hybler, K. Koňata Dolejšová, J. Mach, V. Horecký, J. Nikendey
(2010)

Members of Jára Cimrman's Theatre at the opening of the museum in Příchovice
(2013)

The Jára Cimrman Museum

Let's go back to the moment at which our friend Aleš says: "We'll build Blanka." He found a beautiful spot for the tower above his bed and breakfast, U Čápa, where this large crag juts out of the ground along with lots of smaller rocks. Beautiful beech trees grow there.

And suddenly, Aleš said: "I have a great idea." I was frightened – I know these great ideas from investors all too well. I cowered and waited for a blow over the ears. And it came.

"We'll build a museum of Jára Cimrman too. Don't worry, it'll just be a tiny cabin."

Jára Cimrman is a fictional Czech polymath who is said to have lived during the turn of the 19th and 20th centuries. Among other achievements, he gave the U.S. government the idea for the Panama Canal while also composing the libretto for an eponymous opera.)

I replied: "Aleš, you have to be shitting me. We have a beautiful lonely tower on a beautiful hill and you want to put a Smurf's cabin next to it? You couldn't have pissed me off more."

"Don't worry, you'll think of something."

Completely crestfallen, I thought to myself: "Such a beautiful tower and you're going to fuck it up like that..." And suddenly, something spoke to me: "Why should it be a cabin? There's that beautiful long stone wall running along the path, so we'll just take that and extend it into some beautiful shape." So I sketched it, and, behold – that was it. The museum went as if below ground, with Jára Cimrman's lighthouse jutting out. The way it works is that there is a strange tube inside which forms part of the exhibition. You walk into it and rise through the shaft of the lighthouse up to the viewpoint.

Nobody can imagine what a relief that was. And I have to say that working with the gang around Zdeněk Svěrák is a joy. They're as lovely as you imagine when you know only their performances. It turned out to be a great idea – Liptákov, Jára's favourite village, is nearby, so all we had to do was make a single window in the wall of the museum and we had a view of Liptákov.

The Cimrman lot put a lot of work into breathing life into the place: they came to visit in 19th century clothes on old bicycles, they performed several plays, and during the laying of the cornerstone, Zdeněk Svěrák recited a wonderful poem. I'd be very entertained if people once remembered us and said: "Rajniš, who was that? Oh, right, he worked with the famous builder and architect Kubík on the Jára Cimrman Museum!" I have faith that it might end up that way.

Artefact Kyje – workshop
T. Dvořáková, P. Janáč, T. Svobodová, V. Pošmourný, J. Lank, M. Blažek, E. Müllerová, O. Mráz, M. Mrázová, T. Buryová, J. Daniel
(2014)

With Prince Karel Schwarzenberg by the Artefact in Kyje
(2014)

Builders of the Artefact
M. Sven Nevlida, E. Müllerová, M. Genčurová, L. Lank, T. Kosnar, J. Frenzel, P. Hůlová, J. Smejkal, V. Pošmourný, M. Blažek, M. Utíkal, O. Mráz, T. Dvořáková
(2014)

When I speak about our mountain museum of Jára Cimrman, I can't forget the fantastic people that worked on its construction. It was a group of carpenters led by Vašek Horecký and the excellent Vlasta Pecháč – a Bed and Breakfast owner who took up construction on the side. When you shake his hand, you have to watch out that he doesn't crush it.

When we started building, I told him: "Vlasta, you know what the loveliest way of doing it would be? Like the Dogon people in Mali do it, in Africa. Rocks freely flowing into buildings."

He says: "That's nonsense, isn't it?"

But I kept pleading: "Do it that way, please."

"Okay, we'll try it," he said.

And so the rock became part of the structure and the structure a part of the landscape. It's not a cousin, but a sister of the rock that sprouted from the ground millions of years ago. I have to say it makes me very happy that a person as affluent as Aleš Voverka – whose trousers are even more worn out than mine – could use his obsession (and not

a cent of EU subsidy) to build something that made man and nature better friends.

And there's another benefit too: me and Aleš were friends before we started building and now we're much closer – and that's how it should be. That's why we architects are here – so that we can put things together with our friends and with people who can make money to fund those great projects if it can't be found another way. It's a rocky road, but we haven't taken our last step yet. There are dozens of projects on our drawing tables. Some are secret – they'll be so intoxicating they'll make waves all over central Europe. Hopefully, some will be realised in France, in Tel Aviv, even in Russia. It looks like Pussy Riot will be riding our ferry shouting, "Putin, Putin, get your paws off Ukraine." I myself am curious as to how it'll end. We'll see what surprises this field has in store for us.

Sticks

After playing around with wooden boards, we're now starting to build with sticks. It's strange that in 2014, sticks suddenly appeared in what we were doing. I mean the sticks that can grow on any meadow – they fly in from somewhere, grow roots, and in a few years, they're eight metres tall.

A large portion of my property in the Jizera Mountains cannot be mowed – along streams, between boulders, on hillsides... and that's where these sticks, spread by seed dispersal, are found. Nobody ever thought of them as construction material, so me and Tom Kosnar decided we had to do something about it. We counted up that if you added all the twigs from our place to Scholzberg, they'd make a line six kilometres long!

Meanwhile, fate was getting ready for these sticks of ours. In Prague 14, Černý Most, a friend of ours, the investor Kamil Hošťák, told us: "Boys, I'm preparing a commission for a tower, do you want to send some proposals?" We entered our three-sided and square towers, but I also thought we could draw something with sticks. I made a spiral staircase in the middle and six circular legs

around it. Remembering a number of sea monsters, I started drawing a tangle of legs out of it and reaching up; sticks in both directions, horizontally or a little askew. It was done right away.

Kamil and the mayor and his people looked at the sketches and – without a moment's hesitation – pointed at the drawing with the sticks: "We want this one." Of course I couldn't say "Wait – I have no idea how to do that one. It was just an experiment." I said to myself: "Remember Napoleon." And I heard my falsetto voice say, "Okay then."

I realised that once again, I was on the edge of a precipice, and from somewhere down below, I was being fanned by the icy breath of my professional demise. But me and the boys decided to try it.

"But how do we connect them?"

We tried ropes, leather, lianas, wire, and cables, until Kubík came up with the fact that all these materials would dry out, so we'd have to tighten them periodically. And there's only one reasonable solution for that – threaded rods and a nut with a washer. And we'd add a bulldog so it doesn't slip – a kind of toothed wheel.

We went to the cabin to test-build one leg of the tower – Luboš Lojbl, Kloďák, Tom Kosnar, David Kubík, Vašek Horecký, Mirek Sven Nevlida, Jirka Lank, Martina Genčurová, and I. We marked spots on the ground, Luboš put up some 19th-century scaffolding with incredible speed, and we started weaving. We were awfully nervous – maybe it wouldn't work and we'd have to get on our knees in front of the mayor and explain why we'd have to do one of the other proposals. But suddenly, it started moving and we saw we were on the verge of a huge unexplored architectural landscape where incredible things could be accomplished. We were done in three and a half days.

During that test construction, we connected both the legs at the top, creating a beautiful twelve-metre backside which turned out to be quite the poetic artefact. We put a workshop together and we've since done several more with

Huť architektury exhibition in DOX (2014)

Installation of the roofing at the café of the Museum of Applied Arts in Brno (2016)

Scholzberg Tower
from left to right: M. Rajniš, D. Kubík, J. Mach, D. Baudys, D. Pavlišta, E. Saganová, E. Kosová's boyfriend, E. Kosová, J. Lefler
(2016)

huge success, some of them for the architecture faculties. I made a deal with their administrators: students participating in the workshops would be awarded credits. As always, we promised we'd cook, and for those coming from afar, we'd find accommodation too.

Tom Kosnar did a fantastic job of organising it: in the summer, we started building by the beautiful pond in Kyje, the sun was shining, we kept working and bathing, and in less than a fortnight, a gentle lady's bottom made of sticks towered at the height of a four-storey building. And because you have to honour nature, it even had a cleft in the middle, made of sticks. The students soon understood they were taking part in something nobody had ever done before, or at least not in this way.

It was a little like the Moon landing, backwards – a small step for mankind, but a huge leap for us. Doubravka was built a little differently. We made a boot tree which we use to bend the sticks to create a "doubly ruled surface", as they call it in mathematics. It's just a surface that can't be straightened. Everything goes so fast with this technology, as we tested out on the terrace of the DOX museum, where we installed an exhibition. Kubík called this object "The Elephant's Back".

I should also mention that a month before the show in DOX opened, we boys and girls all went to Paris for the Global Award of Sustainable Architecture. Hah – sustainable architecture, made by an unsustainable architect!

I had to give a talk, so I mentioned that fifty years ago, I was a young vagrant sleeping under the Pont Neuf suffering from terrible diarrhoea, so I befriended all the lady toilet attendants in the area: as if Balzac himself had written the story. And this vagrant – now in a posh get-up with a bow-tie – had made it to the Parisian heavens, where he is being awarded a world prize, on almost exactly his seventieth birthday... Like an American film, isn't it? I still can't rule out the possibility that it's just a crazy screenplay by some director

at the beginning of his career, trying to touch his audience with a totally unlikely narrative...
We accepted the award and hurried back to DOX. The exhibition which Leoš Válka organised mostly because of that famous award of mine went quite well, so we were suddenly making hay. And there was a lot to reap. After we received the award, everyone thought we'd up our prices, but they were wrong. Nobody has to be scared we'll chase them up into high numbers. You see, I think doing good things with good people in good places is still worthwhile. And by good things, I don't mean prisons or police stations, but I also don't mean shopping centres. And the rest? Why not!

Marina Bay Sands hotel, Singapore (2015/2016)

Bathing in the rooftop pool at the Marina Bay Sands hotel, Singapore (2015/2016)

The Future is Knocking at the Gate

The sticks continue their campaign and they will undoubtedly conquer the world – they're sexy to look at and also cheap. We're working on R&D for a machine that would couple them – we'll see. There's a young Scout hidden in every stick, capable of bearing huge loads, connecting with the others, and creating something completely new. Do you also feel the future knocking at the gate? Do you hear, somewhere in the distance, the fragrant winds of beauty and adventure?

I've got my life planned out to the age of ninety, but if something happens, I have a lot of young friends who I've worked with over the years, so I am entirely calm. I know they're ready to work independently, without me. Tom Kosnar, David Pavlišta, Honza Mach, David Kubík, Martin Kloda, Kamila Amblerová, the boys from 4DS, and the amazing guys at ADR. Each of them in their own and different way carries the conviction that it is worth doing top-class architecture at full throttle. That's the best fate you can wish for.

There's no risk of copying. That would piss me off and they don't do it. Architecture, however, is a collective endeavour. I observe how the young ones get up to speed, and I believe they'll push our project further. Perhaps not in precisely the same direction, but these are people filled with determination, courage, and hope, and they're bloody good. Though I have zero social intelligence, I can safely recognise when someone has that flame burning inside them. You see, those are the only people I want to work with.

Although only my name is written on that French award, it should also bear the name of all those I've spent years collaborating with. In short, Czech architecture is returning to the world. Better times are on the horizon, and even though you may sometimes fall prey to hopelessness, it's worth it in the end.

Taking Stock, Death

My beautiful life with Kačenka couldn't last long. One day, she told me: "I've got some sad news for you. It's over."

What should one's reply to sad news be? The art of life consists in softly accepting the hard blows of fate. I practice this discipline every day, and we'll see if I've gotten at least a little farther. I'm sure I have! In the end, I survive even the hardest blows (with some booze and my kind dogs).

My dearest dog Andulka, however, died in the spring of 2015. My first wife Johanka died, Arnošt died, Andulka 2, Judita, my parents died, my grandmothers... But I can't say I feel bad. Quite the opposite. It's a beautiful life.

Like I said at the beginning of this chapter, the third life is there so you can learn to accept death with kindness. So, I'm learning. I have friends. I have – I hope – some work and travel in front of me, and I know that many incredible wonders yet await around the world.

I'm convinced that somewhere in the future, the guiles of fate are still twisting and I'll have to try to squeeze through its knots without being strangled or eaten, like the young Rockefeller whom the Asmat cannibals had for dinner.

Even so... one travelogue from New Guinea says: "The traveller need have no fear of losing his head, for even if he does lose it, his skull will be decorated by so many beautiful beads that – if he could see it – it would bring him great joy..."

That would be a nice ending, wouldn't it?

The Archive of Martin Rajniš

page 12
My father crossing Černá hora on horseback (1934)
page 13
Me on horseback, Prague (1946)
page 14
Aunt Milena, just married to Gerhard von Ströhlin, Prague (1935)
page 15
The house in Římov (2016)
The house on the corner of Rašínovo nábreží after the fatal air raid, Prague (1945)
page 17
At the cabin in Maxov (1949)
Me and Tomík Plzenský, Maxov (1950)
page 18
Grandma Marie and Grandpa Alois Rajniš (1898)
page 19
"Little Nana", my father Ivo, and Aunt Lída (1911)
page 20
My childhood home, Ostrovní Street no. 4
page 21
With my father, Prague (1947)
page 22
The building of the Mánes Union of Fine Artists, Prague (1932)
Mánes, the original interior design of the French restaurant, Prague (1930)
page 23
The empty fountain in the foyer of the Slavia café, Prague (2016)
page 24
My father and his schoolmates, the Italian Riviera (1924)
Italská riviéra (1924)
page 25
My father Ivo, Prague (1985)
Ivo with Andulka, Maxov (1979)
page 26
My parents at the harbour below Vyšehrad (1959)
page 27
My mom with Andulka, Maxov (1970)
page 28
The entrance to the Lucerna cinema, Prague
page 30
Roald Amundsen (1899)
National Library of Norway, photograph by Daniel Georg Nyblin
page 33
The Škoda PV15 steamroller
The Škoda Sentinel with its lowered floor for transporting rubbish bins (1930s)
The funeral of president Edvard Beneš, parade on Národní třída, Prague (September 8th, 1948)
page 34
With Pavel Frieb and his sister Marta at the Točná airport (1953)
page 35
With my schoolmates (1955)
page 36
School photograph, third grade, M.R. is the third from the right in the third row counting from the bottom (1953)
page 37
School photograph, sixth grade, M.R. is in the middle of the first row (1956)
page 40
Glacier, the Arctic (2016)
page 41
The Stalin monument, Prague (1955)
The demolition of the Stalin monument, Prague (1962)
page 42
The funeral of the mass murderer Klement Gottwald, Prague (1953)
A Gottwald postage stamp (1953)
page 46
Football at the cabin (1952)
page 48
With Tom Plzenský in Maxov (2012)
page 49
We from the Scholzberg cabin, Upper Maxov. We've been here for sixty-five years!
By the Brechschmied chapel (October 28th, 2005)
page 50
Poster for the film Salair de la Peur le; The Wages of Fear (1953)
page 51
Graphs of snow cover at Maxov as recorded by Jaroslav Horník (1970–2009)
page 53
The building of my high school in Braník (2016)
page 54
High school class, M.R. third from the right at the top, Petr "Pedro" Kočům fourth from the right at the top (1962)
page 55
High school tableau in Martin Rajniš's graphic layout (1962)
pages 58 and 59
1 Beluga
1a St Helena, 1967–1969
1b Odetta, 1970–1975
2 Pirate, 2011
3 Maia, 1993–2004
4 Wander jola Skua, 1956–1980
5 Salamander – Daisy, 1957–1977
6 Mistral, 1950s
page 62
My certification to navigate small ships (1970)
pages 64 and 65
The "friendly" armies in Prague (1968)
page 68
Judita (1942–1950)
page 70
The photograph in my student index at the technical university (1962)
page 71
Self-portrait (1965)
The photograph in my student index at the Academy of Fine Arts (1969)
page 73
Church of St Martin in the Rock, one of my first projects. The sketch was destroyed by the 2002 flooding, following a wish expressed by Benjamin Fragner, I drew it again in 2010 (1965)

The Archive of Huť Architektury Martin Rajniš

DA Studio Archive

The Archive of Kamila Amblerová

Tom Plzenský

page 67
Maya by the northwestern coast of Mallorca (1994)
Our training sailboat in Davle, Pirát (2016)

Pavel Štecha

page 69
Arnošt (1993–1999)
page 109
Hit in the face on Národní třída (November 17th, 1989)
Beautiful girls gazing admiringly at myself and V. Havel (1989)
page 129
New Delhi (1994)
Devprayag (1994)
page 134
With the A1 Studio in the Himalayas, Kedarmath base camp (1994)
page 186
With Pavel Štecha in the Krkonoše mountains (winter 1988)

Luboš Loibl

page 47
The Maxov cabin (2014)
page 69
Andulka sick at the cabin (2014)
page 165
High Atlas, Morocco, with Luboš Loibl (2013)
page 166
With Luboš Loidl on Inle Lake, Burma (2015/2016)
page 198
Marina Bay Sands hotel, Singapore (2015/2016)
page 199
Bathing in the rooftop pool at the Marina Bay Sands hotel, Singapore (2016)

Milan Pitlach

page 61
Slapy Reservoire (mid-1970s)
At the helm, Slapy (mid-1970s)
Tailwind, Slapy (mid-1970s)

Andrea Thiel Lhotáková

page 135
With the A1 Studio in a pub in Smíchov, Prague (2016)

page 138
Iceland,
A. Thiel Lhotáková, R. Kalmár, M. Steinbachová (1997)
Iceland, Vatnajökul glacier
J. Cigler, M. Steinbachová, R. Kalmár, L. Zemen (1997)
Iceland with the A1 Studio (1997)
page 139
Iceland (1997)
page 166
High Atlas, Morocco, with Luboš Loibl (2013)
page 190
Team Venice in the Prague studio (2010)

Helena Machová

page 69
Andulka II (2007–2015)

Jiří Suchomel

page 81
The SIAL Nursery studio, Jedlová (1970s)
page 82
Karel Hubáček, Míra Masák (late 1970s)
page 83
E. Přikryl, J. Suchomel, Z. Zavřel (1970s)
Mirko Baum at Jedlová (1970s)
Milan Pitlach and Johny Eisler under a painting by Jiří Sopko (1970s)
page 86
Míra Masák, Jedlová (1970s)
page 87
Johny Eisler at Jedlová (1970s)
Drawing Máj at Jedlová (1970s)

The Archive of Jakub Cigler

page 85
Karel Hubáček's birthday party, from left to right: Z. Zavřel, K. Hubáček, M. Rajniš, J. Cigler (1993)
page 125
With Jakub Cigler on the Vltava (2000)
page 136
The Garhwal Himalayas (1994)
The Garhwal Himalayas (1994)
page 137
The Garhwal Himalayas (1994)
The Garhwal Himalayas (1994)

Filip Šlapal

page 124
With Jakub Cígler and students of the A1 Studio (1995)
page 126
My 50th birthday celebration (1994)
My 50th birthday celebration (1994)
page 127
The christening of the first year group of the A1 Studio, Mrač (1995)
The christening of the first year group of the A1 Studio, Mrač (1995)

The Archive of David Kubík

page 187
On the Venice lagoon with David Kubík (2012)
page 191
Team Venice relocating to the boat exhibition (2010)
page 192
Model of Bára, Chrastava (2010)
page 194
Artefact Kyje – workshop

The Archive of Evžen Stein

page 118
Evžen Stein and Karl Glatzel (1991)

The Archive of Jan Nedvěd

page 131
Carpathian Ruthenia with the A1 Studio (1993)
Carpathian Ruthenia with the A1 Studio (1993)
Carpathian Ruthenia with the A1 Studio (1993)

The Archive of Aleš Voverka

page 144
Me on Madre de Dios, the upper tributary of the Amazon (2001)
Aleš Voverka and I in the silver mines inside the Cero Rico mountain at an altitude of over 5000 m MSL, Bolivia (2001)
page 149
Paja brava – a symbol of natural architecture, Altiplano, Bolivia (2001)
page 150
Aleš Voverka and I, photo from the peak, Pisco, Peru (2001)
The peak of Pisco mountain (5650 m MSL), Cordillera Blanca, Huascaran area, Peru (2001)

The Archive of Jiří Žemlička

page 170
Johanka in the Dolomites (1985)
In Gran Sasso (1985)
In the Žemlicka's car, Italy (1985)
page 171
Honza and Dáša Žemlicka, Italy (1984)
Dáša and Honza Žemlička, excellent friends to me and Johanka, whom I continue meeting today, often in the most varied places around the world (1984)
Viktorka and Mirek Jiránek (2005)

Milan Hakl

page 130
Taking the train to Carpathian Ruthenia (1993)

Antonín Kratochvíl

page 188
Neighbours by the café, split Martin (both left and right) (2013)

Vojtěch Kopecký

page 193
Members of Jára Cimrman's Theatre at the opening of the museum in Příchovice (2013)

Tomáš Kosnar

page 196
Installation of the roofing at the café of the Museum of Applied Arts in Brno (2016)
Installation of the roofing at the café of the Museum of Applied Arts in Brno (2016)

Radka Ciglerová

page 165
High Atlas, Morocco, with Luboš Loibl (2013)
page 190
Team Venice in the Prague studio

Martin Rajniš:
Twenty Five Thousand Days
of Memories

Recorded and retold by
Magdalena Šebestová

English translation
Ian Mikyska

English copy editor
Aren Ock

Graphic design
Tomáš Machek, Side2

Typesetting and prepress
Jiří Kristian Počta, Side2

Printed by
Tiskárna Protisk, s.r.o.

Published by
KANT Publishers
Kladenská 29, 160 00 Prague 6

ISBN 978-80-7437-366-4

Appendix

A Selection of Projects and Building Designs

—

The kind reader who has worked through this book, all the way up to here, is perhaps wondering what the aim of this section is. Well, when I was reading and editing this text I noticed that whenever I spoke of architecture, it took the form of boundless pseudo-scientific musings. That's why we ended up including my architectural works in the book as a separate section.

The selection is a result of my subjective feelings. I simply put in what seemed most interesting to me in the summer of 2016; what I love most. This selection represents half a century of work, but if this were all I'd done in that time, I'd be a pretty awful slacker.

This is only a proportion of what I produced during those long years, so please don't mistake this for a serious professional treatise on the subject of "myself and architecture". I hope that in time, that will come too – but ideally written by someone else...

Which of my projects do I love best? They're all my children, and a good parent never says which is the prettiest. It is said that a creator always prefers what he is currently working on. Furthermore, as I'm sure you've understood by now, my slightly restless view of the world is responsible for the fact that the harder a crazy idea is to swallow for the authorities, the closer it is to my heart.

Just to make sure: Architects almost always work in packs (and I've had a number of packs over fifty years!), so you should really list all of those who took part in each project. This, however, is practically impossible, so I'm only presenting things which can more or less be attributed to me, although a number of people participated on most of them. I included them all in a long list. If anyone feels left out, I apologise in advance.

One last thing: so that it looks nice and keeps an internal logic, the pictures are not arranged chronologically. I simply grouped the towers together and arranged the other designs by colour, even though they are from different periods. I hope it's not my last selection – where shall I see my poor babies from 2016 to, at least, 2034?

Martin Rajniš, August 2016

Beer Tower, Prague, CZ, 2016
The beer tower and five other tower projects are among my constructions designed with sticks of anemochorous woods, of which there are millions of kilometres all around Europe. We decided to try and use it for normal structures with all that entails. This tower is part of a project for the brewery in Kbely.

Hexa-feet Tower, Kyje, Prague, CZ, 2014
When I saw how many stems were growing around my cabin, I decided they needed to be put to use. The first structure had six irregular legs and I suddenly realised how wonderfully crooked pieces of wood joined together in three-sided spatial structures.

Doubravka Tower, Kyje, Prague, CZ, 2014
The mayor of Prague 14 expressed an interest in building a wooden tower, and I decided it would have only three legs – fewer legs = fewer concerns, and, presuming equal stability, lower costs. So, the hexa-feet became a triffid, and we named it Doubravka. The sci-fi novel The Day of the Triffids was very popular in its time. This is a late triffid that sailed into our time from the previous century.
Doubravka is among the towers that have a spatial bearing construction from stems.

Artefact, Kyje, Prague, CZ, 2014
I and the boys decided that first we had to test how the two legs would connect. Connecting them (especially since this was in May) produced a bum. That's how the sketch for our student workshop was born – that's where we verified that this crazy structure could really be built.

Pentafeet Tower, Kyje, Prague, CZ, 2014
This five-footer is part of the lineage of development from six legs to three.

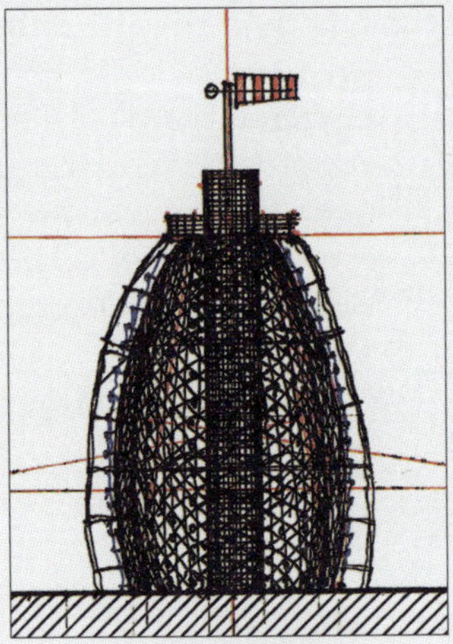
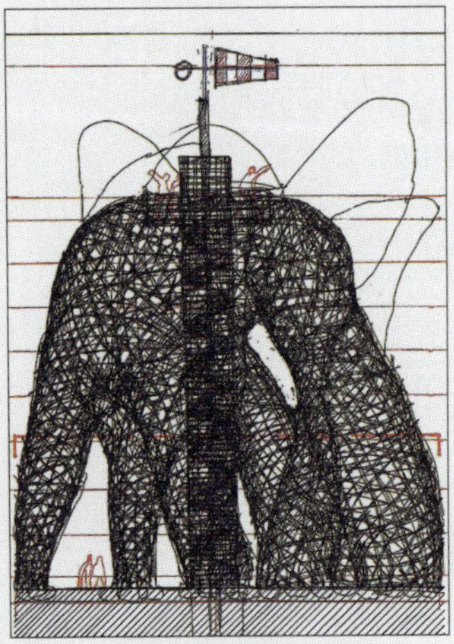
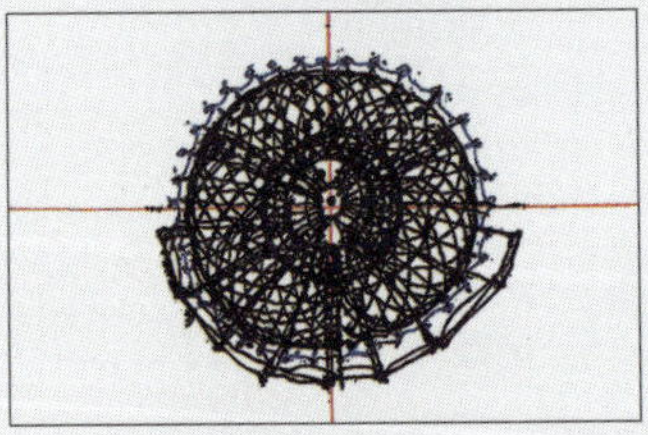
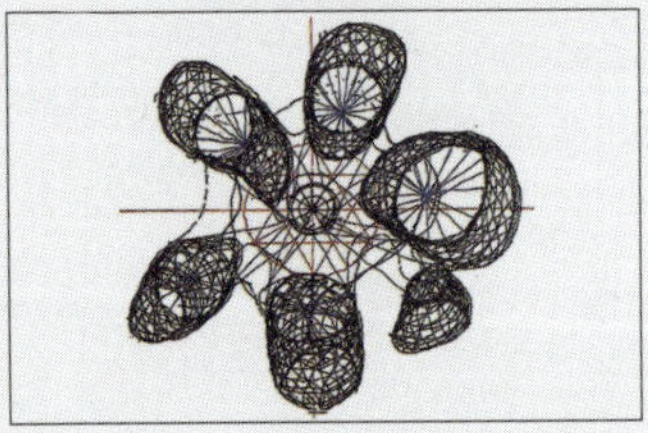
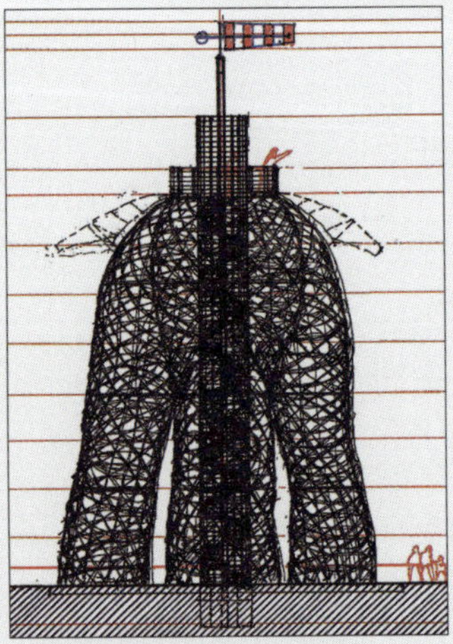
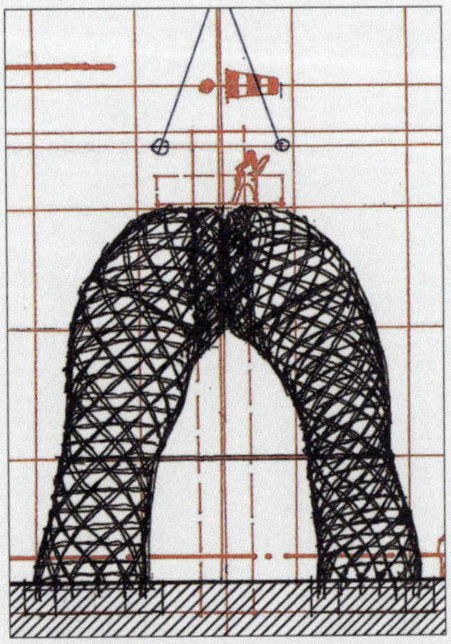
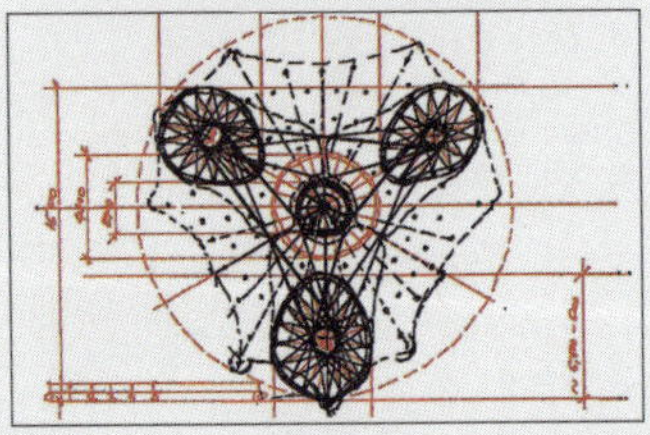
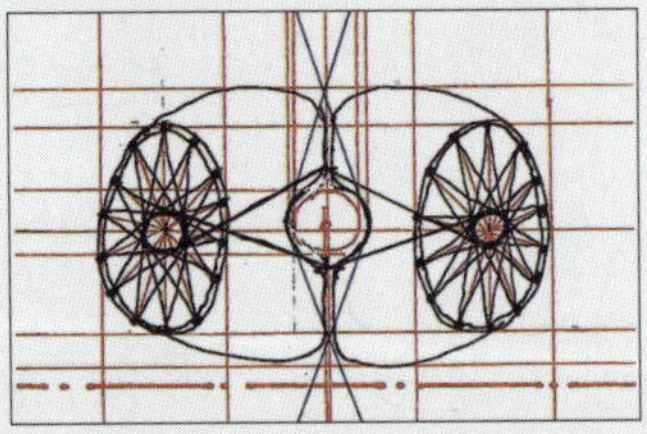

Šišák Tower, 2016

When me and Luboš were sailing down the Irrawaddy, we got an email from Rosťa Koryčánek asking us to make some large sketches for an exhibition he was organising in Brno (by the way, the show has a gorgeous poster). What was originally intended as more or less free graphic work developed through the workings of fate into quite an interesting structure. We're even thinking of building a slightly smaller version at our cabin.

Ecumenical Chapel, Prague – West: Trnová, 2005

The ecumenical chapel was to form part of the senior citizen centre. We created a number of possibilities and discussed many possible locations, but it seems it is not yet time for the chapel. The tower stands out due to the fact that the narrower bottom stone part is "wrapped" in a ring that forms part of the higher wooden structure.

Botanicus Gardens, Lysá nad Labem, 2009

One of several wooden towers on the grounds of the Botanicus Gardens, which stretches out across a small hill. This is where the entrance to the underground is located, as well as the foot of a spiral wooden staircase leading up to the viewing deck.

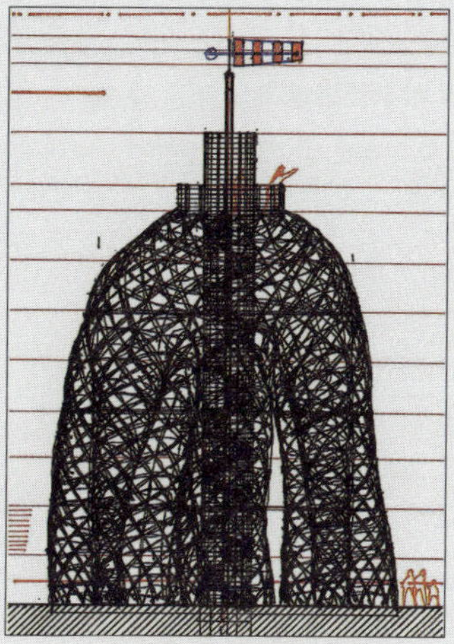

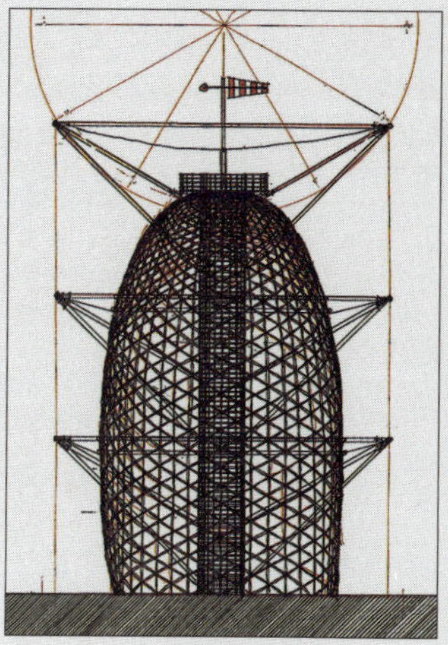

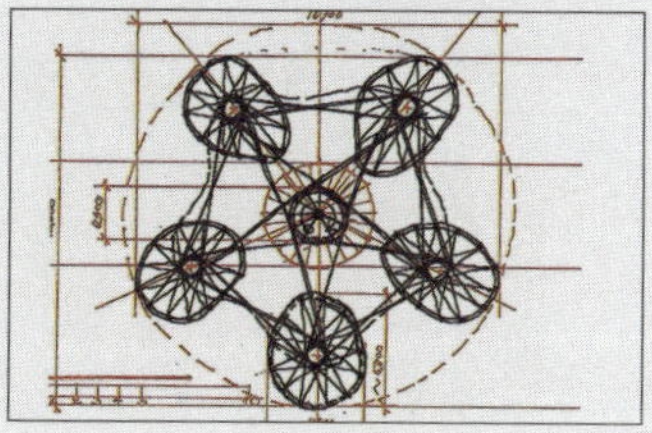

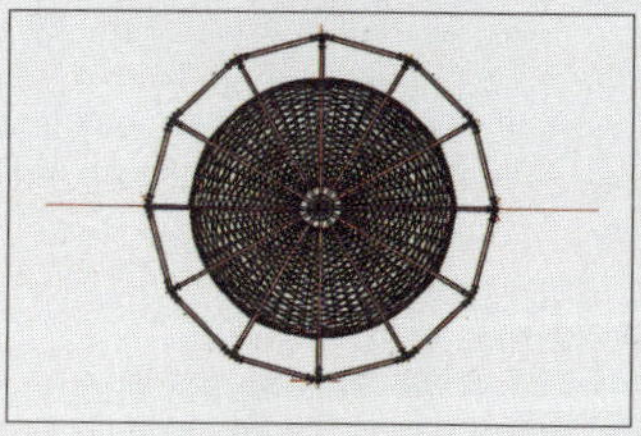

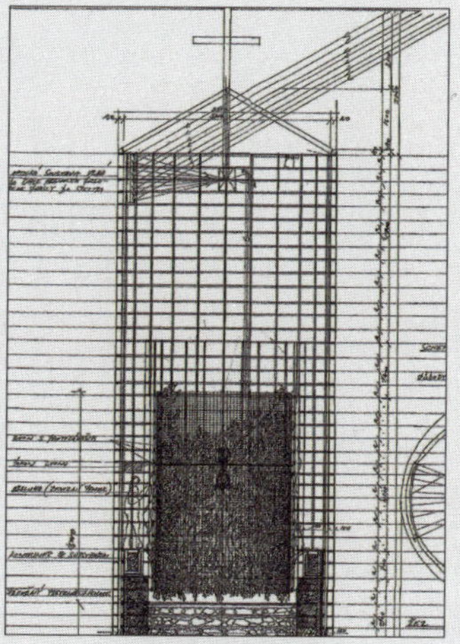

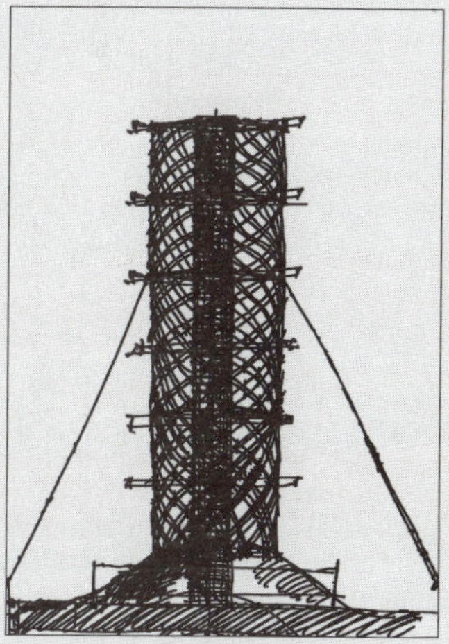

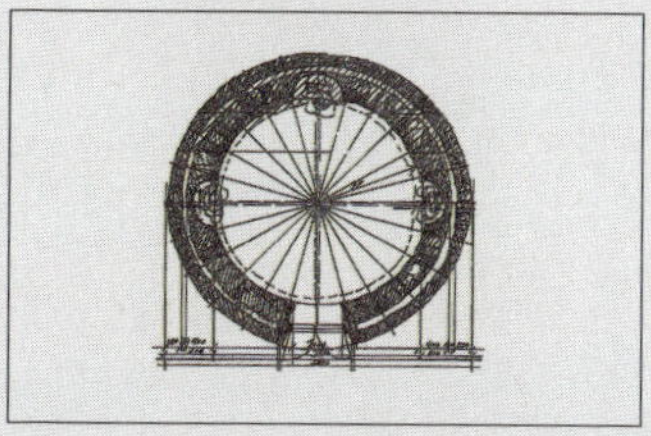

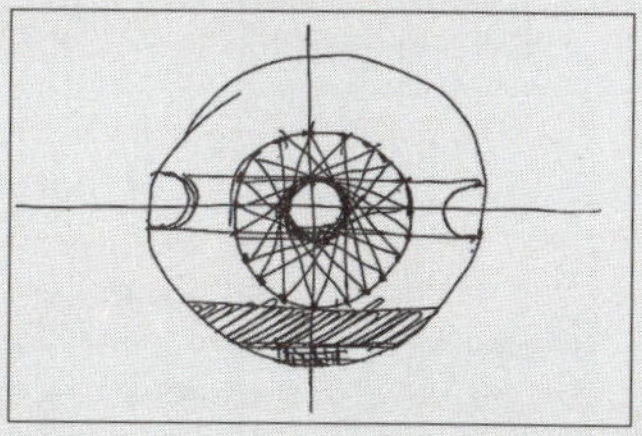

Bára I, Bára II Tower, Chrudim, CZ, 2008, 2009

A book was published on these towers (they're cousins), so I'll just mention some basic facts. This simple three-sided tower built like a stack (by placing boards and sections atop one another) was born during a train ride from Kyoto to Tokyo which I took with Aleš Voverka.

The city of Chrudim announced a competition, to which we submitted drawings for four towers with various ground plans, and we won. So, came Bára I. Four days after opening, however, a serious tornado of F2 strength came through and half-demolished poor Bára I (see pages XX to XX in the main text). We used the insurance money to build its clone, Bára II – more robust, lower, and built to exceed standard resilience specifications. We love them both.

Máminka Tower, Hudlice, CZ, 2015

Radek Olič initiated the construction of this tower. His parents live in a village under Krušná hora, which Máminka towers over. Since he is a native of Hudlice, also home to national revivalist Josef Jungmann, we tried to construct the tower like a memory of the triangulation towers which Austria-Hungary built throughout its territory. Our new tower was named by its initiator, Radek – after his mother. The Máminka tower created an indivisible duo with the nearby Tátovka alleyway.

Scholzberg Tower, Horní Maxov, CZ, 2006

Scholzberg Tower is essentially a cheeky attempt to make a stack like a vertical woodpile without any documentation or money, and with untested technology, so everyone said it would collapse. It didn't, and they didn't come to tear it down either. Our resistance to attack from the building authorities was so strong that they put it right at the bottom of the lowest drawer.

Later, we decided to take the tower apart – it only took us four and a half hours. You see, we made a number of tiny mistakes and the dear tower started tilting and deforming. Since then, we've built a number of other

structures using this method. In time, Scholzberg will have a different, much more beautiful tower.

Doubravka Tower, Prague – Kyje, 2018
What started as wild sketches for a tower made of twigs took four years of designing and experimenting to transform into Doubravka, a real lookout tower – the first structural thin-bone construction in the world.

Lighthouse and Museum of Jára Cimrman , Příchovice, CZ, 2013
I've talked about it already, but I would perhaps mention that the selection committee for the Mies van der Rohe Award for architecture nominated this project. Just like us, Aleš Voverka liked this rounded tower shape, and he decided to build one near his skiing resort and Bed and Breakfast, U Čápa.

That was the genesis of naming it 'Jára Cimrman's Lighthouse', because the Museum of Jára Cimrman is underground. There is a view towards Liptákov from a small window facing south. People love it there and visit often.

Staircase Tower, Post Office on Sněžka, Krkonoše Mountains, 1602 mamsl, 2007
The tower stands apart from the interior, creating an autonomous cylindrical structure. It was the first round tower with a staircase we built. We've made many more since then. When frost forms on the tower, it creates a beautiful ice object.

Residential Tower Klecanky , Prague, CZ, 2013
Our clients had a dilapidated cabin in the wonderful canyon of the right-bank tributary of the Vltava in Klecánky. We agreed we'd build them a family home on the floor plan of the cabin. The project includes several stories: two basements with natural light, a residential floor, a ground floor, and a split-level loft. All this on a floor plan of only a few metres. This is a somewhat idiosyncratic interpretation of what can be done – but with a bit of good will... In order for the owners to feel like nesting birds, they asked for

a terrace with a view of the treetops. However, we haven't entered construction yet – the family has fallen apart, so there's no one to do the nesting.

Giant Wheel, Expo '86, Vancouver, Canada, 1986
We've also spent a number of pages on this project. The entry hall of the exhibition is dominated by the Giant Wheel. It's a poem about speed, steam, and power...

Airplane, Expo '86, Vancouver, Canada, 1986
The Airplane and the four designs that follow are crazy exhibits which dominated the airspace above the actual display. Mad inventors paraded dainty tricks of huge variety. This chance to bring illustrations from Jules Verne novels to life at a realistic scale was among my best designing experiences.

It's a shame that only one of these mad machines survived. I regret not buying them so that I could continue to feast my eyes on them at the cabin. This text is also linked to the helicopter, the eight-winged flying machine, and the monocycle. Back in Vancouver, these won us the "Indian Feather Award".

Pneu Lamp, 1969
With this project, we return to the turn of the 1960s and '70s. It was essentially a SIAL Nursery exercise, and it won me a competition with the well-known Italian light manufacturer Artemide. In fact, I always wished – and I hope it shows – to do not only architecture, but design. Proper architecture, you see, has to include all the elementary aspects of craft – not only grand structures, but also well-planned designs.

Chair, National Gallery in Prague, CZ, 1989
We built this armchair at Mirek Masák's invitation. He was leading the renovation project at the Trade Fair Palace, which belongs to the National Gallery Prague. We provided several pieces of sitting room furniture: the all-wooden

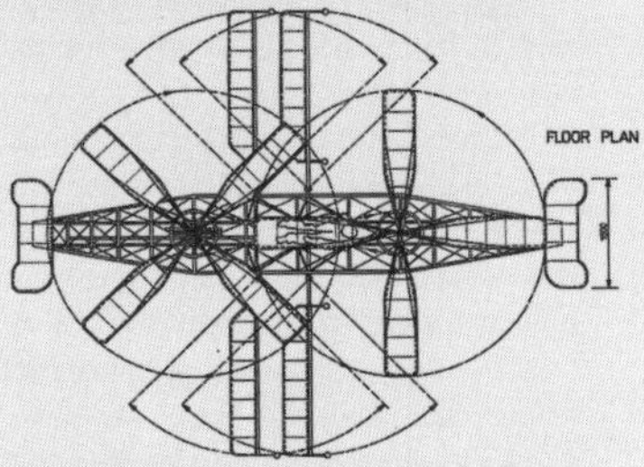

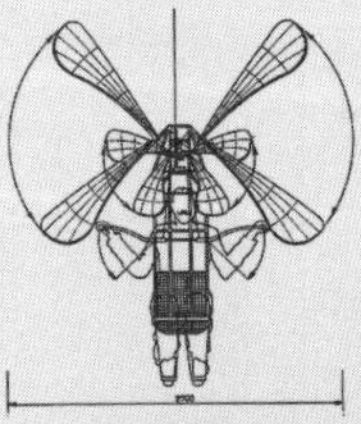
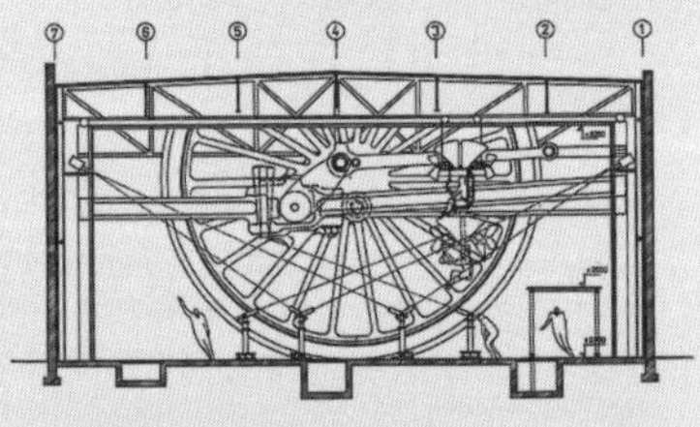

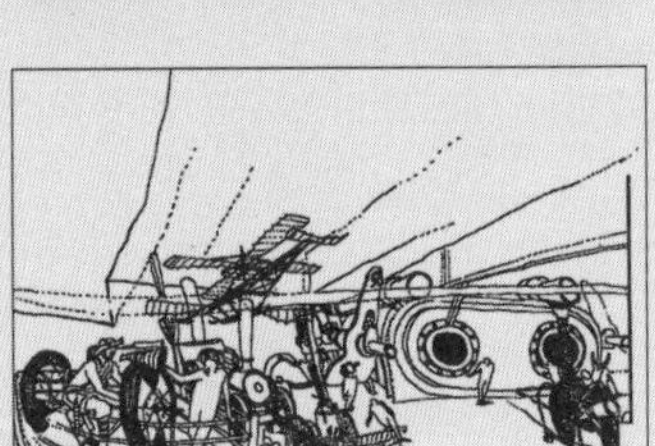

armchair was prototyped with the Tonet company, and the metal one with Jakub Černoch, owner of a lamp factory. With both designs, it's apparent that we were aiming for a classic, balanced, and essentially mainstream modern style. At the time, you see, the idea of the National Gallery awakened in me a hallowed admiration, which has disappeared God-knows-where over the years. But we enjoyed the work.

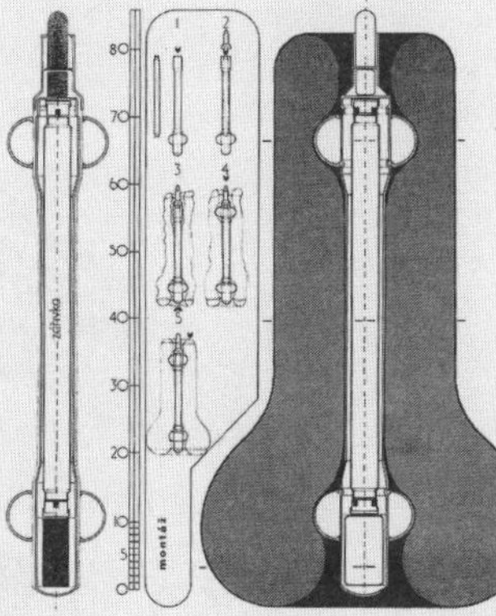

Machinist Armchair, 2014
Machinista is in stark contrast to the National Gallery armchair. It's foldable, cheap, and it seems to have been built by an airplane designer before World War I. Bits of plywood, screws, connecting rods, braced from various directions, a canvas seat you can tighten...

At first it seemed it'd be an easy job. I gave the task to an architecture student in Brno, Nela Gottwaldová, and I was astonished at how complicated it got. We managed in the end though. In a few minutes, the armchair can be taken apart and folded up into a small pasteboard box – IKEA would be amazed.

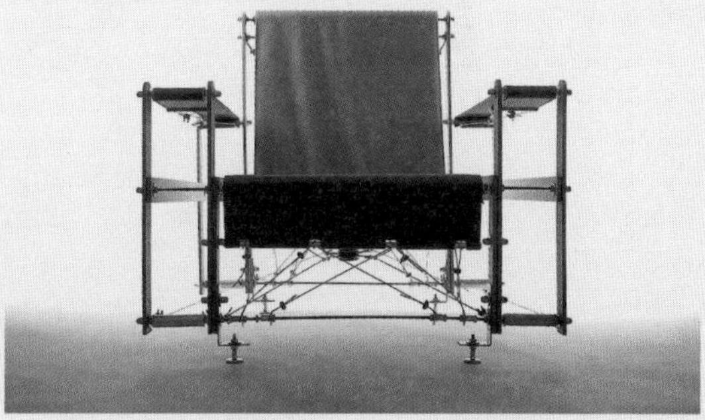

Cast-Iron Park Furniture, Prague, CZ, 1987
When we got back from Canada, we knew all kinds of people from various iron foundries, so we gladly took on the commission to design a range of cast-iron objects for the streets and parks of Prague. Because we were in cahoots with the foundrymen, we prototyped in the real, in cast iron, and we were disappointed we didn't get the chance to realise similar furniture in Prague on a larger scale. The prototypes are still at DH Studio today.

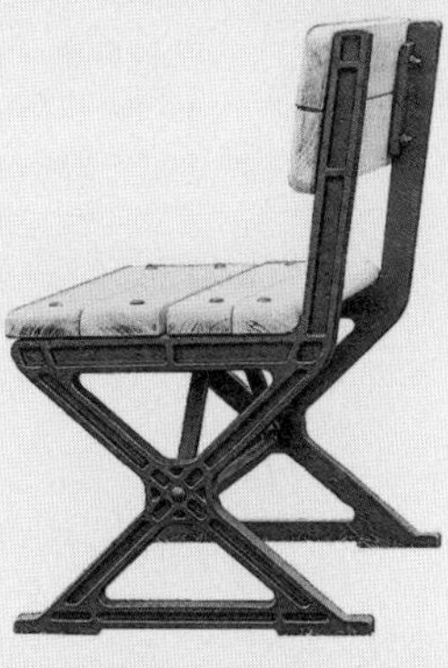

Máj Department Store, Prague, CZ, 1975

Johny Eisler, Míra Masák, and I won the commission mostly thanks to Míra's clever strategy: we placed all the important points of operation that a department store needs in order to operate in the main building rather than the secondary building (which was also part of the project). We were the only team to offer a solution which could be built quickly and actually function.

Both the preservationists and the architectural authorities were horrified: to them, we were little boys in striped trousers. After all, the year was 1972 – some ten years after socialist realism had been called off as the mandatory aesthetic of a socialist society.

Though I stand behind the architecture and craftsmanship, I think Máj is, after all, a little too aggressive for the centre of Prague.

Office Building, Pankrác, Prague, CZ, 1995

This building, erected in the first half of the 1990s, is one of a series of admin buildings for hire that we designed for the Plan & Bau company. Even though the project was set with primarily commercial parameters, it was nominated for the Mies van der Rohe Architecture Award and became the most economically successful building in the Czech Republic in this period. At the time, good economics and good architecture really didn't mix! We even included Jakub Cigler's giant glass pendulum in the costs, which dominated the vertical communications hall.

Lužiny Children´s Healthcare Centre, Prague, CZ, 1990

The doctor Standa Kusý wanted to build an eye hospital for children which they wouldn't be scared of. One was built in Prague 5, another in Prague 6. The one shown here is near the Lužiny metro station. After the series of extracurricular pavilions and exhibitions in Canada, we were happy to be able to implement similar ideas at home. Just as in Canada, we enjoyed an excellent collaboration with Aleš Lamr, whose colour-style for the interior remains just as remarkable today.

SANOPS, Na Mrázovce, Prague, CZ, 1987

The management of SANOPS, which originally belonged to the diplomatic corps and the central committee off the Communist Party, decided to transform this villa into a health centre for their children. I really didn't want to accept the commission, but after all, children are not responsible for their parents...

New Smíchov , Prague, CZ, 1990-2008

I discuss the Smíchov Centre project at length in the main body of the text, so I'll limit myself to a single sentence: It seems like normal life has finally returned to this part of Prague!

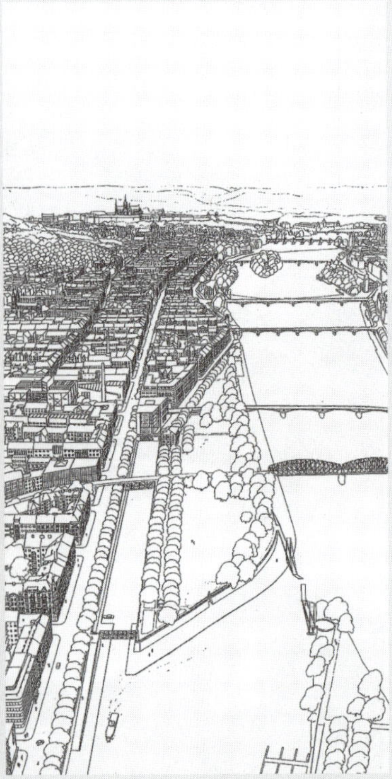

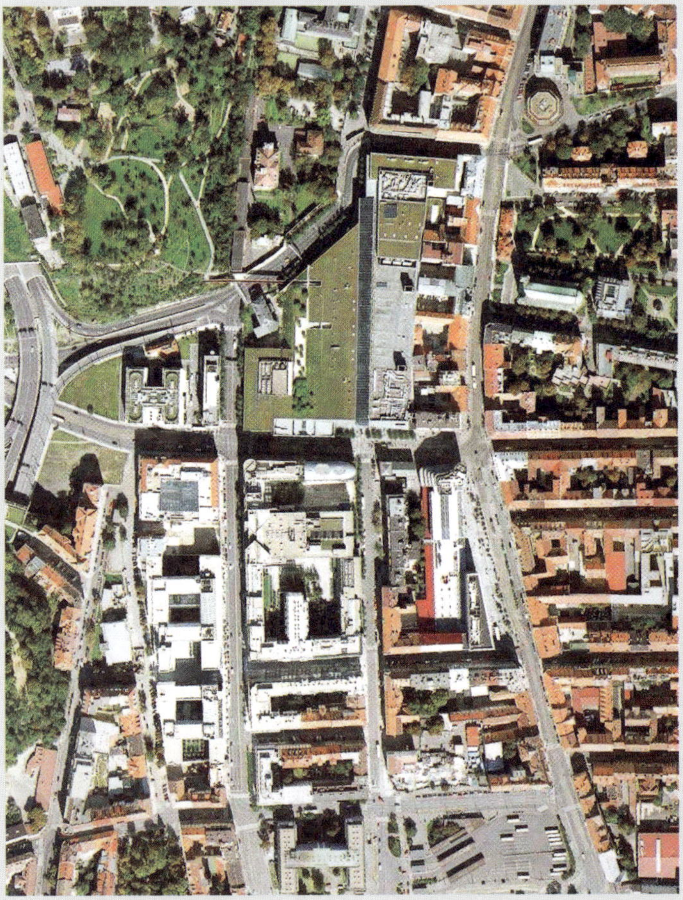

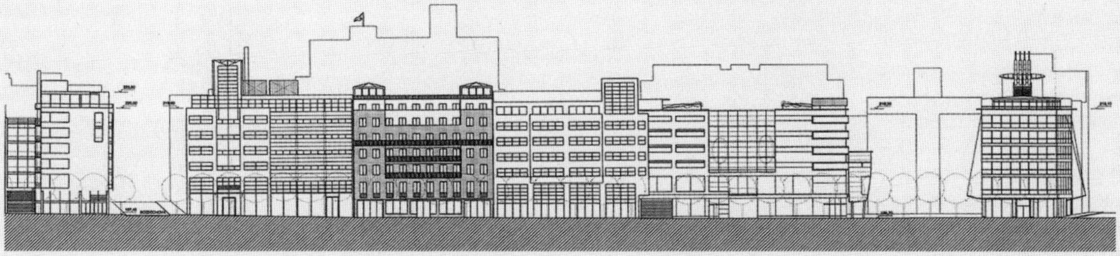

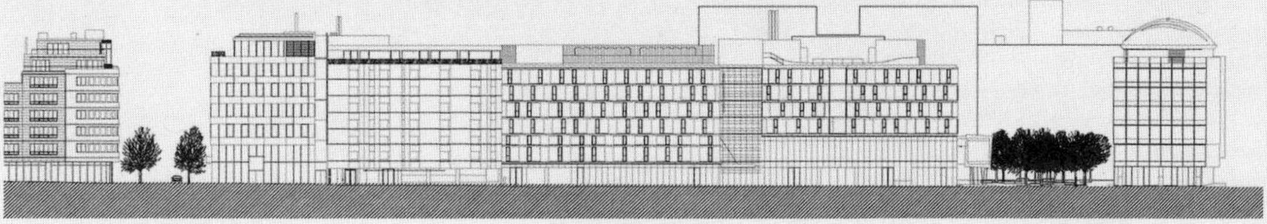

House for Pavel Štecha, Černošice, CZ, 2001

For hundreds of years, a "vejminek" was a commonly found structure in the Czech countryside.

Pavel Štecha – one of my best friends for many years – fell seriously ill and I tried to make myself useful. Because he wanted a wooden house and I'd learnt all about two by fours in Canada, I used that method. The location, size, and arrangement of the house was the work of Pavel and his wife Alice – I just drew it all up.

We left a lot of the structure uncovered and covered the entire south face, with its wonderful view, in glass. Pavel was happy there and this house launched me into my wood period.

Stack at Slavonice, CZ, 2007

The house is located near the village of Stálkov in the centre of the gorgeous natural scenery of Czech Canada in South Bohemia. We were approached by Martin Verner, an editor at Architekt magazine at the time – apparently, ten studios had tried in vain to satisfy his vision for his weekend house. We made our first stack – and it was exactly what he wanted.

We had no experience with this kind of structure, so we resolved a lot of the technicalities as we went. We were all happy when the house was awarded the Ernst A. Plischke Award, which I accepted in the famous hall of the Academy of Fine Arts in Vienna, and I have to say it was a real experience.

Pisek City Forest Administration, CZ, 2009

The commission assignment specified a "modern ecological building", but after we finally arrived at a showing after months of gruelling negotiations, the director retired and the new kings of the castle arrogantly refused the project – even though we were already done with the design! Our exchanges intensified further, and in order to protect myself, I made use of my political contacts, which backfired terribly.

We were trying to accommodate their wishes, especially as concerned economising (often at the expense of the quality of the materials). In the end, the municipal politicians seized upon our conflict and used our poor house to settle their accounts – I've never experienced a campaign as hateful as this one in the Czech Republic. I've been pissed off with Písek ever since.

The House in the Preserve, CZ, 2012

This house is among those joyous projects in which the investor – a builder himself – led the construction of this house set into the picturesque landscape of the Upper Palatine Forest with reason and a steady hand. The investor is a passionate hunter and the entire upper story with its gorgeous southern view is full of trophies from around the world, including Siberia and Africa.

A lot of people hate these kinds of exhibits, but who am I to criticise the investor? The house has a very gentle disposition: on the northern side is a load-bearing wall with little gardens and a transverse supporting system, the southern side is a glass facade with horizontal blinds that make the building look like real architecture. The house seems an integral part of the charming landscape.

Natural Architecture / Exhibition / 12th International Architecture Biennale , Italy, 2010

Aesthetics and art history superstars Jana Tichá and Irena Fialová suggested we could make an exhibition of wooden things, so we created a concept for the Venice Biennale which was based on models of the stacks and towers on a scale of 1:6. I placed mirrors on both walls, mirroring the pavilion to infinity.

Creating a pavilion for Venice was fantastic for my ego but terrible for the accounts – we only had 1.2 million Czech crowns for the entire thing, which took me back to times of destitution. The great Gebrian himself mentioned that this was the first time he didn't have to be ashamed of the Czech pavilion. That offended me – I think we deserved much greater praise.

Sněžka Post Office , Krkonoše National Park, CZ, 2007

Representatives of the Krkonoše National Park and postmistress Skrbková began a discussion on the form of the new post office atop Mount Sněžka. The mayor of Pec pod Sněžkou – the town below the mountain – wanted something unconventional, so me and Patrik Hoffman drafted a simple rectangular building with a flat roof that could serve as a lookout tower. We spent two years fighting for the shape and expression, but in the end, we carried our idea through.

It was a construction kit containing thirty-five thousand pieces which had to be assembled on the spot. The entire shell is covered with slats against light and weather. My friend Tom Plzenský is among those responsible for this atypical, hydraulically operated part of the structure.

Apres Ski, CZ, 2007

As a young man, I went skiing with a beautiful girl in the Dolomites. When they closed the lifts and we still had some time before dinner, we spent a pleasant two hours in the "après ski" lounge. First, I recruited Honza Mach, who included the lounge in his diploma work. And then, on a trip through Albania, I talked my kind friend Aleš Voverka into funding this enterprise.

It's a segment of a rotating toroid (a "tyre"), and Mach and his friends built it in the courtyard of the Technical University in Liberec. However, it did not find favour with various authorities and organisations, so it found its place at the U Čápa Bed and Breakfast, where it looks fantastic.

Factory in Koloděje, CZ, 2004

Jakub Černoch, my cousin five times removed, began building a lamp factory in Koloděje. He's an engineer himself, so he had a construction company draw up the project. Then we went sailing in the Caribbean and he admitted that the poor building was damned ugly. So, we encased it in an elegant wooden construction and all of a sudden – and this is the power of architecture – the ugly duckling became a beautiful, elegant swan.

Jakub originally wanted a villa too, but when he saw his beautiful new factory, he settled with that, dumping the villa even though it was already drafted. The house won a nomination for the Mies van der Rohe Award. It is represented here during construction, because that's when it was most beautiful.

The Scholzberg Dome, CZ, 2013
One time, I was wandering through Copenhagen and I had the idea of making a cupola as a stack. And because I know who to call, me and Tom Foltýn arranged this cupola in the shape of the arch of the Cathedral of Santa Marie del Fiore in Florence. We're glad it has a positive effect on people – there's always a wedding taking place there.

The Brno Dome, CZ, 2013
Nela Gottwaldová, then the director of the Association of Architecture Students, organised a workshop in Brno and talked me into participating. What options does an old man have, other than to oblige? Me and Luboš Loidl made a dome that only widens from about a third of its height, which gives it a certain courageous elegance. Originally, the structure was to be taken apart so it could follow students to various European universities. However, the faculty in Brno liked the dome so much they purchased it and it still stands there today.

Maxov Barn , CZ, 2004

I had always wanted to rebuild the barn which was originally attached to the cabin. In 2005, I decided I'd build it as a stack of wood, but shaped like a house. I never even considered trying to get planning permission – after all, it was just a stack of drying wood. The authorities went mad and I enjoyed it immensely. Negotiations lasted for seven years and they ended up hiding the papers at the bottom of the drawer again. Then, a new building authority director arrived. She paid me a visit and asked for a solution. If they attack, I defend myself, but when they ask me politely, I'm happy to oblige.

So, we legalised it and my stack ended up getting a nomination for the Mies Award. I'm glad to receive photographs from people walking in my footsteps, drying their wood in similar hollow stacks. Perhaps, in my old age, I have become a pioneer?

Clinic in Mladá Boleslav, CZ, 2018

We decided to develop this project, which is not under construction just yet, because it is located in a beautiful spot in the middle of a park, surrounded by sandstone rocks. We designed a house that is partly a gentle segment (slightly bent). Its northern edge is formed by the sandstone, the southern side, which is glass-covered and shaded, opens into a gorge. There is a bridge from the third floor of the building onto the sandstone rock, where a footpath connects to the main entrance of the clinic. I have to say it's a pleasure, once you're over seventy, to win commissions over your younger colleagues... And when you have the opportunity to build in a beautiful spot, more than half the architectural work is done for you.

Brač, Croatia, 2019

Some friends of Tom Kosnar bought a gorgeous ruin of a fisherman's house on the southern side of a beautiful rocky slope in the strictly historically preserved village of Murvica on the Croatian island of Brač. The ground plan showed the remains of five small structures, including a furnace, stables, and two little houses. We conceived of all these structures as a collection of dwelling spaces connected by terraces, covered by pergolas, and overgrown with grapevine.

This entire (non)house is made from stone. For us, it IS a proving ground for working with materials other than wood. This project is extensive and is moving slowly, but we love it very much, as we could hardly imagine a better place to oversee the works!

Transborder in Chrastava, CZ, 2010

In 2010, the town of Chrastava was hit by severe flooding. The adroit mayor Michael Canov made use of his extended remit and arranged construction permits for new bridges, footpaths, and so on. We convinced our friends in ODS to invest in a transborder. The mayor, however, had one tough condition: it had to be operational within twenty-three days, a deadline worthy of an American army engineer in wartime.

David Pavlišta and Jitka Pucandlová put the project together and Vašek Horecký handled the realisation flawlessly. On October 10 2010, a gypsy band boarded the cart, riding back and forth and playing music long into the night.

Transborder in Nantes, France, 2015

After our 2014 exhibition in DOX, we were invited to participate in a competition for a footpath over the River Sevre, a tributary of the Loire. We decided to talk them into a transborder – a cabin which drifts along the structure high above the water, powered by human hands.

The first meetings in the local pub took place under a huge reproduction of a photograph of the original transborder, which was in operation from the end of the 19th century until the 1960s. We told the French architects we'd give a chunk of their beloved history back to them, only in wood, and the competition was over. We are now patiently awaiting instructions from the prudent French administration and cannot wait for the realisation.

Lighthouse and Museum of Jára Cimrman , Příchovice, CZ, 2013

The project of our hearts' desire. Originally, it was just the tower, but Aleš added the idea of the Jára Cimrman Museum – a clever idea. There is a wooden lighthouse on the roof of the museum. The display and its arrangement are partly the work of the Jára Cimrman Theatre group.

Our task was to give the structure an elementary shape and form. We are of the opinion that it is an exhibition of natural architecture: the original rock, and wood from nearby forests – all this symbolises humility and a playful dialogue with the landscape… Just as we like it. The building was nominated for several prizes, including the Mies van der Rohe Award.

Elephant's Belly, Brno, CZ, 2016

Structures of parts of an elephant have become something of a hobby for us – we've built the Elephant's Back, the Elephant's Leg, the Elephant's Trunk, and then, in the Museum of Applied Arts in Brno, we built the Elephant's Belly out of sticks. The workshop lasted a week, it was pouring down with rain, but the students – led by Tom Kosnar and Jirka Táborský – were amazing. The two "elytra" (built on wooden hooves) were hoisted up against the museum wall using cranes, supported by three-sided buttresses made from sticks. There is nothing left of the classical building techniques here!

It was touching that the students received their guláš in little stainless steel bowls, which were then installed onto the wooden structure when we covered it in Mylar. The projected lifespan? A hell of a long time: the membrane has to be changed once every ten years and the sticks will last decades because they're not exposed to the rain!

Golf Club in Kácov, CZ, 2016

For years, we yearned to draw a bigger structure which would be harmoniously embedded into a natural framework, so winning the commission for the golf club in Kácov made us very happy indeed. But serving billionaires turned out to be damn hard: some of our discussions were unpublishable, and I fear I'm not exactly a popular architect among golfers. Nevertheless, we defended the golf club, which ended up more or less as we had imagined it (with the exception of the interiors).

The structure lies atop a ridge rising up above a meander of the Sázava river. The golfers maintain a number of small ponds. We kneaded the terrain into a giant footprint, into whose heel we placed the clubhouse. The vast southern terrace is shielded from the sun by blinds, which – though they are the crowning feature of the entire structure – they had threatened to ditch. We pushed them through in the end, so there's something to look at after all.

Gulliver, a Zeppelin on the Roof of the DOX Centre for Contemporary Art, Prague, CZ, 2016

Leoš Válka (the owner and director of DOX, a gallery in Prague) is certainly among those people without whom art – and especially architecture – in the Czech Republic would suffer considerably. Leoš turned to us to build him something he called "an Ark of Freedom". After long discussions, Leoš proclaimed decisively: "It has to be a zeppelin as imagined by a twelve-year-old boy who wants to take off!"

With the great erudition and fantastic talent of builder and structural engineer Zbyněk Šrůtek, we managed to put together something like a reminiscence of early 20th-century zeppelins, only not in aluminium but in wood.

Building the Ark of Freedom became our most beloved endeavour. The basic ideas – that it would be a zeppelin and that it would be located above the DOX courtyard – came from Leoš Válka.

Leoš is a joy to work with and this was a once-in-a-lifetime experience for everyone who took part. The Gulliver Zeppelin took to the air in the autumn of 2016. Building a zeppelin and then placing it atop an existing structure certainly wasn't easy; just ensuring the structural stability of the wood and steel structures and staircases took over a year.

I believe this complex structure is not sullied by the shadow of laboriousness or premature efforts. I hope it's the opposite – I think the Ark of Freedom is a good ship. It makes me very happy, because as the kind reader – who has now waded their way through my memories – remembers, the freedom which was this structure's birth-right is a property utterly indispensable to my life.

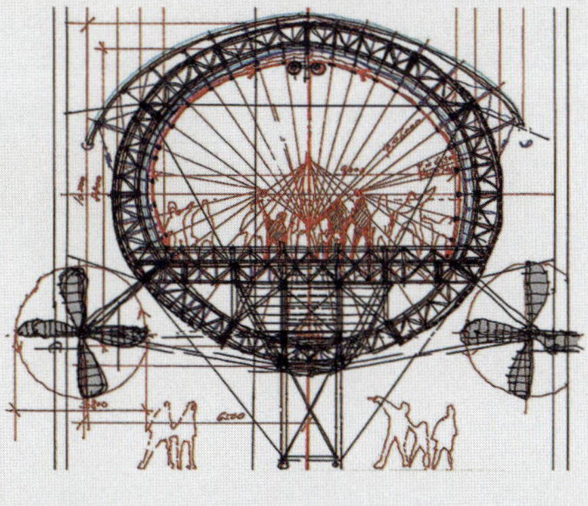

Kbely Brewery, Prague, CZ, 2016

When we were finishing this book in August 2016, the project for a brewery in Kbely was still on the table. We drafted a large roof made of spatial structures from twigs covered in transparent Mylar membranes. As was common in Czech 19th-century breweries, we dressed the slightly renovated buildings with a brick veneer, and we even dared erect two new brewery chimneys, each of which contains a staircase.

The result is a building full of playfulness – you could call it leisure-time architecture. Free time, you see, is something most Czechs associate with beer drinking – a jolly and joyful activity, so the house should feel the same.

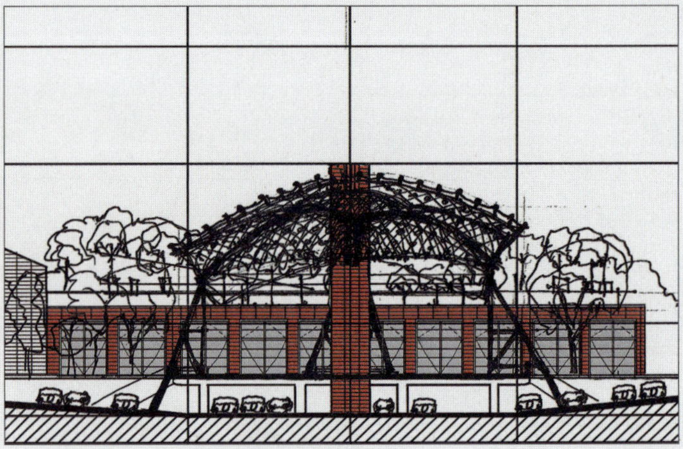

The Zen Cube, Jaroslav Fragner Gallery, the Rašínovo nábřeží quay, private garden, Prague, CZ, 2008
In 2008, we put on an exhibition at the Jaroslav Fragner Gallery, where we wanted to display a finished small structure in real size. Following our design, V. Horecký built the Zen Cube, which we placed in the courtyard in front of the gallery. The cube then travelled through several Czech cities before finally settling down on the roof of a pavilion in Aleš Voverka's private clinic in Prague. Several companies also asked for permission to use the structure in schools, kindergartens, and gardens.

SSBS/prototype W02, Prague, CZ, 2004

The name sounds wild, and our structure is wild too. It's an unusual attempt by our studio to create a wooden construction set that can be easily put together and taken apart. But only if all the necessary pieces are assembled. We later used this system on the Sněžka Post Office, where it was exposed to extreme conditions – to our great joy, it withstood the test.

Studio Above the River, Kamenný Újezdec, CZ, 2009

This small structure is a significant turning point in our attempt to create buildings that have a broad range of adaptations to external conditions. We realised how difficult it is to create a system of mobile vertical isolation slabs, which is why we had to make changes to the structure in the years following its completion. Our attempt at a harmonic connection between the structure and the natural scenery of the Sázava River came off just as we had hoped.

Floating Sauna, Křenovice Forest, CZ, 2012

The recreational centre includes a floating sauna composed of two cylindrical wooden structures with a roof made of translucent membrane mounted on a wooden frame. This poetic little structure was to swim on a forest pond and David Kubík further underlined its romantic nature with what's known as a frog's-eye-view (the perspective of the frog looking out from the depths of the water towards the sauna).

Mourning Hall, Planá, CZ, 2013

After a long break, I allowed myself to be goaded to take part in a competition, and it was a bad decision, as I had, of course, suspected. Never before had I experienced what happened – we got kicked out in the first round. Even so, I am convinced that our proposal was the best and the judges were affected by selective blindness. I have won over thirty competitions during the course of my career, so one loss isn't going to get me down. But really, it's better to get commissions directly, which is – thankfully – usually the case.

1/
Beer Tower, Prague, CZ (Martin Rajniš, David Kubík, Tomáš Kosnar), project: 2016
2/
Hexa-feet Tower, Kyje, Prague, CZ (Martin Rajniš, David Kubík, Tomáš Kosnar), project: 2014
3/
Doubravka Tower, Kyje, Prague, CZ (Martin Rajniš, David Kubík, Tomáš Kosnar), project: 2014
4/
Artefact, Kyje, Prague, CZ (Martin Rajniš, David Kubík, Tomáš Kosnar, Luboš Loibl, architecture students from the Czech Technical University in Prague, the Technical University of Liberec, and the Brno University of Technology), construction: 2014
5/
Penta-feet Tower, Kyje, Prague, CZ (Martin Rajniš, David Kubík, Tomáš Kosnar), project: 2014
6/
Šišák Tower (Martin Rajniš), project: 2016
7/
Ecumenical Chapel, Prague – West: Trnová, CZ (Martin Rajniš), project: 2005
8/
Botanicus Gardens, Lysá nad Labem, CZ (Martin Rajniš, Martin Kloda), project: 2009
9/
Bára II, Chrudim, CZ (Martin Rajniš, Martin Kloda, David Kubík, Vít Mlázovský), construction: 2009
10/
Bára I, Chrudim, CZ (Martin Rajniš, Martin Kloda, David Kubík, Vít Mlázovský), construction: 2008
11/
Máminka Tower, Hudlice, CZ (Martin Rajniš, David Kubík, Martin Kloda, Tomáš Kosnar), construction: 2015
12/
Scholzberg Tower, Horni Maxov, CZ (Martin Rajniš, Jan Mach), construction: 2006
13/
Doubravka Tower, Kyje, Prague, CZ (Martin Rajniš, David Kubík, Tomáš Kosnar), project: 2018
14/
Lighthouse and Museum of Jára Cimrman, Příchovice, CZ (Martin Rajniš, David Kubík), construction: 2013
15/
Staircase Tower, Sněžka Post Office, Krkonoše National Park, 1602 mamsl, CZ (Martin Rajniš, Patrik Hoffman, Jan Mach, Tom Plzenský, David Kubík, Josef Franc), construction: 2007
16/
Residential Tower Klecanky, Prague, CZ (Martin Rajniš, Tomáš Kosnar), project: 2013
17/
Roundhouse, transport history pavilion, Expo '86, Vancouver, Canada, Studio Shape (Studio Shape - J. Hník, M. Rajniš, J.Pšenička, K. Gebauer, M. Kocáb, M.Pavlíček, P.Klikar, P.Skoumal, M.Cajthamlová, V.Jiránek, M.Jiránek, V.Slíva a další), construction: 1986
18/
Pneu Lamp (Martin Rajniš), 1st prize in the Artemide competition, Milan, Italy, 1969
19/
Chair, National Gallery in Prague, CZ, (Martin Rajniš), prototype: 1989
20/
Machinist Armchair, (Martin Rajniš, Nela Gottvaldová), Prague, 2014
21/
Cast-Iron Park Furniture, Prague, CZ, (Martin Rajniš), prototype realised: 1987
22/
Máj Department Store, Prague, CZ (Miroslav Masák, Johny Eisler, Martin Rajniš), construction: 1975
23/
Administrative Building, Pankrác, Prague, CZ (Martin Rajniš, Martin Kloda), construction: 1995
24/
Lužiny Children´s Healthcare Centre, Prague, CZ (Martin Rajniš, DA Studio, Luboš Jíra, Markéta Cajthamlová, Lev Lauermann, Aleš Lamr, and KPÚ project architects Ježková, Jaroš, Kutnar), construction: 1990
25/
SANOPS, Na Mrázovce, Prague, CZ (Martin Rajniš, Markéta Cajthamlová, Lev Lauermann, Jaromír Hník), construction: 1987
26/
New Smichov, Prague, CZ, urbanist study and documentation for the territorial construction proceedings (Tomáš Prouza, Martin Rajniš, Jaroslav Zima, Stanislav Fiala), project: 1995–1998, construction: 1998–2008
27/
House for Pavel Štecha, Černošice, CZ (Martin Rajniš, 4DS - Milan Hakl, Pavel Mikulenko), construction: 2001
28/
Stack at Slavonice, Slavonice, CZ (Martin Rajniš, Kamila Amblerová, Václav Horecký), construction: 2007
29/
Písek City Forest Administration, Písek, CZ (Martin Rajniš, Martin Kloda, David Kubík), construction: 2009
30/
The House in the Preserve, CZ, HAMR (Martin Rajniš, David Kubík), construction: 2012
31/
Natural Architecture / Exhibition / 12th International Architecture Biennale, Venice, Italy, (Martin Rajniš, Jana Tichá, Irena Fialová, Martin Kloda, David Kubík), construction: 2010
32/
Sněžka Post Office, Krkonoše Mountains, 1602 mamsl, CZ (Martin Rajniš, Patrik Hoffman, Jan Mach, Tom Plzenský, David Kubík, Josef Franc), construction: 2007
33/
Apres ski, CZ (Martin Rajniš, Jan Mach), construction: 2007
34/
Factory in Koloděje , Prague, CZ (Martin Rajniš, Patrik Hoffman), construction: 2004
35/
The Maxov Dome, Horní Maxov, CZ (Martin Rajniš, Tom Foltýn), construction: 2013
36/
The Brno Dome, Brno, CZ (Martin Rajniš, Luboš Loibl, Nela Gottvaldová), construction: 2013
37/
Barn in Maxov, Horní Maxov, CZ (Martin Rajniš, Kamila Amblerová, Jaromír Leffler), construction: 2004
38/
Clinic in Mladá Boleslav, Mladá Boleslav, CZ (Martin Rajniš, David Kubík), project: 2018
39/
Brač, Brač, Croatia (Martin Rajniš, Tomáš Kosnar), project: 2015
40/
Transborder in Chrastava, CZ (Martin Rajniš, David Kubík, David Pavlišta, Jitka Pucandlová), construction: 2010
41/
Transborder in Nantes, France (Martin Rajniš, Tomáš Kosnar), project: 2015
42/
Lighthouse and Museum of Jára Cimrman, Příchovice, CZ (Martin Rajniš, David Kubík), construction: 2013
43/
Elephant's Belly, Brno, CZ (Martin Rajniš, Tomáš Kosnar), construction: 2016
44/
Golf Club in Kácov, CZ (Martin Rajniš, David Kubík, Tomáš Kosnar), construction: 2016
45/
Gulliver, a zeppelin on the terrace of the DOX Center for Contemporary Art, Prague, CZ (Martin Rajniš, David Kubík; Leoš Válka), construction: 2016
46/
Brewery, Prague, CZ (Martin Rajniš, David Kubík, Tomáš Kosnar), project: 2020
47/
The Zen Cube, Jaroslav Fragner Gallery, Rašínovo nábřeží quay, private garden, Prague, CZ (Martin Rajniš), construction: 2008
48/
SSBS/prototype W02, Prague, CZ (Martin Rajniš, Patrik Hoffman), construction: 2004
49/
Studio Above the River, Kamenný Újezdec, CZ (Martin Rajniš, David Kubík, Martin Kloda, Jan Mach, Vojta Hybler, Václav Horecký), construction: 2009
50/
Floating Sauna, Křenovice Forest, CZ (Martin Rajniš, David Kubík), project: 2012
51/
Mourning hall, Planá, CZ (Martin Rajniš, David Kubík, Tomáš Kosnar), project: 2013